Casebook in
Child Behavior Disorders

LIST OF RELATED TITLES

Abnormal Psychology
Abnormal Psychology: An Integrative Approach, 2nd edition
by Barlow/Durand
Abnormal Psychology: An Introduction
by Durand/Barlow
Exploring Psychological Disorders, A CD-ROM for Mac and Windows
by Chute/Bliss
Seeing Both Sides: Classic Controversies in Abnormal Psychology
by Lilenfeld
Looking into Abnormal Psychology: Contemporary Readings
by Lilenfeld

Child Behavior Disorders/Child Psychopathy
Abnormal Child Psychology
by Mash/Wolfe

Clinical Psychology
Clinical Psychology: Concepts, Methods and Profession, 5th edition
by Phares/Trull

This text may be ordered together with Mash/Wolfe's *Abnormal Child Psychology,* discount Smart Pak ISBN 0534-77086-x

Casebook in Child Behavior Disorders

Christopher A. Kearney
University of Nevada, Las Vegas

Brooks/Cole • Wadsworth

I⟨T⟩P® *An International Thomson Publishing Company*

Belmont • Albany • Bonn • Boston • Cincinnati • Johannesburg • London • Madrid
Melbourne • Mexico City • New York • Pacific Grove • Paris • Scottsdale • Singapore
Tokyo • Toronto • Washington

Sponsoring Editor: *Marianne Taflinger*
Editorial Assistants: *Scott Brearton,*
 Rachael Bruckman
Marketing Team: *Lauren Harp, Margaret Parks*
Production Editor: *Mary Vezilich*

Manuscript Editor: *Patterson Lamb*
Interior Design: *Vernon Boes*
Cover Design: *Jennifer Mackres*
Typesetting: *Joan Mueller Cochrane*
Printing and Binding: *Webcom Limited*

I(T)P The ITP logo is a registered trademark used herein under license.

For more information, contact:

WADSWORTH PUBLISHING COMPANY
10 Davis Drive
Belmont, CA 94002
USA

International Thomson Editores
Seneca 53
Col. Polanco
11560 México, D. F., México

International Thomson Publishing Europe
Berkshire House 168-173
High Holborn
London WC1V 7AA
England

International Thomson Publishing Japan
Hirakawacho Kyowa Building, 3F
2-2-1 Hirakawacho
Chiyoda-ku, Tokyo 102
Japan

Thomas Nelson Australia
102 dodds Street
South Melbourne, 3205
Victoria, Australia

International Thomson Publishing Asia
60 Albert Street
#15-01 Albert Complex
Singapore 189969

Nelson Canada
1120 Birchmount Road
Scarborough, Ontario
Canada M1K 5G4

International Thomson Publishing GmbH
Königswinterer Strasse 418
53227 Bonn
Germany

Printed in Canada

10 9 8 7 6 5 4 3 2 1

Library of Congress Cataloguing-in-Publication Data

Kearney, Christopher A.
  Casebook in child behavior disorders / Christopher A. Kearney.
    p.   Cm.
  Includes index.
  ISBN 0-534-34643-x (pbk.)
    1. Child psychopathology–Case studies.   I. Title.
  RJ499.K38   1998
  618.92'89–dc21   98-29815
                                                                CIP

To my clients and students

ABOUT THE AUTHOR

Christopher A. Kearney is an associate professor of clinical child psychology at the University of Nevada, Las Vegas. He is also the Director of the UNLV Child School Refusal and Anxiety Disorders Clinic in Las Vegas. Dr. Kearney received his B.A. from the State University of New York at Binghamton and his M.A. and Ph.D. from the State University of New York at Albany. He completed his internship at the University of Mississippi Medical Center. Dr. Kearney's research has focused primarily on the classification, assessment, and treatment of school refusal behavior and internalizing disorders in children and adolescents. He also works with adults with severe developmental disabilities. Dr. Kearney has co-authored and co-edited two books on anxiety disorders in youngsters; in addition, he has written numerous journal articles and book chapters. He is the recipient of the Barrick Scholar Award, the William Morris Award for Excellence in Scholarship, and the Distinguished Teaching Award from the University of Nevada, Las Vegas.

CONTENTS

PREFACE

With the explosion of knowledge about childhood behavior disorders comes a heightened sense of responsibility to appreciate the problems these disorders create for the children, their parents, and others who deal with these children. One goal of this casebook is to synthesize current thinking about childhood behavior disorders with the cases of specific children and their significant others, whether at home or at school. By telling the stories of these children, my purpose is to show how the lives of the children and their families are both painful and disrupted on a daily basis.

 ## Represents the Breadth of Children's Psychopathology

To illustrate the continuum of possible psychopathology in youngsters, a wide variety of cases are presented. You'll find 12 cases that represent internalizing disorders, externalizing disorders, and mixed symtomatology (diagnoses?). To stretch the student's appreciation of how complex real cases are, cases 1 & 14 omit the diagnoses on purpose so that instructors may discuss the issues in the case in class. Case solutions are provided to the instructor in a special supplement. For each case, the student should be able to derive a clinical picture by reading about discussions of symptoms, major assessment methods, causes and maintaining variables, developmental aspects, and treatment strategies. These sections represent the types of information professionals find most important when addressing a particular case. Each case concludes with a series of questions designed to stimulate student review or group discussion of the case. The breadth of these cases is also evident in its examples of how children's presenting symptoms differ from DSM criteria and by substantial differences in the outcome of treatment.

Real Cases Can Be Used in Different Settings, in Different Ways

Although this casebook was primarily designed for undergraduate and beginning graduate students in psychology, the text is written so that persons of other disciplines and interests may find the material useful and appealing. The cases presented are based on actual case histories or composites of cases seen by different mental health professionals. The names and some of the details of the cases have been changed to protect the confidentiality of the people involved. Resemblances to actual people are coincidental because so many of the details have been altered.

An Empirical, Family Systems Approach

In general, this casebook reflects an empirical approach that is derived from a cognitive-behavioral, family systems orientation throughout. This does not imply, however, that other forms of treatment are invalid for a certain population. It is widely recognized that an intricate combination of biological and other interventions is often needed to successfully resolve a particular case of child-based psychopathology.

My thanks for this project go primarily to my former teachers, clients, and students who have taught me so much and who continue to do so. Special thanks go to my wife Kimberlie for her emotional support during the different phases of this project. I would also like to thank several reviewers for their constructive assistance on earlier versions of this casebook's chapters: Natacha Akshoomoff of Georgia State University; Jon Ellis of East Tennessee State University; Sander Latts of the University of Minnesota—Twin Cities; and Marjorie Hardy of Muhlenberg College. Finally, I thank Marianne Taflinger and all the staff at Brooks/Cole who gave me the opportunity to develop this casebook and who helped bring it to fruition.

Christopher A. Kearney

CHAPTER ONE

Mixed Case One

Symptoms

Michael Rappoport was a 9-year-old Caucasian male referred by his parents to an outpatient mental health clinic. At the time of his initial assessment, Michael was in fourth grade. His parents, Mr. and Mrs. Rappoport, referred Michael for what they described as "difficult" and "unruly" behavior. During the telephone screening interview, Mrs. Rappoport said that Michael was not listening to her or his teacher, was failing his subjects at school, and was occasionally aggressive toward his 5-year-old sister. In addition, she hinted that the family had been experiencing conflict and financial problems since Mr. Rappoport had lost his job several weeks before. The Rappoports were scheduled for an intake assessment session that week, but the family either postponed or failed to show up for their appointment three times before attending.

During the intake assessment session, Michael and his parents were interviewed separately by a clinical psychologist who specialized in childhood behavior disorders. Michael was interviewed first, and participated fully in the interview. He was generally polite, social, and responsive to most of the interviewer's questions. For example, he went into detail about his pets, soccer team, and friends in the neighborhood. When asked why he thought he was at the clinic, however, Michael shrugged his shoulders and said that his parents didn't like him very much. In particular, he said that his parents often yelled at him and that his father "hits me when I'm bad." When asked how his father hit him, and how often this occurred, Michael again shrugged his shoulders and did not answer.

The psychologist then asked Michael about the behaviors that his parents considered "bad." Michael said that he would often run and hide in his room whenever his parents fought, which was often, and that his mother didn't like running in the house. In addition, he was usually in trouble for failing to do his homework and for getting poor grades in school. Apparently, Michael was struggling with most of his subjects. He also said that he and his little sister "didn't get along."

1

Michael also complained that his teachers "yell at me for everything." In particular, he said he was often reprimanded for not staying in his seat, for not paying attention, and for not completing his homework assignments. Michael said the work was too difficult for him, especially the reading assignments, and that he could not concentrate on them. As a result of these problems, he usually had to sit close to his teacher during the day and he usually missed recess to make up past work.

The psychologist found it interesting that, as the conversation turned to Michael's behavior, his mood became more downcast and his interaction with her more withdrawn. At one point, Michael began to cry and said that he often felt "lonely and sad." In particular, he felt deprived of time with his friends at school and was embarrassed to bring any of his friends to his house to play. He was also sad that his parents often fought, and he worried about what would happen in the future. Michael denied any thoughts about harming himself but did muse about what his parents would think if he were dead.

The psychologist concluded her initial interview with Michael by asking him what he would like to see different in his life. Michael answered by saying that he wished his father was out of the house because of the constant fighting there. In addition, Michael said he wished he could do better in school and not get into so much trouble. The psychologist asked Michael as well if he wanted to feel any differently, but Michael simply shrugged his shoulders in response.

The psychologist then interviewed Mr. and Mrs. Rappoport. Immediately, it was clear that the two were irritated at one another, as Mrs. Rappoport apologized for the earlier scheduling postponements and indirectly blamed it on her husband. In response, Mr. Rappoport rolled his eyes and said, "Let's get on with this." The psychologist then asked both parents what brought them to the clinic. Mr. Rappoport shrugged, but Mrs. Rappoport quickly listed a series of problems regarding Michael.

Mrs. Rappoport began by saying that Michael was becoming "impossible to control." In particular, he was highly argumentative, boisterous, and noncompliant. Mrs. Rappoport complained that Michael would not listen to instructions and would often yell obscenities at her when she asked him to do something. In addition, Michael would often run around the house during a tantrum, which occurred almost every day. His tantrums, which included yelling, crying, and punching something, were usually set off by parental commands or times when Mr. and Mrs. Rappoport were "discussing something." During these tantrums, Michael would often end up in his room and/or be spanked by his father. This did little to control his behavior, however. Finally, Michael was becoming too aggressive with his 5-year-old sister. On several occasions, for example, he was caught slapping the child. As a result, he was no longer allowed to spend time alone with her.

Mrs. Rappoport also said that Michael was doing quite poorly at school. In particular, he was failing almost all his subjects and was having problems with reading and spelling. This was somewhat surprising, however, as Michael had typically been a good student up to the middle of third grade (last year). In addition, Michael was difficult to control in the classroom, often throwing tantrums and complaining that the work was too difficult for him. He often refused to do his homework and was forced to sit near his teacher during the day so that she could better monitor his behavior. In fact, Michael's academic problems and misbehavior had grown so bad that his teacher, Mrs. Greco, had suggested a referral to special education. Both Mr. and Mrs. Rappoport strongly resisted this suggestion, however.

Mrs. Rappoport completed her comments about Michael by stating that he was often sullen and sometimes "quirky" in his behavior. For example, Michael would often cry when he was upset and withdraw to his room. In addition, he was overconcerned about contracting AIDS (acquired immune deficiency syndrome). Apparently, one of Michael's classmates had returned to class following a bout with hepatitis, and this had triggered a fear of AIDS and other diseases in Michael. As a result, he washed his hands about ten times a day to prevent any possible contagion.

The psychologist then asked Michael's parents about other family matters. Again, Mrs. Rappoport did most of the talking and said that her husband had recently lost his job and that the family was experiencing financial problems. She admitted that she and her husband "sometimes" fought, but did not feel this was related to Michael's behavior. In fact, she insisted that the focus of the interview and later therapy be on Michael, who was displaying the most problematic behavior. Despite several gently prodding questions, she and her husband did not provide any more details regarding their marriage or their disciplinary style.

With permission, the psychologist also spoke with Michael's teacher, Mrs. Greco. She said that Michael had been a relatively good student during the first month of the year but that his grades and behavior had grown problematic since then. Mrs. Greco said that Michael was struggling with many of his assignments even though he was intelligent and could do the work easily if sufficiently motivated. This seemed particularly true for assignments that involved extensive reading and written work. Mrs. Greco also said that she had never recommended Michael for special education, as stated by Mr. and Mrs. Rappoport, but did feel that Michael's parents needed to take a more active role in addressing their son's academic problems. She also speculated that Michael's parents, who were difficult to address in their own right, were a primary cause of many of Michael's problems.

Mrs. Greco noted that Michael's misbehavior was becoming intolerable as well. She complained that her student was often noncompliant, inattentive, and disruptive. In particular, she described how Michael would refuse to do his assigned work by throwing papers, crying, and stomping his feet around the room. As a result, he was sent to the principal's office about once a week. In addition, he was overactive and often needed reminders to sit in his seat. Overall, he demanded a substantial amount of attention from Mrs. Greco, who said that her ability to attend to the rest of her class was suffering as a result.

Based on this preliminary information, the psychologist concluded that Michael and his family had a variety of problems that needed to be addressed. Michael, in particular, seemed to have a combination of internalizing, externalizing, and academic problems. In addition, his family was clearly marked by a high level of conflict and intense life stressors. Potential abuse from the corporal punishment used in the family was also an issue the psychologist felt would have to be explored further.

# Assessment

The general purpose of assessment, or the collection of information on children and their families in a clinical setting, is to answer three basic questions (Eisen & Kearney, 1995):

1. What is the behavior problem?
2. Why is the problem continuing to occur?
3. What is the best treatment for the problem?

These questions may seem straightforward, but they are often difficult to answer. This is especially so in a complicated case like the Rappoports'.

The first question, for example—"What is the behavior problem?"—raises several additional questions that must be considered carefully. First, is there an actual behavior problem that needs to be addressed? This relates to the issue of "disturbed" versus "disturbing" behavior (Algozzine, 1977). With respect to Michael, for example, was he referred for treatment because his behavior was truly abnormal or simply because he upset his parents and teacher? Indeed, some of his behaviors might be considered developmentally appropriate for a 9-year-old. In related fashion, what if the child's behavior problem is an understandable result of family variables like conflict, disarray, abuse, or negative parent attitudes? In other words, what if the "behavior problem" lies more with the family than the child? In Michael's case, for example, it was possible that his parents' fighting led understandably to his sadness. In a situation like this, one shouldn't automatically assume that the child is the one who needs the bulk of attention during treatment.

Deciding what the behavior problem is can also be difficult if one person (e.g., a child) says there is no problem and other individuals (e.g., the parents) insist there is one. Here, the therapist should look for behaviors that clearly interfere with a child's daily life functioning. In Michael's case, several of his behaviors appeared to do so and therefore needed to be addressed. Finally, if the child is assumed to have behavior problems, a decision must be made as to which behaviors are most severe and should be addressed first. In many youngsters referred for treatment, different symptoms from different disorders overlap. In Michael's case, for example, he certainly had a number of overt symptoms, but it was possible that his acting-out behaviors were masking more serious internalizing problems, such as anxiety or depression.

The second question to be answered from an assessment—"Why is the problem continuing to occur?"—is also fraught with difficulty. Here, a therapist must determine what *maintains* each behavior problem in a child. These maintaining variables, as mentioned throughout this casebook, include sensory reinforcement, attention, escape from aversive situations, and tangible rewards like money, among others. Different behaviors could be maintained by different variables, as might have been the case with Michael. For example, his tantrums and aggression toward his sister could be a way of getting attention; his handwashing could be a way of escaping or reducing worry about contamination; his noncompliance could be a way of soliciting bribes from his parents.

These first two questions—"What is the behavior problem?" and "Why is the problem continuing to occur?"—refer to the form and function of behavior. Knowing the form *and* function of a child's behavior makes answering the last major question easier—that is, "What is the best treatment for the problem?" For example, suppose Michael's most severe behaviors were his tantrums at home and school (form). Eliminating this behavior problem might help reduce other behavior problems (e.g., general noncompliance). Suppose also that Michael's tantrums were motivated by attention at home but by escape at school (function). In this case, Michael's parents might wish to ignore his tantrums at home whereas Michael's teacher might wish to work through his tantrums at school and not allow him to leave class.

Various assessment methods can be used to answer these questions; they are described in this casebook. They include interviews, self-report measures, self-monitoring, cognitive assessment, physiological/medical assessment, role-play, parent/family and teacher measures, sociometric ratings, direct observation, and formal intelligence, achievement, and personality tests, among others. In most cases, a multidimensional approach to assessment is necessary to evaluate different areas of functioning (e.g., social, academic, intellectual, emotional) that may be problematic.

In Michael's case, he and his parents were administered the Anxiety Disorders Interview Schedule, a semistructured interview that covers a variety of internalizing and externalizing disorders (Silverman & Albano,

1996). Michael was formally diagnosed with three disorders identified in the *Diagnostic and Statistical Manual of Mental Disorders* (*DSM-IV;* American Psychiatric Association, 1994). One related to an internalizing problem, one related to an externalizing problem, and one related to an academic problem. Each of these disorders was rated as moderate to severe in nature.

Michael was also asked to complete several self-report measures, including the Fear Survey Schedule for Children-Revised (FSSC-R; Ollendick, 1983), State-Trait Anxiety Inventory for Children (STAIC; Spielberger, 1973), Revised Children's Manifest Anxiety Scale (RCMAS; Reynolds & Paget, 1981), Piers-Harris Self-Concept Scale (PHSCS; Piers, 1984), and the Children's Depression Inventory (CDI; Kovacs, 1992). These were given to assess, in more detailed fashion, any internalizing problems that were not discussed in the interview. An interesting result was that Michael endorsed several items on the FSSC-R that indicated a high level of fear for medically related stimuli (e.g., sickness, germs, hospitals, injections), social/evaluative situations (e.g., large crowds, being criticized), and parental arguing.

On the STAIC, Michael indicated that he was often tearful, indecisive, shy, and unhappy in school. He also worried about schoolwork, evaluations from others, and the future. On the RCMAS, Michael's responses showed that he worried about what his parents would say to him and about bad things happening to him. He also had nightmares, trouble concentrating, and various somatic complaints (e.g., feeling sick to his stomach). The PHSCS revealed that his classmates made fun of him, that he hated school, and that he often felt left out of things. On the CDI, Michael indicated that terrible things would happen to him, that he felt alone, and that he could never be as good as other kids. In general, Michael seemed anxious and depressed about different areas in his life. Areas of most concern included his current family situation, medical status, social evaluations, and future events.

Michael's parents, Mr. and Mrs. Rappoport, were asked to complete the Child Behavior Checklist (CBCL; Achenbach, 1991a), Family Environment Scale (FES; Moos & Moos, 1986), Parental Expectancies Scale (PES; Eisen, Spasaro, Kearney, Albano, & Barlow, 1996), and Dyadic Adjustment Scale (DAS; Spanier, 1976), which is a measure of general marital satisfaction. On the CBCL, Mr. and Mrs. Rappoport endorsed high levels of attention problems and aggressive behaviors regarding Michael. In particular, they emphasized their son's impulsivity, nervousness, poor school performance, arguing, meanness, disobedience, screaming, temper tantrums, and demands for attention. Few internalizing symptoms were endorsed. On the FES, Mr. and Mrs. Rappoport indicated that their family had substantial conflict and was somewhat detached. On the PES, Mr. and Mrs. Rappoport confirmed their high expectations that Michael would take a lot of responsibility at home. However, they were quite disappointed in his performance there.

Finally, on the DAS, Mr. and Mrs. Rappoport indicated that they frequently disagreed with one another in several areas, especially finances. In addition, they revealed that they rarely had positive conversations with one another or showed affection for one another. These responses contrasted somewhat with their verbal reports during their interview. In general, the Rappoport family was clearly in distress, but Mr. and Mrs. Rappoport continually saw their son's externalizing behaviors as the main problem. They referred especially to his noncompliance and disruptive behavior.

Other assessment instruments used in this case included the Teacher's Report Form (TRF; Achenbach, 1991b), a continuous performance test, and the third edition of the Wechsler Intelligence Scale for Children (WISC-III; Wechsler, 1991). Michael's teacher, Mrs. Greco, completed the TRF and emphasized Michael's social and attention problems, keying especially on her student's regressive behavior, crying, lack of concentration, impulsivity, disorganization, and underachievement. A continuous performance test, which measures impulsivity, indicated that Michael's speed of responding resembled that of children with attention deficit/hyperactivity disorder. Finally, his WISC-III score was in the high average range, suggesting that his academic problems were not the result of an intellectual deficit. Instead, Michael was performing far below his ability.

After gathering this information, the psychologist saw that Michael had a variety of behavior problems that could not be clearly defined. In addition, many of these problems were maintained by different functions. On top of all this, Michael's family situation was obviously marked by marital tension, conflict, financial stress, and even possible abuse. Thus, any treatment program would likely have to involve the entire family and a complex strategy.

Causes and Maintaining Variables

Most childhood behavior problems, as noted in this casebook, are caused by different variables that interact during the course of the life span. Mash and Dozois (1996), in describing the general etiological theories regarding child psychopathology, outlined some of these major causal variables. For example, psychodynamicists emphasize inborn sexual drives and intrapsychic personality conflicts in the creation of later psychopathology. In addition, attachment theorists speculate that a caregiver's failure to provide for an infant's needs could lead to future psychopathology in that child. These theories may have some relevance for youngsters, but the validity of both has been called into question.

A more widely held etiological theory, and one that is mentioned throughout this casebook, is the behavioral model. Proponents of the behavioral model claim that children learn, or are reinforced for, abnormal behaviors. Examples include parents who inadvertently reward noncompliance, family members who provide sympathy for depressive behaviors, and peers who reward delinquent behaviors in a youngster. In related fashion, social learning theorists propose that children imitate or model the inappropriate behavior of others. Examples include increased child aggression following parental spanking and substance abuse after watching others drink alcohol or use illegal drugs.

In Michael's case, these learning models did seem to explain some of his behaviors. For example, his aggression toward his sister was reinforced by the attention he received from his parents. In addition, Michael's medical anxieties, fear of AIDS, and handwashing were apparently triggered by social learning. Several of Michael's classmates had discussed the student who had hepatitis, describing his hospital stay, isolation from others, injections, and constant need for cleanliness. Like many 9-year-olds, they exaggerated the stories. Michael, however, took them quite seriously and became fearful and somewhat compulsive in his handwashing as a result.

Another popular etiological theory of child psychopathology is proposed by cognitivists, who hold that distorted thought processes trigger or maintain a behavior problem. Examples include (1) anxiety and depression from irrational thoughts of negative evaluations from others, and (2) an eating disorder maintained by irrational beliefs about beauty and weight loss. In related fashion, affective theorists claim that some people have difficulty regulating their emotions and subsequently have trouble with motivation, behavior organization, or communication with others (Mash & Dozois, 1996). In people who have been abused, for example, ongoing anxiety or arousal from cues that remind the person of the abuse could lead to posttraumatic stress disorder and its long-term effects.

In Michael's case, distorted thought processes were not clearly an issue, although he did have a number of worries about present and future events. However, his emotional state was excitable, and Michael therefore had some problems regulating his own behavior. As a result of his excitability and impulsivity, he had difficulty concentrating on his schoolwork, organizing his materials, maintaining conversations with others, and controlling his temper tantrums. All these led to his poor grades, feelings of isolation from others, and punishment for disruptive classroom behavior.

Biological models are also commonly used to describe the etiology of child psychopathology. Causal mechanisms from this model include genetic predispositions, chromosomal aberrations, central nervous system changes, neurochemical imbalances, and stress and temperament. For example, evidence supports a genetic predisposition for several disorders, including depression. In addition, chromosomal aberrations like Down syndrome often lead to moderate mental retardation. Similarly, central nervous system changes can lead to specific developmental disabilities like learning disorder or more general disabilities like autism. Neurochemical imbalances, stress, and difficult temperament have also been implicated in problems as diverse as social anxiety and attention deficit/ hyperactivity disorder. In Michael's case, a general medical examination revealed no outstanding problems. However, his misbehaviors may have been partially explained by less obvious problems like changes in the brain or ongoing stress.

Finally, family systems models have been developed to explain childhood disorders that apparently result from inconsistent parenting or family dysfunction. In Michael's case, his parent's ongoing conflict may have sparked his behavior in several ways. For example, the stress of the conflict may have triggered his sullenness, withdrawal, and isolation from others. In addition, his parent's verbal threats to one another regarding harm or divorce might have fueled Michael's worries about the future. Such depression and worry could then lead to difficulties in concentration, lack of motivation, and poor schoolwork. Finally, Mr. and Mrs. Rappoport's fighting took time away from disciplining Michael for his behavior. As a result, his tantrums and other disruptive behaviors were often ignored until they became quite severe.

Each of these theories—psychodynamic, attachment, behavioral, social learning, cognitive, affective, biological, and family systems—holds that specific causal pathways are responsible for childhood behavior disorders. However, no one theory successfully explains all aspects of any childhood disorder. Instead, the complexity of childhood disorders demands an integrative approach. Combinations of variables from these different perspectives, or multiple causal pathways, are needed to explain fully the etiology of any disorder. In Michael's case, for example, different child, parent, peer, and teacher factors influenced his behavior. The presence of multiple causal pathways suggests also that treatments for children with behavior problems will have to involve many targets.

Developmental Aspects

Developmental psychopathology refers to the study of the antecedents and consequences of childhood behavior disorders and how such disorders compare to normal behavior development (Wenar, 1994). An important task of developmental psychopathologists is to identify *pathways* that lead to normal development, mental disorder, or some fluctuation between the two in children. For example, a developmental psychopathologist may wish to discover what child and family factors lead to depression. In addition, he or she might want to know what factors prevent the development of depression, what factors help a person with depression return to mental health, and what factors maintain depression over time.

An important task in developmental psychopathology involves discovering whether behavior problems in youngsters are stable over time and whether they lead to problems in adulthood (Hechtman, 1996a). Some childhood behavior problems are *very* stable over time. Consequently, they almost always interfere with a person's functioning in adulthood. Examples include pervasive developmental disabilities like autism, profound mental retardation, and aggressive forms of schizophrenia. Severe forms of late adolescent problems like conduct disorder or substance abuse may also carry into adulthood and create ongoing difficulties.

Other childhood behavior problems remain *fairly* stable over time. They may or may not lead to problems in adulthood depending on the severity of the disorder and whether early intervention is administered. Examples include attention deficit/hyperactivity disorder (ADHD), learning disabilities, aggression, school refusal behavior, eating disorders, pediatric conditions, and effects from abuse. Finally, other childhood behavior problems tend to be *less* stable over time. These may dissipate on their own, but they could still cause problems over time if they are aggravated by negative environmental events. These problems include fear and anxiety, depression, and elimination disorder, among others.

Note, however, that although childhood behavior disorders may be stable over time, the symptoms of the disorders may not remain the same. For example, children with ADHD tend to become less active as they mature, but their ongoing restlessness and lagging social development create other problems in adolescence. Similarly, a child who wants to coerce items from family members may do so by noncompliance in childhood but with aggression in later adolescence. In addition, a child who is behaviorally inhibited as a preschooler may avoid new social situations in childhood and become depressed in adolescence.

This type of change was evident in Michael's case. Although his problem behaviors were somewhat different now compared to his preschool days, some of his general behavior *patterns* remained the same. For example, his parents described Michael as an "ornery" child who was fussy and who often complained about what he had to eat. Mrs. Rappoport also said that Michael was a "very sensitive child" who overreacted to criticism and inadvertent contact from others. To some extent, these general characteristics were imbedded in Michael's current behavior problems. For example, his temper tantrums were a regressive way of dealing with stress and his sudden fear of disease was an overreaction to his classmate's stories. Although his behaviors were different over time, his behavior patterns were fairly stable.

What variables determine the stability of a childhood behavior problem? Mash and Dozois (1996) summarized some of these variables, which can be generally divided into proximal and distal factors. Proximal factors are those close to a child that have a more direct impact on his or her behavior, such as these:

1. Development of a disorder early in life, especially one that affects language
2. Major changes in the child's brain or other physical status
3. Early and ingrained learning patterns
4. Strong biological predispositions triggered by early environmental events
5. Ongoing experiences that threaten the child's self-esteem and social and academic competence
6. Obstacles that lead a child to pursue more maladaptive behavior patterns

With respect to the latter, obstacles like family conflict or sexual abuse could initiate an adolescent's noncompliance or increased alcohol use.

In Michael's case, he didn't appear to have any major stressor or biological problem early in life. However, he did learn early that one of the best ways to get parental attention was to act inappropriately. Over time, Michael effectively trained his parents to give him attention whenever he was noncompliant, aggressive toward his sister, or problematic in school. Michael also experienced several obstacles when he tried to build long-term friendships, such as loss of recess at school and discomfort at bringing potential friends into his house. These obstacles then led to maladaptive behaviors like social withdrawal and depressed mood.

Other factors that affect the stability of childhood behavior problems are distal ones, or those that indirectly affect a child, such as these:

1. Poverty and/or homelessness
2. Marital conflict and/or inconsistent or neglectful parenting
3. Loss of a parent early in life
4. Severe family dysfunction
5. General community disorganization (Mash & Dozois, 1996)

In Michael's case, marital conflict was most pertinent. Some of Michael's tantrums were triggered by his parent's fighting or were done deliberately to get his parents to stop fighting.

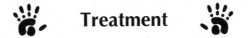

Treatment

Treatment for the Rappoport family initially got off to a rough start. Mr. Rappoport became progressively more withdrawn and, after 3 weeks, stopped attending therapy altogether. He did agree, however, to speak with the psychologist by telephone and to help his wife with the therapy procedures. In addition, Mrs. Rappoport remained adamant about maintaining the focus of treatment on her son. The psychologist, in response, spent the first four sessions describing the family mechanisms behind many of Michael's behaviors and the necessity of including Mrs. Rappoport and Michael's teacher in the therapy process. Only after this 4-week period did Mrs. Rappoport reluctantly agree to participate in therapy. She also agreed to consider the psychologist's recommendation that she and her husband pursue separate marital therapy.

During this 4-week period when Mrs. Rappoport was considering her role in therapy, the psychologist worked with Michael individually. Here, Michael's fear of disease and excessive handwashing were addressed. First, Michael was fully educated about the transmission of disease in general and AIDS in particular. A focus was made on external causes and internal effects of illness, and Michael was fascinated by this material. His self-reported anxiety regarding illness and general medical procedures declined somewhat during this time.

The psychologist also focused on Michael's handwashing, which was often triggered by sitting next to someone who "looked sick." The psychologist first had Michael sit next to different people in the clinic's waiting area. He was allowed to wash his hands only if someone next to him sneezed. Otherwise, he was taken to the psychologist's office and not allowed to wash for at least an hour. In this period, Michael saw that his anxiety declined without handwashing. In subsequent sessions, Michael was required to wait even longer before washing. He was then asked to practice waiting before handwashing in real-life settings. His response to this approach was immediate and positive. By the end of the 4-week period, he was washing his hands for a normal amount of time each day.

As mentioned before, Mrs. Rappoport agreed to play a more active role in treatment at this time. However, she insisted that the first area of focus be on Michael's noncompliance, tantrums, and aggressive behavior. The psychologist explained that Michael would often react to his parent's fighting by acting out, and Mrs. Rappoport and her husband agreed to hold their "discussions" in private as much as possible. Both parents were also shown that they waited too long to respond to Michael's misbehaviors. Instead, one parent or the other was to place Michael in time-out for 10 minutes if he was noncompliant following a request. This was thought to be a good alternative punishment to spanking as well. Further assessment had yielded no evidence of abuse, but everyone agreed that spanking was not a preferred option. Therefore, 3 weeks of therapy focused on using time-out following noncompliance. During this time, Michael did heed his parents more, although it was unclear whether he was compliant simply because of the extra parental attention he received.

Michael's tantrums also decreased a[...]
again that reduced parental fighting and in[...]
encing his behavior. However, his aggression [...]
in this initial stage of therapy. The psychologi[...]
that Mr. and Mrs. Rappoport increase their super[...]
sister when they were together. This way, much of[...]
prevented. If aggression did occur, spanking was 1[...]
cause children often model the aggressive response[...] psychologist advised Mr. and Mrs. Rappoport to ignore M[...]ter he hit
his sister and to give their daughter a lot of "sympathy and extra attention. This combination worked moderately well during the next 3 weeks.

At this time in therapy, Michael's parents decided to separate and Mr.
Rappoport left the house. Somewhat surprisingly, Mrs. Rappoport continued to participate in Michael's treatment despite her depressed mood. The
psychologist at this point decided to provide support to Mrs. Rappoport
and to fine-tune therapy recommendations from previous sessions. In this
way, Mrs. Rappoport would not be overwhelmed with new treatment responsibilities but would still be able to control Michael's behavior. Fortunately, Michael's response to his father's absence was not too negative
because the two spent time together on the weekends. Michael also promised to help his mother with the household responsibilities, as his father
was no longer there to assist.

Given Mrs. Rappoport's emotional state, a new emphasis was placed
on Michael's school-related problems. This shift of focus let the psychologist spend about half the therapy time with Mrs. Greco, Michael's teacher,
who had graciously offered to attend. Because Mrs. Rappoport would not
allow Michael to be medicated for his behavior, the psychologist set up a
token economy system based on a card system. Specifically, Michael was
to be given a warning for acting-out behavior; if he did not stop, he would
have to change his card from green to yellow. If he continued to act out, he
would receive another warning and then a red card. A red card meant that
Michael would have to spend the rest of the day doing his schoolwork in
the principal's office. A green card for the entire day was rewarded with
different prizes or classroom privileges.

Over a 5-week period, however, no change was seen in Michael's
acting-out behaviors. In addition, Mrs. Greco reported that the token economy was difficult for her to maintain consistently. Part of the problem was
defining exactly what acting-out behaviors should be considered. The focus of the token economy was therefore changed to Michael's academic behaviors. Michael was required to stay in the classroom regardless of his
behavior; instead he was rewarded or disciplined primarily for the
amount of work he completed. Unfortunately, this strategy also brought
no changes in Michael's homework or grades.

lack of change may have been due to Michael's family situation worsened. Mr. and Mrs. Rappoport decided to divorce, and Mr. Rappoport suddenly moved to a job in another state. Within 3 weeks, he was gone and had no face-to-face contact with Michael or the other family members for some time. As a result, Michael went through a month-long period of sadness and lack of motivation regarding school, friends, and sports. He eventually rebounded to some extent when his father resumed direct contact with him, but he remained uninterested in therapy.

As a result of what was happening in the family, Mrs. Rappoport and Michael attended therapy only intermittently during the next 6 weeks. Eventually, despite urgings from the psychologist, Michael and his mother no longer visited the clinic. Mrs. Rappoport did consult with the psychologist occasionally by telephone over the next year and reported that the family situation and Michael's home behavior had stabilized. However, Michael's academic problems and school-related misbehaviors continued to some extent.

 # Discussion Questions

1. Which of Michael's behaviors do you think may have been more "disturbed" and which do you think may have been more "disturbing" to his parents and teacher? Which of Michael's behavior "problems" might be fairly normal for a 9-year-old?

2. What were Michael's *primary* behavior problems? Identify five that you consider most important and explain your reasoning. In addition, as mentioned in the case, three *DSM-IV* diagnoses were assigned to Michael. Which ones do you think were most pertinent? Defend your answer.

3. In a case like Michael's, the family may be as problematic as the child. How would you explain to parents and others that their behavior must also change if the child's behavior is to change? Also, how would you convince a family to stay in treatment if you believed they could greatly benefit from doing so? Should you do so if the family made it clear they were no longer interested in therapy? Why or why not?

4. A key goal for developmental psychopathologists is to identify pathways that lead to, and away from, mental disorder. Choose a childhood disorder or behavior problem and develop a causal model for it. In particular, form a theory about why some children develop that particular problem and others do not. Be sure to discuss "protective" factors that help children avoid such misbehaviors. In addition, outline the factors that might move a child away from maladaptive behavior or at least improve his or her prognosis for the future.

5. Outside of the Rappoport family members and Michael's teacher, which people might be important for addressing Michael's behavior problems? What would you want to ask or say to these people? Why?

CHAPTER TWO

Social Anxiety/Withdrawal

Symptoms

Bradley Mavin was a 12-year-old Caucasian male referred to a specialized clinic for youngsters with social anxiety and social withdrawal. At the time of his initial assessment, Bradley was in seventh grade. His stepfather and mother, Mr. and Mrs. Nelson, had referred Bradley to the clinic after reading a newspaper advertisement calling for participants in a group therapy project. The project was designed to test an assessment and treatment protocol for youngsters with social problems. During the telephone screening interview, Mrs. Nelson said that Bradley was having trouble adjusting to his new middle school and had seemed depressed and withdrawn. In addition, he seemed upset about her recent divorce and remarriage. As a result, Bradley was missing more school than usual and his grades were beginning to suffer.

During the initial intake session, Bradley was interviewed by an advanced doctoral student in clinical child psychology. At first, Bradley was cautious and unsure of himself, avoiding eye contact and speaking very softly. The student, who was experienced with shy and socially anxious children, first talked with Bradley about a variety of topics that he seemed to enjoy. These included his pets, school projects, and sisters. Following this development of rapport, Bradley seemed more relaxed. The student then questioned Bradley about his recent social problems.

Bradley explained that his new middle school was quite different from the elementary school he had been in since kindergarten. He stated first that many of his friends from elementary school had been zoned for a different middle school, so he didn't know very many people at his current location. In fact, he wanted to transfer to the other middle school so that he could be with his old friends. In addition, Bradley claimed that few of his new classmates spoke to him or invited him for lunch or other activities. However, the interviewer discovered that Bradley rarely initiated contact with others in school. Bradley also said that he "hated" physical education class, where everyone "made fun of him" for his size (he was slightly smaller than his peers). In general, he felt lonely, sad, and "left out."

Bradley also complained that he now had to give oral presentations in his English class, an assignment he'd never had before. He reported that his first oral presentation went badly. He was supposed to give a presentation on the history of automobiles, but became quite anxious when asked to stand in front of his classmates. Bradley claimed that he trembled and had trouble breathing, which made his hands and voice shake noticeably. He noticed that some of his classmates were snickering at him, and he decided then that he would not give another presentation. Unfortunately, he was required to give three others and his failure to do so would result in an "F."

As a result of these experiences, Bradley was starting to refuse school. He began by occasionally skipping his physical education class, but in the past month had missed one or two full days of school per week. When skipping school, Bradley would stay home and do his homework and watch television. He had already asked his parents to transfer him to a new middle school or place him in home schooling.

The remainder of the interview focused on other areas of Bradley's social life. Bradley said he was active with friends from his neighborhood but avoided anyone new. In addition, he appeared to have a good relationship with his mother and two sisters. His relationship with his stepfather, however, was strained. Bradley reported that his stepfather was strict in his discipline and not afraid to spank him for various offenses. Bradley also reported that his stepfather was livid about his refusal to go to school, and that his parents often fought about this issue. They had immediately called the number in the newspaper when they saw it was for children with social problems.

During their interview, Mr. and Mrs. Nelson largely confirmed Bradley's report. Mrs. Nelson said that Bradley had always been a well-behaved son until about 2 years ago, when she and her first husband had separated (Bradley's biological father was currently out of state and had no contact with the family). At that time, Bradley became quite withdrawn and unwilling to play with other children in his neighborhood. Contrary to Bradley's report, he still avoided many of his old neighborhood friends and spent much of his free time doing homework or playing videogames. He did participate in family dinners and outings, but generally preferred to stay close to his mother and sisters.

Mrs. Nelson said that Bradley's situation had grown worse during the past 3 months while he was in seventh grade. She confirmed Bradley's fears about his physical education class and oral presentations and agreed that he had made few, if any, new friends. She also confirmed that Bradley wanted to be placed in home schooling, and she was about to do so when she saw the clinic's advertisement in the newspaper. Mrs. Nelson then decided that Bradley might benefit more from therapy than home schooling, and she wanted the advice of clinic staff members on this matter.

Mrs. Nelson said that Bradley was an excellent student who was generally quite shy. He seemed to enjoy working on his school projects as much as other kids enjoyed playing baseball. In general, he was a "loner" who rarely interacted with other children his age and who preferred to play with his two younger sisters. Otherwise, he was a normal child who was compliant, polite, and dutiful with respect to his household responsibilities.

Mr. Nelson added that his relationship with Bradley had always been difficult, and that the two "just didn't seem to connect." Mr. Nelson was adamant about Bradley's return to school but deferred to his wife when she recommended therapy. He said he wanted to help Bradley with his problems but wasn't sure he could, given his own outgoing nature. Instead, Mr. Nelson hoped that therapy would help Bradley become more self-confident and would improve their relationship.

With Mr. and Mrs. Nelson's permission, the therapist also interviewed Bradley's teachers at school. All generally indicated that Bradley was a fine student with excellent potential but one who was very shy and withdrawn. Bradley's English teacher, Mrs. Arnot, said that her student had done well on all of his assignments up to the oral reports. His first oral report had not gone badly, but Mrs. Arnot said it was clear that Bradley had physical symptoms of anxiety. She also said she had a strict class rule that students could not make jokes or laugh when anyone was giving an oral report, and generally no one did during Bradley's report. However, Bradley had approached her after class and cried profusely, asking to be relieved of his remaining oral presentations.

Bradley's physical education teacher echoed this report, although it was clear that Bradley was being teased to some extent. The teacher said that Bradley needed to "grow up," interact more with the other kids, and become more assertive. Conversations with Bradley's other teachers and guidance counselor confirmed that Bradley avoided many social situations, especially those that required meeting new people, working cooperatively with others, and performing in front of an audience. Based on these early reports, the therapist made a preliminary conclusion that Bradley was moderately socially withdrawn and met criteria for social phobia/social anxiety disorder.

Assessment

According to the *DSM-IV*, the essential feature of social phobia or social anxiety disorder is a "marked and persistent fear of social or performance situations in which embarrassment may occur" (American Psychiatric

Association [APA], 1994, p. 411). In general, social functioning with people known to the person, such as family members, is good, but the social fear occurs whenever the person interacts with unknown others or during situations in which he or she might feel negatively evaluated, humiliated, or embarrassed. In addition, the person usually has a panic attack or panic symptoms when exposed to these social situations. In youngsters, this may be evidenced by "crying, tantrums, freezing, or shrinking from social situations with unfamiliar people" (APA, 1994, p. 417). Those with social phobia, though not necessarily children, recognize their fear as unreasonable, and even so, they endure social situations with great distress if they cannot avoid them. Finally, the disorder must significantly interfere with one's daily life functioning, last at least 6 months, and not be due to a general medical condition or substance. Social phobia is considered generalized if most social situations are feared.

In Bradley's case, he appeared to meet these criteria. He was fearful and anxious when meeting new people and was reportedly "nervous and sick" in large social situations. In particular, Bradley was uncomfortable in situations where he was most closely evaluated by others, such as physical education class and oral presentations. Bradley reported nausea and trembling during these situations and was convinced that others could see him become upset. As a result, his level of social anxiety and withdrawal was clearly interfering with his academic functioning. However, Bradley's social interactions with his family and relatives were appropriate.

The assessment of youngsters with social anxiety typically includes interviews, self-report measures, self-monitoring, parent and teacher measures, and physiological evaluation. Multiple measures are often used because results from them are not always highly correlated. In stressful situations, for example, a child may report no cognitive symptoms of anxiety but still have a lot of physiological arousal.

Semistructured interviews for children with anxiety disorders are available; one of the most common is the Anxiety Disorders Interview Schedule for Children (ADIS-C; Silverman & Albano, 1996). The ADIS-C is often used in clinical research settings to identify anxiety symptoms and other pertinent problems in youngsters. Bradley was seen in a specialized research clinic, and the ADIS-C was used.

With respect to social anxiety, the ADIS-C has questions regarding (1) concerns about the evaluations of others and (2) feelings of embarrassment or shame in social situations. In addition, the child is asked about his or her level of fear in social situations such as answering a question in class, taking a test, eating in front of others, and dating. Fear of these situations is rated on a 0 to 8 scale where 8 represents the greatest amount. Questions are also raised as to (1) whether the child's social fear declines when certain (e.g., younger) people are present, and (2) how much the social anxiety interferes with the child's daily life functioning.

Bradley said he was afraid he would do something "stupid" or clumsy in different social situations, especially when meeting new people or performing in front of others. As noted earlier, he was also concerned about the snickering of others and feeling embarrassed at these times. When asked to identify the social situations that made him feel most nervous, Bradley chose oral reports, physical education class, eating in the cafeteria, starting or maintaining conversations, and answering questions in class.

The assessment of youngsters with social anxiety also includes self-report measures like the Social Phobia and Anxiety Inventory for Children (Beidel & Randall, 1994) and the Social Anxiety Scale for Children-Revised (SASC-R; La Greca & Stone, 1993). The SASC-R contains items that address fears of negative evaluation and social avoidance and distress. Bradley rated several SASC-R items very highly. These included worry when he was doing something in front of others, worry about being teased, worry about what others thought of him, nervousness when talking to others not well known to him, feelings of shyness, feelings that others were making fun of him, and difficulty asking others to play.

The therapist who handled Bradley's case also asked him to self-monitor several behaviors. In particular, Bradley was to write down any social situation during the day that caused him to feel nervous or sick. In addition, he was asked to rate, on a 0 to 10 scale, how nervous and sad he felt during these situations. The therapist also described various thoughts that Bradley might have during these situations and asked him to record the presence of these as well. Finally, Bradley was to note any other concerns that he had during the course of the day.

Over a period of 2 weeks, Bradley's self-monitoring revealed two interesting findings.

1. His social anxiety was highest when he entered school, went from class to class, and ate lunch in the cafeteria. He did not rate his physical education and English classes as highly anxious *unless* he had to perform individually in front of others.

2. Bradley's thoughts during unpleasant social situations were somewhat distorted. For example, he believed that others were often watching him closely and evaluating him negatively. More darkly, Bradley indicated that he thought others were plotting to "gang up on him" and steal his books and other materials.

Parent and teacher measures are also used to evaluate children with social anxiety, most notably the Child Behavior Checklist and Teacher's Report Form (CBCL and TRF; Achenbach, 1991a, 1991b). Mr. and Mrs. Nelson, for example, rated Bradley high on the CBCL subscale of "social problems," noting especially their son's clinging, clumsiness, preference for younger playmates, and reports of being teased by others. In addition, Bradley's English teacher, Mrs. Arnot, recorded Bradley's crying and hurt feelings during evaluative situations. Physiological assessments (e.g., heart rate, sweat indices) are also sometimes used to assess youngsters with social anxiety, but these were not used in Bradley's case.

The assessment of children who are considered more socially withdrawn may additionally include sociometric measurement and direct observation. Sociometric measurement involves soliciting peer ratings of a child suspected of being rejected or neglected. Sociometrics may include nominations, when children simply list the names of classmates they would most or least like to work and play with. In addition, teachers or children can give general rankings of each child in a classroom. This is done to identify one particular child's level of popularity and social interaction (Bierman & Welsh, 1997). Paired rankings, where each child is directly compared to every other child, may also be examined. Sociometric measures must be done carefully, though, so that some children are not singled out for further rejection. Sociometric measures were not solicited in Bradley's case, however.

Instead, Bradley's therapist conducted a direct observation of her client during selected times at school. Although Bradley knew the therapist would be entering the school to observe him at some time, he did not know when. The therapist observed Bradley during his lunchtime and outside during his physical education class. At both times, the therapist noticed that Bradley generally stood alone, rebuffed interactions from others, and seemed emotionally depressed. The therapist confirmed that Bradley was anxious in these situations and lacked some basic social interaction skills.

Causes and Maintaining Variables

The causes of anxiety and withdrawal in youngsters are still not entirely clear, but they appear to involve a combination of biological vulnerability to high arousal, family factors, stressful life events, and child characteristics like social apprehension, uncontrollability, and behavioral inhibition. With respect to biological vulnerability, data indicate that some people have a genetic predisposition toward unusually high arousal and therefore develop certain anxiety disorders. For example, studies indicate greater concordance for social phobia among identical than fraternal twins, and the risk for social phobia is greater for relatives of someone with the disorder than the general population (Black, Leonard, & Rapoport, 1997). However, it is possible that these individuals are inheriting a tendency for general negative affect and not a specific disorder. In addition, genetic data, while crucial, may partly reflect an environmental factor: how anxious parents raise anxious children.

Indeed, general family factors do seem to have a strong influence on the development of social anxiety and withdrawal in children. For example, anxious children tend to model perceptions of environmental threat from their parents (Ginsburg, Silverman, & Kurtines, 1995). In other words, they watch the carefulness, caution, and avoidance shown by their parents and imitate the behavior in their own social situations. In Bradley's case, this seemed to be true. His mother was a shy and reserved woman who reportedly enjoyed the traditional role of wife and mother. As such, much of her social life involved her husband and children, and she infrequently associated with others. In addition, she herself appeared anxious when meeting new clinic staff members. Thus, Bradley may have been adopting many of his mother's withdrawn, anxiety-based social interaction behaviors.

Other family variables that are related to social anxiety in children include overprotection, lack of parental warmth, and disrupted attachment (Albano, Chorpita, & Barlow, 1996). In Bradley's case, his mother was clearly overprotective, often demanding to know where her son was at different times of the day and even picking out his clothes in the morning. She also kept him physically close to her when shopping or working outside. However, Bradley's relationship with his mother was affectionate and his early attachment with her was secure. He did have more difficulty getting along with his stepfather, as was the case with his biological father, but this did not seem too relevant to his current social anxiety or withdrawal.

Children with anxiety disorders may also have parents with anxiety disorders, depression, or substance abuse. For example, Bradley's biological father had alcoholism and possible depression. Bradley's mother, Mrs. Nelson, also reported that she felt depressed and would retire to her room when "down in the dumps." Possibly, Bradley was modeling this behavior in addition to the others noted above.

Various stressful life events, especially those related to social trauma, can also influence the development of anxiety and withdrawal. In Bradley's case, this happened recently when he had troubles during his oral reports and physical education class. However, discussions with Bradley and his mother revealed that Bradley's friendships had generally declined in number since fourth grade and that this decline may have been related to some events at *that* time. For example, many of his early school-age friends moved out of town when the main industry in the town relocated. In addition, Bradley was teased in first and second grade for occasional wetting in school.

Other precursors to child social anxiety and withdrawal include characteristics of the child per se. These characteristics include social apprehension, feelings of uncontrollability, and behavioral inhibition. With respect to social apprehension, many children come to expect the worst possible outcome to occur in social situations. In Bradley's case, this was certainly true. When faced with social or evaluative situations, Bradley would complain that others were out to harm him or did not like him. For example, he was convinced that peers would ridicule his oral presentation even though no evidence supported this belief. In addition, Bradley reported that he didn't ask others to play or work with him because they would "probably push me or steal my stuff."

Children with social anxiety often report feelings of uncontrollability as well. This refers to a general sense of learned helplessness in which the children feel that their actions will have little impact on their surrounding environment. This may explain why many children with anxiety also have symptoms of depression. Bradley showed feelings of uncontrollability when he said it was pointless to start conversations with others or try to relax when speaking in class. In addition, the therapist had observed that Bradley often stayed by himself and walked with his head down. This behavior suggested that Bradley did not think he could make any positive change in his social situations.

By far, however, the one variable that has received the greatest amount of recent attention by researchers of child social anxiety/withdrawal is behavioral inhibition. Behavioral inhibition may be defined as an "enduring temperamental trait characterized by quiet, withdrawing, and timid behavior; reluctance to speak; and a state of neurological arousal in response to novel situations, including interaction with unfamiliar adults" (Black et al., 1997, p. 501). Behavioral inhibition affects about 10% to 15% of youngsters and may be related to various childhood anxiety disorders. This is so because the behavior is associated with basic themes of escape, avoidance, dependence, and passivity. In Bradley's case, these behaviors were clearly evident. He was timid and shy in situations involving people outside his family, and he withdrew quickly from situations that were unfamiliar to him. In addition, he seemed overly dependent on his mother for emotional support and was relatively unassertive. In fact, it was difficult to say whether Bradley's lack of social interactions were the consequence of a specific anxiety disorder or a general personality pattern.

Various factors thus conspire to cause social anxiety and withdrawal in youngsters. In many cases, the problem begins with an irritable, withdrawn temperament and a moderate biological vulnerability to high arousal. As the person grows, a series of negative social events may predispose him or her to develop a sense of learned helplessness or uncontrollability about the surrounding environment. These events may also trigger the biological arousal. The person may then become socially apprehensive as he or she scans the environment for potential threats. Subsequently, the person avoids more and more social situations (Albano et al., 1996; Stein, 1995).

Social anxiety or withdrawal can also be maintained by several factors. For example, a child may complain to his parents about social mistreatment at school and, as a result, receive a lot of positive attention from them. Such attention may be in the form of sympathy, verbal praise, or physical affection. Conversely, a child may want to escape different situations that involve added work or stress (e.g., helping a parent at a party). Claims of social anxiety and negative physical symptoms (e.g., stomachache) might help get a child out of certain responsibilities. In Bradley's case, both attention-seeking and escape-motivated behaviors were evident.

Developmental Aspects

Several longitudinal studies indicate that one of the core aspects of social anxiety and withdrawal, behavioral inhibition, has a stable course (Chess & Thomas, 1996; Kagan, Reznick, & Snidman, 1988). For example, inhibited or temperamentally difficult infants often show irregular eating and sleeping patterns, withdrawal from novel situations, poor adaptability, irritable mood, and intense reactions to aversive stimuli (e.g., loud noises). Conversely, less inhibited or temperamentally "easy" infants are marked by more positive mood and good adaptability.

These characteristics—inhibition and adaptability—seem to remain core aspects of an individual's personality with age. For example, inhibited children tend to become more shy, fearful of others, cautious, and introverted during their preschool years. In addition, they become quieter and cling to adults more over time (Albano et al., 1996). This is especially so when new social situations arise. Inhibited children also show more adverse physiological arousal (e.g., increased heart rate) and emotional reactivity in these situations than adaptable children.

Rubin and Stewart (1996), in their developmental model of social withdrawal, stated that these early inhibitions make school-age children more hesitant to explore new social situations outside the home. In turn, this reluctance negatively affects normal play behaviors and prevents the children from acquiring the social and cognitive skills they will need to develop advanced social relationships. The children thus become more anxious during social interactions, avoid them, and feel isolated. Recognizing this social failure, such children may also develop a sense of insecurity and poor self-esteem. They may be predisposed to develop conditions like separation or social anxiety disorder.

Mrs. Nelson reported that Bradley was a somewhat "fussy" baby but not one who was overly difficult to care for. She also said that Bradley played appropriately with others during preschool and was never aggressive. However, she did recall that Bradley's preschool teachers said he was shy and waited for others to approach him before he would interact with them. Exceptions included adults, whom Bradley seemed to like more than his peers. This was demonstrated by his sometimes excessive politeness, compliance, and sensitivity to adult feedback. In addition, Mrs. Nelson admitted that her marital problems sometimes led her to be overprotective and emotionally dependent on her son. As a result, she often kept him physically close to her.

During Bradley's elementary school years, Mrs. Nelson reported some separation anxiety on her son's part, but this seemed to fade over time. Of greater concern, however, were her marital problems, which worsened and caused great disruption in the family. These problems were magnified after the arrival of Bradley's two younger sisters. Mrs. Nelson admitted that her husband's failure to help her with the children caused her to rely more on Bradley, who became responsible for some of the feeding, laundry, and general housecleaning chores. As a result, time that might have been spent developing friendships was instead put toward fulfilling family responsibilities. In addition, these stressful family events reinforced the emotional bond and dependence between Bradley and his mother.

During Bradley's later elementary school years, these patterns deepened. Mrs. Nelson divorced her husband and shifted even more household responsibility onto Bradley. In addition, Bradley was relying more on his schoolwork as a source of self-esteem, which took time away from church group activities, participation in sports, and other social events. Bradley's therapist speculated that Bradley lost some opportunities to build better social skills during this time and therefore had trouble understanding how to approach others or how to maintain conversations.

The developmental aspects of specific play behaviors have also been charted and may have important ramifications for treating children who are socially anxious and withdrawn. With respect to age, for example, very young children are highly egocentric, adult focused, and rule oriented. In the later preschool period, however, cooperation, sharing, and appreciation of others become more evident. For example, a child playing a game learns to wait for another child to take his or her turn before proceeding. Because these behaviors are often the foundation of later social skills development, treatment for socially withdrawn children may be crucial at this time.

Indeed, the successful development of these early play behaviors is intimately tied to later social behaviors like delaying immediate gratification, listening to others, appreciating the viewpoint of others, understanding the concept of friendship, solving problems without aggression, communicating effectively, and being assertive (Cartledge & Milburn, 1995). Children who lack these skills are likely to become deficient in social relationships and perhaps require treatment. In Bradley's case, his self-discipline and conversational skills with adults were well developed but his understanding of peer relationships was not. For example, he was not very knowledgeable about how many friends most people had or even how friendships developed in the first place. In addition, he didn't link the development of friendships to better quality of life. Bradley's communication skills with peers, especially his articulation, needed improvement as well.

Gender differences have also been noted in the development of play and social behaviors. Hops and Greenwood (1988) noted that preschool boys are more likely to play with blocks and movable toys, whereas girls tend to prefer dramatic play and table activities (p. 272). In addition, girls are more likely to play with toys that are traditionally thought of as masculine or feminine, whereas boys prefer toys that are primarily masculine. Boys also tend to be more physically active and spend more time outdoors than girls, which leads to competitive but more frequent and durable social contacts. As noted earlier, however, Bradley often stayed indoors or close to home during his preschool and elementary school years. This may have prevented the establishment of some peer social contacts.

Cartledge and Milburn (1995) also noted that boys, more so than girls, tend to (1) use hostility and coercion in social interactions, (2) become angry when trying to solve a problem, (3) prefer competitive team sports, and (4) become sensitive to peer influence. In Bradley's case, however, his social profile was more traditionally feminine. For example, he was meeker, more adult oriented, and more attracted to solo activities than most boys. The therapist speculated that these characteristics contributed to Bradley's rejection by his male peers.

What about the long-term developmental profile of a child with social anxiety or withdrawal? Social isolation and poor social skills development seem related to various problems in adolescence, including depression, negative self-esteem, and loneliness (Rubin & Stewart, 1996). Other possible consequences include substance abuse, ongoing academic and occupational difficulties, and increasingly poor interpersonal relationships. These potential long-term effects, however, can be mediated by a warm family environment, academic competence, and perceptions that one is sufficiently involved in social activities. In Bradley's case, these mediators were present and could blunt any ill effects of his early social withdrawal. For example, his academic prowess and family support may allow him to become a "late bloomer" and develop more lasting friendships in high school and college.

 **Treatment**

When treating a child who is socially anxious or withdrawn, it is important to note whether the problem is primarily due (1) to a lack of social skills or (2) to social anxiety that blocks the display of already-developed social skills. In Bradley's case, he was originally referred for group therapy regarding his social skills. Because his immediate problem was social phobia and school refusal behavior, however, Bradley first began a program of individual therapy to address his anxiety in specific situations.

Therapy for youngsters with social anxiety often involves exposure to anxiety-provoking social situations and building skills for coping with or reducing the anxiety. In addition, cognitive therapy may be used to help the youngster think more realistically in these social situations. Initially, a common strategy is to build a "social hierarchy" or a list of specific interactive situations that the person avoids. These are usually arranged in order from least to most anxiety-provoking. In Bradley's case, he listed four situations: entering the cafeteria to buy and eat lunch, participating in physical education class, meeting new people, and giving an oral presentation (the last being the most aversive).

The youngster then addresses each item on the social hierarchy in the therapeutic setting, beginning with the lowest anxiety-provoking item. In Bradley's case, the initial item involved his cafeteria behaviors. Bradley discussed his fears about this setting, including dropping food, going too slowly in line, not having enough money to pay the cashier, and being stared at while eating. The therapist first helped Bradley identify thoughts that seemed to have no basis. For example, the therapist asked Bradley if any of the "in-line" behaviors he mentioned had ever happened before. They had not. The therapist thus demonstrated that Bradley did not have enough evidence for his thought and should therefore come up with a more realistic one. Bradley then said he might drop some food or fail to have enough money, but agreed this was unlikely. In addition, the therapist pointed out that Bradley rarely looked at anyone else while eating and therefore should not expect that others were looking at him. To confirm this, the therapist took Bradley to a local cafeteria, where he was shown that no one else was watching him eat.

The therapist then addressed the more difficult items on Bradley's hierarchy, emphasizing the immediate concerns of physical education class and the oral reports. Bradley discussed his fears of each situation, which were remarkably similar: he believed that others were unfairly dismissing him or making rude comments about his performance. In physical education class, for example, Bradley complained about not being picked for a team even though he was good athletically. In English class, he complained that his classmates were either not paying attention to him or were belittling his oral report. In both cases, the therapist pointed out Bradley's tendency to overestimate others' harsh evaluations and criticism, as he did in the cafeteria setting. In addition, she pointed out that Bradley's self-imposed withdrawal perhaps made other youngsters wary or avoidant of him.

The therapist asked Bradley to approach more classmates in his physical education class and ask to be picked for a team before class. To ease this situation, the therapist helped Bradley practice different lines of conversation he could use to introduce himself and let people know of his skill in a particular area (e.g., basketball). Also, with Bradley's permission, the therapist contacted the physical education teacher to ask whether Bradley could make team selections more often and assume a leadership role when possible. Somewhat surprisingly, Bradley adapted to this new situation quite well, and his anxiety during physical education class diminished sharply.

A greater concern was Bradley's refusal to do another oral report. The therapist therefore instructed Bradley to give a series of oral reports to her in the office. At first, this consisted of reading newspaper and magazine articles. Later, brief reports on a topic were assigned by the therapist and researched and given by Bradley. During these reports, the therapist gave Bradley extensive feedback on his presentation skills, especially his voice projection, eye contact with the audience, enunciation of syllables, and control of physical anxiety symptoms. With respect to the latter, for example, Bradley was taught to tense and release different muscle groups that seemed most problematic during his talks. These included tense facial and jaw muscles as well as trembling legs.

After frequent therapy sessions in a one-month period, Bradley's oral presentation skills in the office were good. He was then subjected to a greater audience of unknown people, some of whom had been instructed beforehand to engage in distractions like sighing, not paying attention, and snickering. Bradley found these distractions quite upsetting at first, but subsequently worked through them and gave his reports without much trouble. Cognitive therapy was also used so that Bradley would not "catastrophize" the situation. For example, Bradley eventually acknowledged, after watching his classmates, that not all of them laughed during the oral presentations. In addition, he saw, with the therapist's and teacher's help, that even when people did laugh, the consequences were not dreadful. Following this process, Bradley was asked to give his oral reports in class (the teacher had graciously put off all his remaining reports until last). Bradley was able to give three reports in a 3-day period and, though his performance was only fair, his anxiety did decline with each presentation. In addition, Bradley resumed full-time school attendance.

Following this individual treatment regimen, Bradley participated in group therapy with other children with social skill deficits and social withdrawal. The main purpose here was to build Bradley's skills for meeting new people. For example, all group therapy members were instructed in how to approach someone and introduce themselves. To practice, each group member turned to the one on his or her left, looked that person in the eye, said hello and his or her name, and offered a handshake. Most of the group members found this to be quite anxiety-provoking, but all did at least a fair job. Over time, they developed other skills including the ability to maintain a conversation, compliment others, exit a social situation with grace, and control physical anxiety symptoms. In addition, the group engaged in social outings to practice their skills in real-life settings. Finally, each group member was assigned the task of joining two social activities in their church, school, or neighborhood.

Group therapy for people with social anxiety/withdrawal has two primary advantages: (1) discovering that others have a similar problem, and (2) experiencing a sense of social support. In Bradley's case, both were especially comforting and two members of his group became his good friends. Over the course of his 6-month therapy program, Bradley improved substantially in specific areas of concern, such as speaking in front of others and maintaining a conversation. However, he remained somewhat shy overall and still avoided some social situations when he was anxious. As a result, he was invited for several booster sessions over the next 2 years. By the end of this time, Bradley's overall social functioning was determined to be fair to good.

 ## Discussion Questions

1. What do you think differentiates children who are (a) naturally shy, (b) socially anxious, (c) socially withdrawn, (d) neglected, or (e) rejected? Be sure to explore family and peer factors as well as child characteristics.

2. What characteristics make one child more "popular" than others?

3. Do you think Bradley's social anxiety and withdrawal were due primarily to personal or to family factors? What could a parent do to encourage more appropriate social behaviors in his or her child? What activities would be most effective in helping a child develop positive social skills? What social skills do you think are most important for a child to have?

4. What gender expectations do we generally have regarding social behavior in children? Explore activities that are often considered "off-limits" for boys and girls. How might this harm the development of social skills?

5. What aspects of your own social behavior do you wish you could improve on? What might be the best way to do so? How would you enlist the help of others? How might you help someone who is shy but wants to be more socially active?

6. How might you respond to a child who had no friends but reported that he or she didn't care about it?

7. How might you address a child who had decided to join a gang or hang out with the "wrong crowd?" What are the advantages and disadvantages of this type of social behavior?

8. What else might you have added to Bradley's treatment program? In particular, how might you have included his family members in treat-

ment? How might you improve Bradley's social relationship with his stepfather?

9. What do you think can or should be done in schools to help children with social anxiety or social withdrawal?

CHAPTER THREE

Depression

 Symptoms

Anna Thompson was a 16-year-old African-American female referred to the adolescent unit of an inpatient psychiatric hospital. She was referred by her mother, Mrs. Thompson, who had discovered her daughter bleeding from her wrists in her bedroom. The amount of blood was not substantial, but Mrs. Thompson had brought Anna to a hospital emergency room anyway for treatment. The attending physician had said that Anna was not seriously injured but recommended that the teenager be committed to an inpatient psychiatric hospital for evaluation. Given Anna's recent depressive behaviors, Mrs. Thompson consented to a short-term commitment of her daughter. The next day, Anna was interviewed by a psychiatrist who specialized in adolescent behavior disorders.

Anna was initially hesitant about talking and quite angry at her mother for committing her. After some initial discussion, however, she was more forthcoming. Anna said she had recently moved to a new school in the area following her mother's divorce, and that no one at the school seemed to like her. In particular, she was upset at being in the racial minority and at having developed few friendships. When asked if a specific recent event had upset her, Anna said she felt that other teenagers were making derogatory remarks about her weight as she ate alone during lunch (Anna was quite overweight). Anna could not be more specific, however, and it was unclear whether any remarks had actually been made about her.

Anna stated further that the past 13 months had been difficult ones. Her parents, following a period of marital conflict, had separated and eventually divorced. For reasons that Anna didn't completely understand, her mother had moved out of state with Anna, thus separating her from her father and 13-year-old brother. This was traumatic for Anna, as she had been close to her father and brother but was no longer allowed contact with either one. Anna was enrolled in her new school in August and began attending in September. However, she missed about one-third of school days in the first 2 months, and had not gone at all in the past 2 weeks. Anna complained that she was quite lonely because her mother was often working and because she had not developed any new friendships.

Over the past 2 weeks, Anna reported that her mood was becoming worse. She greatly missed having her entire family together and lamented not being able to spend Thanksgiving with her father and brother (her mother had already said it was impossible). As a result, she had become less active, lying around the house, watching television, and surfing the Internet to chat with others. In the past week, she had gone out of the house only twice, and she was overeating and oversleeping. Her mother was at work a lot and hadn't talked to Anna much in the past 2 weeks. When she did converse, it was usually to try to persuade Anna to go back to school.

The psychiatrist also raised the topic of Anna's injuries from the day before. Anna said she was feeling bad and wondered what it would be like if she committed suicide. In particular, she wondered how her family would feel and who would come to her funeral. She said she was not optimistic about the future and that suicide sometimes seemed preferable to living. Anna insisted, however, that her behavior was not an actual suicide attempt. Instead, she claimed she made a few scrapes with a butterknife to see what would happen. She did get herself to bleed to some extent but did not feel that the injuries were serious (the medical report confirmed Anna's statements). Anna said that her mother came into her room, saw the blood, and "freaked out." Anna was then ordered to get into the car and go to the emergency room. The attending physician had asked about her injuries, and Anna had told him truthfully what she had done. She was then transferred to her current unit with a person sitting outside her room to watch her.

The psychiatrist asked Anna if she had any current thoughts about harming herself, and Anna said no. She reiterated that she had not wanted to kill herself the day before and that she now wanted to leave the unit. She also asked to see her mother, and was told she would see her that evening. Anna promised the psychiatrist not to harm herself on the unit and to speak with him immediately should she have any suicidal thoughts or impulses. Anna was then placed on a mild sedative and slept for the remaining afternoon.

The psychiatrist also interviewed Anna's mother, Mrs. Thompson, who provided more information about the family situation. Mrs. Thompson said that she and her husband had had many arguments in the past about several issues, most notably his alcohol use and the family's financial status. The last straw came, however, when Mrs. Thompson caught her husband leaning over Anna as she slept in her bed. Although never proven, Mrs. Thompson suspected that Anna was sexually abused by her father. Anna denied this in conversations with her mother, but Mrs. Thompson felt it was best that she and Anna leave the state. Mrs. Thompson indicated that she parted company with her son as well because he was unruly and because they had a poor relationship.

With respect to recent events, Mrs. Thompson confirmed some of Anna's reports. For example, she confirmed that she was quite busy at work and not able to devote the kind of attention to Anna that her daughter was used to. However, the two did share time together on the weekends, though not in the past 3 weeks, and they had good rapport. Mrs. Thompson also confirmed that she and Anna had little contact with Anna's father and brother. This would include, she said, the upcoming holiday season.

Mrs. Thompson also verified that Anna had missed a lot of school in the past 2 months and did not seem too successful at making new friends. Both women were concerned about Anna's weight, and Mrs. Thompson knew this was a major source of embarrassment and frustration for her daughter. Despite these situations, however, Mrs. Thompson said she was shocked to find Anna bleeding in her bedroom. The possibility of suicide had never been considered by Mrs. Thompson, but the apparent seriousness of the situation led her to agree to the inpatient commitment.

With Mrs. Thompson's permission, the psychiatrist also spoke with Anna's guidance counselor at school. The counselor, Mrs. Deetz, was quite upset about Anna's condition and revealed that Anna had made a comment about suicide one month earlier. Apparently, Anna had come to Mrs. Deetz's office and complained that several students in her physical education class were making fun of her weight. Anna began to cry, complained that she was unable to make any friends, and said "I wish I was dead." Mrs. Deetz then changed Anna's schedule so that she wouldn't have to attend that particular physical education class. She also made several recommendations regarding extracurricular activities, but Anna dismissed them because she would be in the racial minority. Mrs. Deetz insisted, however, that Anna's concerns about social rejection were unfounded. She remained concerned about Anna and offered to assist the psychiatrist in whatever way possible.

The psychiatrist interviewed Anna again the next day and confirmed that she had no current suicidal thoughts or impulses. He placed her on a low dose of antidepressant medication and asked her to attend group therapy sessions that morning and evening. Anna agreed, and the psychiatrist noted that her mood was somewhat improved from the day before. However, given the information received so far, the psychiatrist suspected that Anna had just experienced a major depressive episode and should be kept on suicide watch.

Assessment

According to the *DSM-IV*, the essential feature of a major depressive episode is "a period of at least two weeks during which there is either depressed mood or the loss of interest or pleasure in nearly all activities. In children and adolescents, the mood may be irritable rather than sad" (APA, 1994, p. 320). During this 2-week period, the person must experience five of the following symptoms to qualify for the disorder: constant depressed mood, lack of interest in previously enjoyable activities, significant weight loss or gain, difficulty sleeping or oversleeping each day, restlessness or feeling very slowed down, daily fatigue, feelings of inappropriate guilt or worthlessness, difficulty concentrating or making decisions, and suicidal thoughts or attempts. In addition, the symptoms must cause significant interference in daily life functioning; must not be linked to mania; and must not be due to substance use, a medical condition, or an understandable reaction to life events like a death in the family.

In Anna's case, many of these symptoms seemed to apply. For example, her mood over the past month had been quite depressed, and she rarely initiated activities for fun. She did not show appreciable weight gain, but was overeating and oversleeping. This latter activity, known as hypersomnia, is common to persons with depression who want to escape aversive life events. Early-morning wakenings are also common in this population, but were not reported by Anna. In addition, Anna said she felt "very slowed down" and often tired. Further conversations revealed that she felt guilty about her parent's breakup as well, even though this was not warranted. Difficulties in concentration were not reported, but this may have been because Anna was not regularly attending school. Each of these depressive symptoms, in combination with Anna's suicidal thoughts and gesture, led the psychiatrist to his initial diagnosis.

The assessment of depression in adolescents can take many forms, including laboratory testing, interviews, self-report measures, and direct observation. While Anna was in the inpatient hospital, she underwent various medical tests to identify different conditions that might explain her depression. Several neurological and medical conditions can produce symptoms of depression, including sleep apnea, Addison's disease, diabetes, parathyroid disorders, infections, and lead intoxication, among others (Kashani & McNaul, 1997). A variety of substances can also produce symptoms of depression. In Anna's case, however, none of these conditions or substances were evident.

One specific laboratory test for depression that is sometimes used for adults, but less so for youngsters, is the dexamethasone suppression test (DST). Here, a person is evaluated for his or her ability to suppress cortisol secretion. Persons with depression tend to have high levels of cortisol, a stress-induced hormone. Unfortunately, the DST is not very useful or reliable for youngsters (Compas, 1997). For example, a positive finding does not necessarily mean a person has depression, only that one marker is present. In Anna's case, however, a negative DST result was found.

An interview is particularly important when assessing individuals with possible depression. This is true not only for the information that is obtained but also for developing rapport with someone who may be initially unwilling to share very personal issues. Structured interviews are available for this population, including the Schedule for Affective Disorders and Schizophrenia for School-Aged Children (Kaufman et al., 1997). However, most mental health professionals, including the psychiatrist in this case, rely on their own unstructured interview. This is done so that characteristics unique to a certain case can be explored in depth.

In an interview of someone with possible depression, a number of topics should be explored. These topics include symptom description, history of symptoms, family history, and associated problems like anxiety, substance use, and acting-out behaviors. The youngster's perception of his or her own symptoms, overall situation, and others should be discussed as well. In addition, of course, an interviewer should assess whether someone with depression has thoughts about harming himself or herself. Many people who attempt suicide are willing to communicate their intent beforehand and accurately convey their plan for doing so. In general, the more detailed the suicide plan, the more the person is at risk for harm. Other important signs should be examined as well, including sudden changes in behavior and recent environmental stressors (e.g., loss of a relationship).

Anna's symptom history was described earlier, and her perceptions of her situation and significant others in her life were generally discussed during inpatient group therapy sessions. Anna was reportedly confused by recent life events, especially by her mother's quick departure from Anna's father and brother. She said she missed the rest of her family and former friends. She also admitted feeling scared and upset on the psychiatric unit, but acknowledged that she had more social contact now than she had had in the past 6 weeks.

In many inpatient and outpatient settings, self-report measures are also commonly used to assess depression. Primary examples include the Reynolds Adolescent Depression Scale (Reynolds, 1987), Children's Depression Scale (Tisher & Lang, 1983), and Children's Depression Inventory (CDI; Kovacs, 1992). In Anna's case, she was administered the CDI during her inpatient stay and during her later outpatient counseling. The CDI is a 27-item measure of recent depressive symptoms like feeling sad, crying, self-blame, indecisiveness, fatigue, eating and sleeping problems, and loneliness.

At the time of Anna's admission to the psychiatric hospital, her CDI score was in the clinical range (27). She gave several items high ratings, particularly those related to feeling sad, tired, lonely, and unmotivated. By the end of her 3-week stay, however, her score was reduced to 15 (in the normal range). Anna was also assessed for hopelessness, a construct often associated with depression in general and suicide in particular. A common measure for this is the Hopelessness Scale for Children (Kazdin, Rodgers, & Colbus, 1986), a 17-item true-false instrument that emphasizes the youngster's feelings about the future. Anna did not complete this scale, but her answers to the psychiatrist's questions indicated her level of hopelessness to be moderate to high.

Direct observation of behavior may also be used to assess those with depression. In particular, assessors should look for these characteristics:

1. sad facial expressions
2. decreased social and motor activity (i.e., less talking, game-playing, interactions with others)
3. solitary behavior (e.g., reading, watching television by oneself)
4. slow speech
5. decreased eye contact
6. arguing
7. poor affect in the form of frowning, complaining, or lack of smiling.

(Matson, 1989)

Initially, hospital staff members noted some of these characteristics in Anna. For example, they saw that Anna kept to herself unless someone encouraged her to attend group activities. In addition, Anna often looked sad and talked softly to others.

Other forms of assessment for this population include peer and adult ratings (Kazdin, 1988). In Anna's case, peer ratings were not obtained because her classmates didn't know her very well. However, Mrs. Thompson's ratings on the Child Behavior Checklist were obtained during later outpatient treatment (Achenbach, 1991a). These ratings indicated a moderate to high degree of loneliness, sadness, crying, and guilt on Anna's part.

Causes and Maintaining Variables

Many cases of depression are caused by a mixture of biological/genetic and psychological factors. As indicated earlier, those with depression sometimes have neuroendocrine changes like abnormal cortisol regulation or reduced growth hormone secretion. Changes in the neurotransmitters norepinephrine and serotonin have been implicated in depression as well. Low levels of each have been noted in this population, and drugs that increase the levels of these neurotransmitters are good antidepressants. Other studies have looked at the role of melatonin and acetylcholine in causing adolescent depression (Kashani & McNaul, 1997). In Anna's case, no major physical abnormalities were present, although it is possible that some undetected physiology was responsible for some of her depressive symptoms (e.g., oversleeping). In addition,

Anna did not respond much to antidepressant medication, suggesting that her depression was more environmentally based, or exogenous, than biologically based, or endogenous.

Genetic factors may also predispose some adolescents toward depression. Studies indicate that identical twins are about twice as likely to share depressive symptoms than fraternal twins. Youngsters whose natural parents had depression are also more likely than controls to show depression themselves, even when raised by adoptive, nondepressed parents. In addition, family studies of depressed adolescents reveal that immediate family members are more likely to be depressed than the general population. This is especially true if the youngster's depression develops early and if his or her relatives have alcoholism (Carlson & Abbott, 1995). One should keep in mind, however, that genetic studies do not explain all the variance associated with adolescent depression. Environmental factors are often needed to trigger biological predispositions toward depression.

In Anna's case, her family history regarding depression was spotty. Mrs. Thompson apparently had some depressive symptoms herself, but it was unclear whether these were simply normal reactions to recent life events. Anna's father was also thought to have a history of depression and alcoholism, but Anna's mother did not know whether he'd ever experienced a major depressive episode. In addition, Anna herself had never experienced major depression earlier in life. Possibly, then, her current state was more environmentally based. However, few additional family members were known to Anna or her mother, so a more detailed family history of depression was not available.

Psychological theories of depression may have been more pertinent to Anna's case. Psychodynamic theory alleges that depression results from an early development of overdependence on others. Subsequently, when an overdependent person loses someone close, either through perceived loss, death, abandonment, or, in Anna's case, separation, that person will engage in introjection. Introjection is a process whereby the person internalizes feelings of anger and hatred toward the lost one. As a result, feelings of self-blame and worthlessness occur and depression begins.

A more widely accepted psychological model of mood disorder is a behavioral one. This model holds that depression generally results from (1) decreased reinforcement for active, prosocial behavior and (2) increased reinforcement for depressed behavior. For example, an adolescent may do all the things expected of him, like going to school, finishing chores, completing homework, and working at a part-time job. If these behaviors are taken for granted by others, however, the youth receives little positive attention. Conversely, if the adolescent becomes depressed and his or her performance in these activities slips, then others may take notice, provide sympathy and support, and inadvertently reward the depressive symptoms. In addition, suicidal gestures, like the one displayed by Anna, may be done for attention.

Anna was not depressed solely for attention, but she did relish the social contact that her situation brought. During her inpatient stay, for example, she said that her mother was now more interested in her life than before. In addition, she came to enjoy talking to the other adolescents and staff members on her inpatient ward. In fact, some of the nurses grumbled that Anna was a general nuisance as her discharge approached; she constantly asked them personal questions and wondered aloud if she could maintain contact with them. Mrs. Thompson and the psychiatrist noted this as well and agreed that Mrs. Thompson would have to encourage and reward Anna's future social behavior with peers.

A related behavioral theory of depression holds that poor social skills are central to the disorder (Lewinsohn, 1974). However, Anna was capable of talking and making friends when she was motivated to do so, as she was on the inpatient ward. In addition, Rehm's (1977) self-control model stipulates that people with depression selectively attend to negative life events, overpunish and underreward themselves, and focus on unrealistic goals and short-term outcomes. This model did apply somewhat to Anna, who focused almost exclusively on the negative aspects of her family and her social life. In addition, when Anna focused on the future, it was often in the form of "pie-in-the-sky" expectations. For example, Anna thought that she and her mother would eventually reconcile with her father, and that she could meet all of her high school obligations after entering college.

One of the most popular psychological models of depression is Beck's cognitive theory, which emphasizes dysfunctional ways of viewing oneself, the world, and the future (Beck, Rush, Shaw, & Emery, 1980). For example, some youngsters with depression have cognitive distortions about surrounding events and think that things are worse than they actually are. An adolescent may believe, for instance, that everyone will laugh at him during an oral presentation, despite clear evidence to the contrary. This is known as catastrophization. In Anna's case, she displayed personalization, or the attribution of external events to oneself without cause. For example, she thought that classmates who were whispering in the hallway were necessarily talking about her and making rude remarks. However, no evidence existed to support this thought.

A related cognitive theory of depression is learned helplessness, which links sadness to inaccurate attributions about different life events (Abramson, Seligman, & Teasdale, 1978). In particular, those with depression are thought to attribute the causes of negative events to internal, global, and stable factors. For example, failure on a test might result in negative self-statements regarding the situation's internality (e.g., "It was my fault"), globality ("I am a failure at everything"), and stability ("I will always fail these tests"). Such thinking is often the result of past experiences in which a person felt or had little control over environmental events. In Anna's case, she often blamed negative, uncontrollable life events like her parents' divorce on herself. She was also quite pessimistic about her future social life. However, thoughts like these are often true of nondepressed adolescents as well. Therefore, assessing cognitive symptoms of depression in adolescents is sometimes difficult.

Other factors can also be related to the onset and maintenance of depression, such as the following:

unassertiveness	ineffective coping styles
impulsivity	poor school performance
anxiety	detached parents
low peer attachment	disorganized or hostile families
poor social support	negative reactions to life stressors
unpopularity	economic disadvantage
problem-solving deficits	(Hammen & Rudolph, 1996)

Several of these applied to Anna, especially her troublesome family situation, impulsive behavior, lack of friendships, and her belief that she had little support from others.

Several theorists have combined many of the factors just described into an integrative model of depression (e.g., Birmaher et al., 1996; Hammen & Rudolph, 1996). Some people are likely have a genetic predisposition toward depression as well as troublesome family experiences, poor interpersonal skills and coping styles, and feelings of inadequacy. These biological and psychological predispositions may be triggered later by stressful life events to produce depression. The severity of a person's depression can be mediated, however, by stress hormones, attributions, social contacts and support, and degree of hopelessness, among other variables. In Anna's case, a general predisposition toward depression may have developed from her negative family interactions. Then, a stressful move to a new school, lack of social support, and cognitive distortions may have conspired to help produce her major depressive episode.

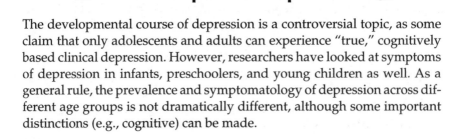

Developmental Aspects

The developmental course of depression is a controversial topic, as some claim that only adolescents and adults can experience "true," cognitively based clinical depression. However, researchers have looked at symptoms of depression in infants, preschoolers, and young children as well. As a general rule, the prevalence and symptomatology of depression across different age groups is not dramatically different, although some important distinctions (e.g., cognitive) can be made.

In very young children, for example, "depression" may be in the form of more behavioral symptoms like social withdrawal or indiscriminate attachments (e.g., *DSM-IV* reactive attachment disorder of infancy or early childhood). Greenspan (1997) has noted other developmental problems in infants that may provide a basis for later emotional difficulties as well. Such problems include deficits in self-regulation, curiosity, communication, behavioral organization, and representational capacity.

In preschoolers, depression becomes somewhat easier to identify as children show advanced motor behavior and talk more about basic emotions. In general, depression in preschoolers is marked by withdrawal, slow movement, crying, lack of growth, and somatic complaints like stomachaches. However, these symptoms could be due to other disorders, and symptoms of depression are sometimes manifested by oppositional behavior at this age. Therefore, a diagnosis of depression is often difficult to make in preschoolers.

During the school-age period, children become more able and willing to express themselves when they feel emotionally distraught. Typical depressive symptoms in 6- to 12-year-olds include somatic complaints like headaches and stomachaches, declining school performance, poor concentration, crying, irritability, unhappy mood, fatigue, insomnia, increased or decreased motor activity, worry, and low self-esteem (Mitchell, McCauley, Burke, & Moss, 1988). In addition, suicidal thoughts and attempts become more prevalent as children age. However, these symptoms are sometimes more indicative of other disorders. Also, some children with depression show no overt symptoms. For example, Mrs. Thompson reported that Anna never had any obvious behavior problems.

Depression in adolescence and adulthood is closer to the "classic" depression represented by *DSM-IV* criteria. Specifically, adolescents and adults tend to show more depressed mood, psychomotor retardation, and sleep problems than preschoolers or school-age children. In addition, depression in adolescents and adults is more likely to be marked by psychotic features, whereas depression in preschoolers and school-age children is more likely to be marked by separation anxiety disorder (Kovacs, 1996). Depressed appearance, somatic complaints, and low self-esteem are also not as prominent in older persons with depression as they are in younger ones (Carlson & Kashani, 1988).

Other symptoms common to adolescents with depression were evident in Anna. For example, she was socially withdrawn, especially after her move. Those with depression sometimes shy away from new stimuli or lack the energy to cope with new interpersonal situations. Anna seemed to enjoy social contact, but she was inhibited by fears of rejection and humiliation. Indeed, symptoms of worry and anxiety are common to adolescents with depression. Anna constantly worried about her life situation, in particular the family's finances, her social status, and her mother's general welfare. In fact, Anna technically met diagnostic criteria for generalized anxiety disorder, which involves pervasive worrying. Anna's cognitive distortions, which were mentioned earlier, tended to exacerbate these anxiety symptoms as well.

Other symptoms particularly common to adolescents with depression include disruptive behaviors, somatic complaints, low self-esteem regarding body image, and suicidal ideation (Hammen & Rudolph, 1996). Anna did not have any acting-out behavior problems but did have somatic complaints like headaches and stomachaches. In addition, she was highly concerned and depressed about her weight. Anna had gained a substantial amount of weight in the past few months and felt socially rejected as a result. However, her continued overeating and lack of participation in group activities were not helping matters. Therefore, weight management became an important part of her outpatient treatment plan. Finally, Anna was obviously having thoughts about suicide, and her suicidal gesture indicated that she was at greater risk than the general population for harming herself. The psychiatrist felt that Anna's gesture was largely the result of a desire for attention and was related to Anna's sometimes impulsive behavior.

In general, the average length of a major depressive episode in adolescents is 16 to 36 weeks (Del Medico, Weller, & Weller, 1996). The length of an episode may be related to the severity of life events, degree of suicidal ideation, and presence of comorbid disorders. With respect to the latter, for example, a depressive episode will tend to last longer if it is associated with anorexia, oppositional defiant or conduct disorder, an anxiety disorder, or substance abuse. As mentioned earlier, Anna did have substantial anxiety. In addition, the length of a major depressive episode increases with the presence of family dysfunction, as was the case for Anna. In particular, a high level of expressed emotion, or open hostility among family members, aggravates depression in youngsters. Low self-esteem and low self-confidence also serve to lengthen their depression (Del Medico et al., 1996).

Data indicate that 40% of those who have experienced one major depressive episode will eventually experience a second episode within 2 years. About 70% will eventually experience a second episode within 5 years (Birmaher et al., 1996). A large percentage of those with a depressive episode will also continue to display dysthymia, or ongoing depressed mood without major interference in daily life functioning (Keller, Lavori, Endicott, Coryell, & Klerman, 1983). In Anna's case, for example, she continued to experience occasional depressed mood and social withdrawal even after outpatient therapy.

The average recovery time from a major depressive episode in adolescents is 7 to 9 months, and several factors are related to good recovery (Kovacs, 1996). Two important ones are early referral to treatment and later age of onset of the first major depressive episode. Both of these factors were present in Anna's case. Ongoing access to treatment and family and social support are also key predictors of whether an adolescent will remain depressed. In Anna's case, as discussed next, referral to outpatient therapy and the development of peer support were critical aspects of her recovery. The latter was especially pertinent because Mrs. Thompson continued to deny Anna any contact with her father or brother.

Treatment

Treatment for adolescents with depression may occur in both inpatient and outpatient settings, as it did for Anna. Inpatient therapy is usually designed to reduce severe depressive symptoms, suicidal ideation, and imminent harm. Treatments to accomplish this, in addition to individual and family therapy, include antidepressant medication, group therapy, and milieu therapy. Milieu therapy involves setting up an environment that encourages a client to take responsibility for his or her recovery and participate actively in treatment activities. In Anna's case, for example, the psychiatrist, nurses, and other staff members encouraged her to attend group therapy sessions and maintain good personal hygiene.

Group therapy typically focuses on building social support as well as social, conversational, and problem-solving skills (Kashani & McNaul, 1997). In an inpatient setting like Anna's, short-term group therapy is the norm. Anna's stay on the unit was 3 weeks, as it was for many of the other adolescents there, so group therapists emphasized discussion and support. During this time, Anna spoke about her recent problems and fears, and she discovered that her concerns often overlapped with concerns of others in the group. None of Anna's primary problems were completely solved, but her mood did generally improve during her hospital stay.

Antidepressant medications for adolescents include tricyclic antidepressants, selective serotonin reuptake inhibitors (SSRIs), and monoamine oxidase (MAO) inhibitors. Several tricyclic antidepressants are available, including imipramine, amitriptyline, nortriptyline, and desipramine. However, data indicate that these are not much better than placebo treatment for depressed adolescents. The SSRI studied most in adolescents with depression is fluoxetine (Prozac), and data indicate this drug to be slightly more effective than placebo, especially for those with anxiety symptoms. Finally, MAO inhibitors are sometimes used if tricyclic and SSRI antidepressants do not work, but they must be used carefully given their potentially dangerous side effects. Tranylcypromine is a common MAO inhibitor, and some positive response to the medication has been shown in youngsters.

Anna was placed on a low dose of fluoxetine while in the hospital. Over the course of her 3-week stay, she told the psychiatrist that her mood improved, but it was unclear whether this was due to the drug or Anna's increased social contact. Anna did report, however, a substantial decrease in anxiety, which may have been the result of the fluoxetine.

Following her brief stay in the hospital, Anna was referred to a clinical psychologist for outpatient therapy. Outpatient therapy for adolescent depression often involves a behavioral approach, which may be supplemented by medication. In Anna's case, her psychological therapy was supplemented with fluoxetine for 6 months, after which the drug was discontinued. Behavior therapy for clients with depression often includes scheduling additional activities, increasing positive reinforcement from others, building social skills, and practicing social skills in different settings.

At the beginning of outpatient therapy, the psychologist, Anna, and Mrs. Thompson discussed several treatment goals, including resumption of school attendance, improved mood and socialization, and weight loss. The psychologist also made a verbal contract with Anna regarding suicide. Anna agreed to contact her mother or the therapist whenever she had thoughts of suicide or was tempted to hurt herself.

After developing a good rapport with Anna, the psychologist helped her develop ways of increasing her self-esteem and socialization. Using a problem-solving approach, the two decided that Anna could join a local weight-loss clinic, resume school attendance part-time, and participate in at least one peer activity. Anna adopted these solutions and within 2 months had lost some weight, received partial academic credit through an after-school program, and started singing in the school choir. In addition, the therapist worked with Mrs. Thompson to increase her time with Anna on the weekends and participate in at least one activity with her daughter outside the home. Mrs. Thompson also encouraged Anna to ask others to visit the house for dinner.

The therapist also focused on Anna's social skills, which were good but needed "fine-tuning." For example, Anna had difficulty approaching people she didn't know well, especially boys. The therapist worked with Anna to help her start and maintain conversations, integrate verbal and nonverbal behavior, and apply these skills to those she met at school. Anna had little difficulty talking to people once she knew them, and she was eventually able to connect with some of the members of her choir and after-school class. At times, Anna relapsed by avoiding these situations and spending more time with her mother, but the therapist and Mrs. Thompson continuously encouraged Anna to maintain her social contacts with her peers.

Over the course of therapy, Anna's psychologist recognized that some deeper problems needed to be addressed as well. For example, Anna continued to put herself down, complain about her family situation, and suspect others of wrongdoing. The psychologist felt that Anna was intelligent and capable of absorbing some aspects of cognitive therapy, and this became a major focus of her later stages of treatment. Cognitive therapy often involves several steps. In general, clients are taught to do the following:

1. Self-monitor their thoughts
2. Understand the connection between their thoughts and their behaviors
3. Evaluate each thought for its accuracy
4. Substitute more positive and realistic thoughts for inaccurate ones

As mentioned earlier, one of Anna's ongoing cognitive distortions was personalization, or her belief that others were purposely acting against her. Initially, the therapist asked Anna to keep a daily log of times when she felt that others were making derogatory statements or otherwise being rude to her. In the meantime, the therapist pointed out how Anna's thoughts were sometimes related to her avoidant behavior and depression. For example, Anna might see classmates snickering and looking at her, and think they were talking about her. Anna would then overgeneralize the incident to other people she knew and subsequently avoid certain social situations. As her social withdrawal increased, she would become depressed. From Anna's log, the therapist identified other examples of how Anna's thoughts could lead to depressive behaviors.

Next, the therapist asked Anna to challenge her negative thoughts directly. Specifically, Anna was asked to examine any evidence for and against each thought. If Anna could not find any credible evidence to support her thought, then she was asked to find a more logical and realistic explanation (e.g., the girls are talking about something else). In addition, the therapist helped Anna think about what to do even if someone *was* acting rudely toward her. Over time, Anna's suspiciousness and depressive symptoms gradually declined.

Anna remained in outpatient therapy for about a year, after which time the therapist thought she was functioning well enough to end treatment. Some issues did remain unresolved, however. For example, Mrs. Thompson remained adamant about the current family situation, continuing to ban Anna from seeing her father and brother. Anna felt occasionally sad about this but had adapted well to her new lifestyle and now had some good friendships. Telephone contact with her 6 months after therapy revealed no recurrence of major depression or suicide attempt.

Discussion Questions

1. Do you believe that depression truly exists in infants, preschoolers, and school-age children? Defend your answer. What symptoms do you feel are most indicative of depression at different ages?

2. Why do you think more girls than boys display depression? Be sure to explore issues of socialization. Also, do you think that women report being depressed more than men? If so, why might this be the case?

3. Why do you think that males tend to choose more lethal methods for committing suicide than do females?

4. What type of person is most likely to commit suicide by making the act seem like an accident? What do you suppose his or her motivations for doing so would be?

5. What questions would you most want to ask someone who seems depressed? How would you go about discovering whether the person is thinking about suicide, and what would you do with this information?

6. Everyone seems to get depressed at one time or another. What life events cause you to feel sad or "down in the dumps?" What separates "normal" depression from "abnormal" depression? Was Anna's depression normal or abnormal? Why do you think so?

7. What are the major ethical issues involved in giving medication to children or adolescents with depression? Given that depression is often a "warning sign" that something is wrong, explore how medication might prevent one from solving serious life problems.

8. How might you treat an adolescent with depression who does not want to talk with you? How might you change your treatment plan for a teenager with depression if he or she also had a drinking problem, was the victim of abuse, or had symptoms of conduct disorder?

CHAPTER FOUR

Eating Disorder

Symptoms

Andrea Weston was a 17-year-old Caucasian female referred to a clinical psychologist who specialized in anxiety, depressive, and eating disorders. At the time of her initial assessment, Andrea was a senior in high school. She was referred by her parents, Mr. and Mrs. Weston, for what they described as "very unusual behavior." During his initial telephone conversation with the psychologist, for example, Mr. Weston said that Andrea was recently caught by her sister eating a large amount of sweet foods. The incident was especially worrisome because Andrea had then struck her sister in the face, an act she had never committed before. Mr. Weston also claimed that Andrea was becoming more irritable, withdrawn, and argumentative. In particular, her relationship with her boyfriend was tempestuous and a source of tension between Andrea and her parents. Mr. Weston also said that Andrea was reluctant to enter therapy and had agreed to do so only if the entire family was involved.

During the initial interview, the psychologist found Andrea to be somewhat gaunt and diminutive, but not seriously underweight. Instead, her major symptoms initially seemed depressive in nature. Andrea reported that, over the course of the school year (it was now early February), she had experienced a number of stressful events that felt overwhelming. She said her parents were constantly interfering with her life, giving her advice on how to look, act, and work toward the future. In particular, her mother often "poked her nose" into Andrea's affairs, especially her appearance, schoolwork, social life, and dating. In addition, Andrea said that she was doing poorly at school, claiming a severe case of "senioritis." On top of this, Andrea said she felt lonely and rejected as many of her friends seemed to be joining other social groups.

Andrea was asked about recent events that triggered her father's call to the psychologist and said that both her parents were unhappy with her boyfriend of the past 5 months. Both objected to his older age (20 years), rough demeanor, and questionable status, characteristics that Andrea seemed to relish. When asked for more details, Andrea simply responded that this was her first real boyfriend and that her parents "just don't want me to have any independence." Andrea did not openly admit that annoying her parents was a fringe benefit of dating her boyfriend, but her tone led the psychologist to this conclusion.

The psychologist also asked Andrea about various depressive symptoms, and she appeared to have several. For example, she was sad, often felt tired, had low self-esteem, and occasionally thought about suicide. The psychologist then made a contract with Andrea in which she promised to contact the psychologist following suicidal ideation or prior to any suicide attempt. Andrea was also quite concerned about her weight and body size, which she described as "chubby" and unappealing to others. The psychologist saw that Andrea was a bit thin, but that her weight was generally appropriate for her age, gender, and height. Andrea said that her parents, especially her mother, made frequent comments about her weight as she grew up. For example, they sometimes said she needed to watch her figure if she was going to fit in with her social group. As a result, Andrea was particularly sensitive about her weight and felt bad whenever she gained a few pounds or "felt fat."

When asked about her recent episode of binge eating, Andrea became tearful and spoke softly. She said she began dieting about 3 months earlier while dating her current boyfriend. He had made an offhand comment about her weight, which Andrea took immediately as a threat that he would not see her unless she lost weight. She then lost weight by eliminating certain foods from her diet and by eating substantially less than before. Andrea lost about 20 pounds, reaching her current weight of 100 pounds, and said that she felt more attractive but still inadequate. She also felt anxious about her relationship with her boyfriend and other friends. In particular, she felt they were becoming more distant from her and tended to blame this on her weight.

As Andrea lost weight, however, her sense of sadness and anxiety did not go away, and she often felt hungry. At this point, about 2 months ago, she began to binge secretly. The binges usually consisted of sweet foods like ice cream, cake, candy bars, and soft drinks. Andrea said the binges occurred only once every other week, but the psychologist suspected that they occurred more frequently. Andrea also reported that the binges made her feel "gross and fat," so she started vomiting afterward. Andrea said that she vomited only twice and that she no longer binged or vomited, but again the psychologist found this doubtful.

The psychologist then interviewed Mr. and Mrs. Weston, who confirmed much of Andrea's report but made the situation sound more dire.

For example, Mrs. Weston revealed that Andrea had been hospitalized for a suicide attempt the previous year and was continuing to show symptoms of depression. Further questioning revealed that the "suicide attempt" was actually a car accident involving Andrea as the driver. Andrea had said afterward that she wished she had died in the accident, but it was unclear that she had actually tried to kill herself. The psychologist took note of Mrs. Weston's tendency to make events like these sound quite dramatic.

Mr. and Mrs. Weston also described some recently upsetting events regarding Andrea. At the top of their list was her relationship with her boyfriend, whom the parents described as a "bad seed." Further questioning revealed that Andrea's boyfriend had a history of drug use and had been arrested for theft twice in the past 4 years. In addition, Mr. and Mrs. Weston felt that Andrea was now sexually active with her boyfriend and worried about the possible consequences. They said their attempts to dissuade Andrea from dating the man were unsuccessful. Mr. and Mrs. Weston also noted that Andrea's grades were suffering, that her social life was shrinking, and that her participation in family activities was declining. Both parents had argued vehemently with Andrea about these issues in the past few months, but their concern had produced no change in their daughter's behavior. Both, however, described their relationship with Andrea as "excellent."

The psychologist also asked about Andrea's weight and eating habits. Mrs. Weston repeated the "binge" story given earlier by her husband, and added that she felt Andrea was too fussy about the way she looked. Mrs. Weston said that her daughter had always had a weight problem, and that she, Mrs. Weston, had always tried to control Andrea's diet. Specifically, Mrs. Weston said that Andrea's weight "fluctuated like a yo-yo" as her moods changed. (The psychologist noted the paradox in Mrs. Weston's behavior: She claimed that Andrea was too fussy about appearances but emphasized such appearances herself.) Both parents became more concerned when Andrea revealed her recent pattern of binge eating, and speculated that she was vomiting as well. Their primary treatment goal, however, was to "help Andrea overcome her feelings of inadequacy."

With Mr. and Mrs. Weston's permission, the psychologist also spoke with Andrea's schoolteachers. All indicated that Andrea was normally a good student but that her grades had slipped recently because of incomplete homework. They also noted that Andrea seemed preoccupied with other matters and speculated that her home life was the cause of her recent academic problems. Based on this early information from Andrea, her parents, and her teachers, the psychologist made a preliminary conclusion that Andrea had subclinical anorexia nervosa of the binging/purging subtype as well as subclinical depression.

Assessment

According to the *DSM-IV*, the essential features of anorexia nervosa are these:

1. Refusal to maintain a minimally normal body weight
2. Intense fear of gaining weight
3. Significant perceptual disturbance regarding one's body shape or size
4. Amenorrhea in postmenarcheal females (APA, 1994, p. 539).

Specifically, those with anorexia maintain their body weight at less than 85% of normal weight for age and height. In addition, they commonly fear weight gain even when they are underweight, base their self-worth on weight, and/or deny that a problem exists. Female amenorrhea in anorexia refers to the absence of three consecutive menstrual cycles.

Anorexia nervosa may be of (1) the restricting type, in which a person has lost weight and is not binging or purging, or (2) the binge eating/purging type, in which a person engages in binge-eating as well as purging through vomiting, laxative abuse, or excessive exercise. According to the *DSM-IV*, a binge is defined as "eating in a discrete period of time an amount of food that is definitely larger than most individuals would eat under similar circumstances" (p. 545).

In Andrea's case, diagnosis was difficult. The psychologist tentatively refrained from a diagnosis of bulimia nervosa because Andrea's binge eating and purging was found to occur too infrequently to meet diagnostic criteria. *DSM-IV* criteria for bulimia nervosa mandate an average of two binge-purge episodes a week for 3 months. This left a possible diagnosis of anorexia nervosa with binge-eating/purging features, a common finding in those with eating disorders. Andrea was not ameorrheic or more than 15% underweight, but she had lost 20 pounds in the past several weeks. If she continued on this path, as she seemed inclined to do, then she'd be seriously underweight in a short period of time.

The psychologist initially preferred a diagnosis of anorexia nervosa as well because of Andrea's fear of weight gain and worry about losing her boyfriend. Andrea was convinced that her boyfriend and other friends would abandon her if she gained weight, and that her parents would comment on her "obesity." She also felt she would look "ugly." In addition, the psychologist noticed that Andrea was oblivious to the negative consequences of losing more weight and seemed to judge her self-worth almost solely on the way her body looked. According to the *DSM-IV*, those who meet most but not all the symptoms of anorexia nervosa, like Andrea, may receive a diagnosis of "eating disorder not otherwise specified." The psychologist also felt that Andrea had depressive symptoms that needed treatment, although she didn't meet criteria for a major depressive episode.

The assessment of those with anorexia nervosa should initially begin with a medical examination, as severe physical complications and even death can result. According to Herzog and Beresin (1997), anorexia may result in a number of common physical problems:

Gastrointestinal distress	Dry skin
Bloating	Edema
Dizziness	Anemia
Dehydration	Cardiovascular abnormalities
Electrolyte imbalances	Renal dysfunction
Lethargy	Atypical neurological patterns

For those who induce vomiting, erosion of the dental enamel may also be evident. In Andrea's case, however, no major physical symptoms were present and no medical examination was conducted.

According to Garner and Garner (1992), a psychological assessment or interview of those with eating disorders should concentrate on the following:

1. Attitudes toward weight and body shape
2. Characteristics of binging and purging
3. Feelings of loss of control, distress, anxiety, and depression
4. Impulsive behaviors
5. History of abuse
6. Maladaptive personality traits
7. Social and family functioning
8. Reasons for seeking treatment and motivation for change

With respect to the first point, Andrea said that she and her mother had always paid close attention to weight and that Andrea's self-worth was closely linked to her weight. In fact, Andrea kept daily records of her weight and eating habits and agreed to provide the psychologist with this information. Keeping such a diary is a common form of assessment in this population.

With respect to characteristics of binging, assessment should focus on what the person ate, length of the binge, related emotions, and what conditions preceded and came after the binge. The psychologist discovered that Andrea's binges usually came after school and before she saw her boyfriend. Apparently, Andrea would come home from school sometimes feeling isolated, inadequate, or hungry and would occasionally binge on items that were easily bought and quickly eaten (e.g., soft cake). Typically, no one was home at this time. Following this binge and dinner with the family, Andrea worried that the ingested food would cause her to gain weight and look inferior to her boyfriend. She would then purge prior to dates with him. The psychologist instructed Andrea to keep a record of her binges and purges as well.

The psychologist also found that Andrea's moods were often tied to food. For example, she ate and binged when she was anxious or depressed, and she purged when she felt guilty, fat, or ugly. In general, Andrea had few moods that were not tied to eating, and she often ate impulsively and with little control. The psychologist also covered other areas mentioned by Garner and Garner (1992) but found no major patterns of borderline personality traits, aggression, or substance abuse. In addition, no history of physical or sexual abuse was reported. These findings support the belief that no one pattern of symptoms necessarily fits all those with anorexia nervosa.

The psychologist also focused on the link between Andrea's social and family interactions and her eating behaviors. In particular, Andrea had distorted thoughts that she would be abandoned by others if she gained weight and that she would be popular if she lost enough weight. An in-depth discussion with Andrea and her parents also revealed a pattern of vacillating enmeshment and conflict. In other words, Andrea and her parents would often become overinvolved in one another's lives and would then fight about this. For example, Andrea and her mother would spend hours shopping and talking about Andrea's appearance. Subsequently, Andrea would complain that her mother was "trying to control me." Similar patterns were also seen with respect to Andrea's girlfriends, though not her boyfriend.

The psychologist also explored the family's reasons for seeking treatment and their motivation for change. An interesting observation was that no one focused much on Andrea's eating habits, preferring to complain instead about each other's role in the family. Eventually, with a prompt from the psychologist, Mr. and Mrs. Weston did acknowledge their concern about Andrea's weight, and the issue became a centerpiece of the family therapy conducted later.

Interviews for those with eating disorders can also focus on social skills, sexual behavior, and menstrual history, but these were not discussed at length in Andrea's case. In addition, assessment in this area may include rating scales like the Eating Attitudes Test (Garner & Garfinkel, 1979; Maloney, McGuire, Daniels, & Specker, 1989); standardized family assessments like the Family Environment Scale (Moos & Moos, 1986); and a consideration of cultural factors that impinge on a particular case (Foreyt & Mikhail, 1997). However, these assessment directions were not taken in Andrea's case.

Causes and Maintaining Variables

The cause of eating disorders in general and anorexia nervosa in particular involves a mixture of physical, psychological, and sociocultural factors. In addition, the causes of eating disorders may overlap with those for depression. With respect to physical factors, for example, anorexia nervosa and depression are associated with changes in cortisol as well as the neurotransmitters serotonin and norepinephrine (Herzog & Beresin, 1997). A noteworthy finding in Andrea's case was Mrs. Weston's report that several of her relatives suffered from depression.

Other biological causes of eating disorder may include genetics and taste differences. Studies show the concordance rate for anorexia nervosa in identical twins to be about eight times the rate in fraternal twins (e.g., Holland, Sicotte, & Treasure, 1988). In addition, family members of people with eating disorders are more likely to have eating disorders themselves compared to the general population (Strober, 1995). Those who binge also tend to have a greater sensory response to high-calorie foods (Sunday, Einhorn, & Halmi, 1992). These factors did not seem pertinent to Andrea's case, however.

Several individual psychological characteristics have been associated with anorexia nervosa as well. For example, young people with anorexia tend to be compliant, conforming, obsessive, and stoic. Those who binge and purge also require approval from others, show mood swings and impulsivity, and like novel stimuli (Strober, 1995). In Andrea's case, some of these characteristics were evident; others were not. For example, Andrea was dramatic in her behavior, a characteristic not typical of those with anorexia. In addition, she was moderately noncompliant and seemed to enjoy irritating her parents.

On the other hand, Andrea clearly needed approval from others, especially her friends and boyfriend. The opinion of her parents, despite her objections, seemed important to Andrea as well. In addition, Andrea was known for her mood swings and impulsive behavior, a fact that greatly concerned her parents. In particular, Andrea sometimes said and did things with little thought, such as driving fast and buying clothes impetuously. Finally, it was clear that Andrea obsessed about her relationships with other people and about her weight. She also had perceptual and cognitive distortions regarding her weight, insisting that she was "ugly and fat" even as she lost weight, and claiming that other people were often talking about her weight behind her back.

Cognitive-behavioral models of eating disorder, especially binge eating, tend to focus on cycles of emotions and obsessional thinking (Rosen & Leitenberg, 1985; Wilson, Fairburn, & Agras, 1997). One possible scenario, for example, is that stressful situations, low self-esteem, and worries about one's body shape and weight lead to general feelings of apprehension. Binge eating may then follow to temporarily reduce this anxiety and tension. However, as guilt and shame gradually develop after the binge, the person purges to reduce these emotions. Unfortunately, stressful events and a sense of low self-esteem remain in the person's life, and the cycle is repeated. This scenario applied to some extent to Andrea, who sometimes binged following a stressful day at school. However, as she felt regret and distress over the binge, including possible weight gain, she purged by vomiting.

Other psychological theories of eating disorder emphasize family variables. A classic developmental/psychodynamic/object relations view holds that anorexia nervosa is a manifestation of internal conflict. Here, anorexia is seen as a compensatory behavior for satiation or separation problems during the oral stage of psychosexual development. A related view is that anorexia results from a problematic mother-child attachment. In this case, the mother gratifies the physiological but not the emotional needs of the child. This may derive from the mother's insecurity or hostility toward the child, but the end result is a child who feels insecure, rejected, and possibly vulnerable to depression and eating disorder.

Other family theories of eating disorder focus on interactions among all family members. For example, some families of adolescents with anorexia are enmeshed (Minuchin, Rosman, & Baker, 1978). This means that family members are overinvolved in one another's lives, to the point that even minor events (e.g., daily dress) become a source of great attention. Perhaps an adolescent in this case, feeling dominated by his or her parents, rebels by overcontrolling a very personal aspect—weight. In addition, weight loss and its related medical complications may be exploited by an adolescent to draw extra attention from an enmeshed family.

In Andrea's case, she certainly had a strange and contradictory relationship with her parents:

1. Andrea valued their opinions but then claimed to reject them.
2. She sought advice from her parents but then complained of being overcontrolled.
3. She professed love for her parents but greatly enjoyed needling them.

In addition, Mrs. Weston often gave Andrea mixed messages:

1. Mrs. Weston dismissed the importance of appearance and weight but then gave Andrea extensive advice in the area.
2. She told Andrea she loved her while avoiding eye contact.
3. She blended criticisms of Andrea with compliments.

As a result, Andrea was probably confused about how her parents and others felt about her. Possibly, she then developed low self-esteem and the mistaken belief that weight loss was a key way of getting affection from others.

Some families of adolescents with anorexia nervosa are also character- ized by overprotectiveness, avoidance of conflict, poor problem-solving skills, and negative communication and hostility. All of these were present to some degree in Andrea's case. Her family was often sarcastic, critical, and reluctant to discuss certain problems. In addition, some theorists hold that children model a parent's preoccupation with weight reduction (Wil- son, Heffernan, & Black, 1996). In Andrea's case, her mother appeared to be quite particular about her own appearance, and the psychologist dis- covered that Mrs. Weston also weighed herself and dieted on a regular ba- sis. Possibly, Andrea imitated this behavior as she grew up.

Another popular model of eating disorder is a sociocultural one. Pro- ponents of this model claim that the glorification of thinness in the media provokes many young women to diet. Indeed, the image of the "ideal" fe- male body size in popular literature has gradually become thinner in past decades. This could lead to anorexia in two ways. First, as more young women feel pressured to diet, more of them could trigger a biological pre- disposition toward anorexia nervosa. Second, failure to meet societal de- mands for thinness could lead to depression, low self-esteem, and unusual eating patterns (Wilson et al., 1996).

A sociocultural perspective might explain why abnormal eating pat- terns are seen more in adolescent females from higher-income families in Western countries. Interestingly, these characteristics matched those of Andrea and her family. In addition, the psychologist in this case noted that Andrea and her mother subscribed to several women's fashion magazines. Both often matched their appearances to the models in the magazines as well.

Developmental Aspects

Several developmental variables are related to the onset, course, and treat- ment of adolescents with eating disorders. One developmental variable that may explain why girls show anorexia nervosa more than boys in- volves physical development. As they grow during adolescence, females tend to increase their amount of fat tissue at a greater rate than males, and this obviously moves them away from the "ideal" body size portrayed in the media. It may explain as well why anorexia and bulimia nervosa are more commonly seen in adolescents than children. Other physical factors that seem related to the onset of eating disorder include early menarche and breast development (Striegel-Moore, Silberstein, & Rodin, 1986). Parental reactions to these events are also critical.

In this case, the psychologist found that Andrea was an "early developer" and was teased by her classmates for being so. Andrea found this to be humiliating and became sensitive about showing her weight and figure. This attitude, combined with her mother's comments noted earlier, led Andrea to be very self-conscious about her appearance. She was nearly obsessed with how others looked at her, and tended to "catastrophize" even minor flaws in her appearance (e.g., wrinkles, skin blotches). Some claim that insecure female adolescents often construct their identity based solely on physical features (e.g., Striegel-Moore, 1993), and this seemed to be the case with Andrea. When the psychologist asked Andrea to list her positive aspects, Andrea mentioned her figure, weight, height, and others' reactions to her appearance. Little mention was made, however, of her role as a student, daughter, or girlfriend.

According to Wilson et al. (1996), dieting is also a key developmental aspect of eating disorders. They define dieting as a "rigid and unhealthy restriction of overall caloric intake, skipping meals, and excessive avoidance of specific foods in order to influence body weight and shape" (p. 559). They noted that chronic dieting actually induces some people to eat more high-calorie foods, which can then trigger binging and other eating disturbances. Patton (1988) found that 21% of teenage girls who had been dieting developed an eating disorder one year later. This applied to only 3% of nondieters, however.

Wilson et al. (1996) noted that as people diet, their metabolic rates are reduced and weight loss becomes more difficult. Subsequently, they may diet even more vigorously and become more vulnerable to binge eating. As this behavior develops, biological and psychological vulnerabilities to eating disorder are triggered. In addition, the dieters may feel increasingly "out of control" and decide that purging is the only way to moderate the effects of binging. The cognitive-behavioral cycle described earlier (Rosen & Leitenberg, 1985; Wilson, Fairburn, & Agras, 1997) can then serve to maintain the disorder. For those with restrictive anorexia, dieting may start by eliminating certain foods from their daily menu (e.g., sweets). As the disorder progresses, however, more and more foods (e.g., meat, bread) are added to the "forbidden" list, and the person's daily caloric intake and weight decline steadily.

In Andrea's case, both she and her mother had a long history of dieting. Andrea was reportedly frustrated over the "yo-yo" effect of dieting, often losing weight to fit into certain clothes or to attend social functions, then adding the weight back on in subsequent weeks. The addition of her boyfriend to her life and his comment about her weight, however, seemed to give her dieting a new sense of urgency. As noted earlier, Andrea had lost 20 pounds in the past several weeks and was now terrified that the lost weight would return. This fear had caused her to restrict her diet even more so than in the past, but this aggravated her feelings of social isolation, depression, and hunger. Thus, her binging and purging had recently begun.

The development of eating disorders over time can also be influenced by a person's level of concurrent depression. For example, Smith and Steiner (1992) compared adolescent females who had anorexia nervosa with those who had anorexia nervosa and depression. Following a 2-year period, the authors found that adolescent females with anorexia and depression showed greater psychopathology and poorer prognosis than those with anorexia only. The presence of depression may therefore be a significant impediment to effective treatment for this population.

In Andrea's case, her level of depression, while not severe, did extend the length of her treatment. Her low self-esteem and general feelings of worthlessness, for example, led to cognitive distortions about her "ugly" body size and weight. In addition, Andrea occasionally mused about suicide, which required its own intervention. Finally, Andrea's depression was preventing her from interacting with her girlfriends, which ironically led to Andrea's impression that no one wanted to socialize with her. Her subsequent feelings of rejection later increased her desire to diet, binge, and purge.

What about the long-term future of those with eating disorders? Data indicate that various directions may be taken over time. Some with anorexia, for example, have only one episode of weight loss and soon return to normal patterns of eating and weight control. Others experience a gradual course of weight loss and gain that is not marked by any serious symptoms. Still others enter a severe period of weight loss that leads to treatment and subsequent improvement. About 10% to 15% of those with anorexia, however, eventually die from the disorder because of heart failure, electrolyte imbalance, or suicide.

The long-term pattern of bulimia is slightly different as this disorder usually develops later in life. The best available evidence indicates that symptoms of bulimia alternately improve and worsen over time. The course of the disorder appears to change favorably after treatment, although relapse rates are high (Mizes, 1995). In particular, many people with bulimia continue to show low-level eating disturbances like extensive dieting, laxative use, and exercise.

The prognosis for those with eating disorders depends on several factors. Factors associated with poor outcome include substance abuse, borderline personality disorder, severe disturbance in the perception of one's body size, and clinical anxiety and depression (Mizes, 1995). However, good outcome may be associated with cognitive-behavioral treatment and reduced isolation (Fairburn, Jones, Peveler, Hope, & O'Connor, 1993).

What about Andrea? In general, her long-term outcome is probably good and is almost certainly better than that of most people with eating disorders. This is largely because she received treatment relatively early in her disorder, whereas those with anorexia or bulimia nervosa sometimes hide their behavior for several years before entering therapy. In addition, Andrea's therapist was experienced in treating eating disorders and utilized cognitive-behavioral methods. Andrea's eating disorder was also rather limited in scope, and her family, though problematic, was motivated to resolve their recent difficulties. Finally, Andrea's level of depression was not clinical, and it generally dissipated as individual and family therapy for her eating problems progressed.

Treatment

Treating people with eating disorders can involve both inpatient and outpatient therapy. Inpatient treatment is usually applied to severe cases of eating disorder, especially anorexia nervosa. For example, inpatient treatment is best when the medical complications of anorexia are dire or a person's behavior is life-threatening. Major medical complications include substantial loss of ideal body weight (>25%), electrolyte imbalance, cardiac problems, and severe dehydration (Stevenson, 1989). In addition, severe symptoms of depression and suicidal behavior must sometimes be addressed.

During hospitalization, the main goal is to stabilize a person's health and increase weight and nutrition. In particular, staff members set a "target weight" that should be met prior to discharge. Interventions can include these:

1. Structured eating sessions with staff and family members
2. Education about eating disorders
3. Reconstruction of proper eating and nutritional habits
4. Group therapy
5. Medication for physical complications or depression

In Andrea's case, given her relatively moderate eating problem, hospitalization was not necessary.

Outpatient therapy for those with anorexia nervosa often involves drug, group, individual, and family therapy. Drug therapy for this population includes antidepressants like amitriptyline or fluoxetine (Prozac). These are sometimes effective because the drugs successfully reduce obsessive-compulsive and depressive behaviors that trigger or aggravate anorexia. In addition, anti-anxiety drugs sometimes reduce tension and the temptation to binge and purge. As noted by Herzog and Beresin (1997), however, when drug therapy is used, it should start at a low dose, relevant family members should be educated about the use of medication, and side effects should be monitored. In Andrea's case, the use of antidepressants was initially discussed but later abandoned. Instead, an emphasis was placed on individual and family therapy.

According to Garner and Garner (1992), important goals of individual therapy for those with anorexia nervosa involve several elements:

1. Developing rapport with the client
2. Increasing the client's motivation for behavior change
3. Normalizing the individual's weight and eliminating binging and purging
4. Modifying the person's cognitive distortions about weight and body size
5. Addressing other conditions such as depression

Treatment within a cognitive-behavioral framework is usually recommended.

In this case, the psychologist spent considerable time developing a positive therapeutic relationship with Andrea. Because she felt isolated and sometimes distrusting of others, it was important for the therapist to recognize her concerns and offer no judgments of her behavior. As a result, the first three sessions concentrated on the development of a positive working relationship as well as education about proper eating habits. For example, the psychologist and Andrea designed a daily eating schedule that was largely fat-free, but also nutritious. In addition, they agreed that Andrea's weight could fluctuate between 100 and 110 pounds, but no lower. Andrea also agreed to weigh herself in front of the psychologist during each weekly visit. Andrea's response to this treatment was quite rapid, as she rigorously adhered to her new diet and did not lose any more weight. Her motivation to deal with her binging, purging, and social and family problems also seemed to increase.

The tougher part of individual therapy for this population is to eliminate binging and purging and modify cognitive distortions about body size. A reduction in binging and purging sometimes happens when the behavior is out in the open and the person and those around him or her actively monitor the behavior. This was the case with Andrea, who had binged and vomited only three times since her parents became more aware of the problem. A therapeutic method of eliminating binging and purging is to have the person eat high-calorie foods in a therapist's office and then prevent the subsequent purging response (Rosen & Leitenberg, 1985; Wilson, Fairburn, & Agras, 1997). This approach is similar to one used for obsessive-compulsive symptoms and assumes that the person's anxiety will eventually decrease as he or she is prevented from purging. In that way, the person realizes that the binge-purge cycle is unnecessary for reducing stress.

The psychologist outlined this therapy technique to Andrea, who agreed to give it a try. Andrea consumed a fair amount of ice cream, candy bars, and cupcakes within a half-hour period and was then asked to wait. She was not allowed to use the bathroom, and the psychologist taught Andrea how to relax. In addition, the psychologist reminded Andrea that self-induced vomiting was an ineffective way of negating the binge, as many of the calories were quickly absorbed by the body anyway. Andrea reported some anxiety following this process, but was able to relax. She said she didn't want to try it again, however, out of fear of weight gain. Instead, she agreed to have her family members closely monitor her behavior for any signs of binging and purging. Over the next several weeks, they reported no such incidents.

Individual therapy for people with eating disorders may also address cognitive distortions. Such distortions may involve food, weight, and body size as well as themes of abandonment, loss of autonomy, and guilt (Garner & Garner, 1992; Robin, Bedway, Siegel, & Gilroy, 1996). In Andrea's case, the psychologist focused on helping Andrea develop more realistic thoughts about (1) what would happen if she lost or gained weight, (2) her ideal and real body size, and (3) isolation from others.

To start, the psychologist explored with Andrea the probable consequences of weight loss and gain. For example, she was shown that her friends would not notice much or change their opinion of her as her weight fluctuated slightly. In addition, Andrea was given feedback about the way she perceived her body and about the effect her negative thoughts had on her social relationships. Andrea came to realize, for example, that her fears of abandonment by others led to her withdrawal and even greater feelings of isolation. Therefore, a series of outdoor activities were planned with Andrea's friends to dispel these beliefs, increase her social interaction, and reduce her depression.

Family therapy was also a main component of Andrea's treatment regimen. In particular, the therapist explored the enmeshed patterns of the family, concentrating especially on Mrs. Weston's tendency to overcontrol her daughter's appearance and social life. Fortunately, Mrs. Weston was responsive to this and allowed Andrea a fair amount of free time with her friends and boyfriend under certain conditions (e.g., curfew). In addition, Andrea agreed to eat dinner with her family at least five times a week and to allow her parents to monitor her weight and possible binging and purging.

Other issues related to Andrea's boyfriend, school performance, and future educational status were also discussed. For example, Mr. and Mrs. Weston relayed their concerns about Andrea's dating, and Andrea admitted that she saw her boyfriend in part to annoy her parents. As therapy progressed, Andrea did start dating other people. In addition, Mr. and Mrs. Weston encouraged Andrea to put more effort into her classes, which she did, and to develop a plan for attending college in the fall.

Andrea and her family participated in therapy for 4 months. Following therapy, Andrea's overall functioning was thought to be good. Some issues did remain unresolved, such as Andrea's sexual activity. However, her eating problems were no longer evident and her mood had greatly improved since the beginning of therapy. In addition, the psychologist felt that the family had developed improved insight into their own dynamics and their effects on one another. Family members were also more motivated to work together to solve future problems. Informal telephone contact with Andrea 6 months later indicated no recurrence of eating problems or depression.

 ## Discussion Questions

1. What distinguishes people with anorexia nervosa, the binge-eating/purging type, from those with bulimia nervosa? Explore not just diagnostic criteria, but social, family, and other variables as well.

2. Eating disorders appear to be largely specific to Western societies. Why do you think this is so? What societal changes might lead to a reduction of anorexia and bulimia nervosa in the general population? What might be done to prevent the disorders?

3. Eating disorders also appear to be largely specific to females. Why do you think this is so? Give specific examples of messages from the media, family members, and peers that might promote this disorder in young women.

4. Do you feel that your eating behavior is often tied to your emotional state? How so? What changes in how you handle stress, if any, could lead to an improvement in your eating habits?

5. Devise a treatment plan for someone who wanted to lose weight responsibly. What kinds of foods, shopping and food preparation behaviors, eating times and places, activities during eating, and other variables would you focus on?

6. Would you say anything to someone who appeared dangerously underweight? If so, what might you say to that person? What prejudgments would you want to avoid?

7. What influence do you think Andrea's boyfriend had on the development and maintenance of her eating problems? Would involving her boyfriend in the therapy process be a good idea? Why or why not? If yes, how might you do so?

8. What is the danger in placing someone treated for anorexia back with family members? What could be done to prevent a relapse in this situation?

9. What could or would you do if a person was in danger of losing his or her life from anorexia but refused treatment?

CHAPTER FIVE

Elimination Disorder

Symptoms

Amber Dillon was a 7-year-old Caucasian female referred to an outpatient mental health clinic for children and families. At the time of her initial assessment, Amber was in second grade. She was referred to the clinic by her father, Mr. Dillon, who was quite upset about his daughter's problems. During the telephone screening interview, he reported that Amber was wetting her bed more at night and often needed to urinate during school. She was also experiencing minor academic problems. The family was scheduled for an appointment one week later.

The intake interviews were conducted by a marriage and family therapist with a master's degree in clinical psychology. At the initial assessment session, Amber was accompanied by both parents and her 2-year-old brother, Daniel. The therapist interviewed Amber alone first, but the girl was initially very quiet and made no eye contact. In addition, she didn't respond to any of the therapist's questions, even to those that had nothing to do with her reported problem. After 20 minutes of soliloquy, the therapist asked Amber if she wanted to return to her parents and go home. Amber nodded yes to this question but agreed to come again the following week. The therapist rescheduled the appointment with Mr. and Mrs. Dillon and made it clear that the change was not due to any in-session misbehavior on Amber's part. The therapist noticed that Amber was quite attentive to the therapist's discussion with her parents.

During the second assessment session the following week, Amber seemed more relaxed. The therapist again interviewed her alone, and this time she was more cooperative but still quiet. Following several minutes of general conversation and reassurances of confidentiality, the therapist asked Amber why she thought her parents had brought her to the clinic. Amber shrugged at first, and the therapist gently encouraged her to answer. Amber said that she was getting into a lot of trouble at home and that her parents were mad at her. When asked why they were mad, Amber said she wasn't doing well in school and that she felt "nervous." The therapist was careful to praise Amber for her answers.

Over the course of the session, Amber became more relaxed but still avoided eye contact and spoke in a hushed tone. She said her grades had been getting worse over the course of the school year and that she was having trouble concentrating on her assigned work. She had apparently been a very good student the year before, especially in reading, but was now struggling with different subjects. The therapist found that she had to ask a lot of "yes/no" questions to get information from Amber, who was clearly uncomfortable about the subjects of conversation. As a result, the therapist intermittently switched to lighter topics to maintain rapport.

When the therapist felt that Amber was comfortable enough, she broached the subject of the girl's alleged wetting. Amber said she wet her bed at night about once or twice a week. In addition, she often had to use the bathroom at school, going about three or four times a day. This was apparently a source of annoyance for her team teachers, Mrs. Thelmisa and Mrs. Mayberry. On one occasion, Amber said that she didn't make it to the bathroom in time and slightly wet her pants. Fortunately, this was not noticeable, but Amber was quite embarrassed about the incident. In fact, she now placed a wad of toilet tissue in her underwear to diminish the results of any possible mishaps in the future. The therapist also discovered that Amber's wetting had increased from the year before, when she wet the bed only "once in a while" and didn't have any problems at school. When asked if there were other reasons why she was brought to the clinic, Amber shook her head and became quiet. The therapist praised her for answering tough questions and asked her to wait outside while she spoke with her parents.

During their interview, Mr. and Mrs. Dillon first said they were greatly concerned about Amber and wanted to know more about her problems. Both parents agreed that Amber had wet the bed about twice a week since October (it was now February), but had done so almost every other night in the past month. They were quite surprised by this, as Amber had been having more dry nights since kindergarten. At that time, she was wetting the bed about three times a week at night and never had an accident during the day. A medical checkup during kindergarten had revealed no major problems, and the pediatrician had told Mr. and Mrs. Dillon then that the wetting would likely clear up within a year. This seemed to be the case during first grade and part of second grade, as Amber wet the bed only about once a month.

Mr. and Mrs. Dillon were also concerned about their daughter's school performance, which had declined steadily since October and more rapidly since Christmas. They said that Amber was unmotivated, depressed, and withdrawn; also, she was eating less than usual. No major acting-out problems were reported, and Amber was described as a generally compliant and talented child. In addition, Mr. and Mrs. Dillon had just met with Amber's teachers and principal, who reported that Amber was doing adequately in school but certainly not reaching her potential. The school officials had apparently recommended that the family seek counseling.

This latter statement signaled the therapist to ask if any significant changes were going on at home. The question seemed to strike a nerve, as both parents paused and looked at each other nervously before answering. Finally, Mr. Dillon said that he and his wife had been having marital problems within the past year and that they were fighting more than usual. In fact, the possibility of divorce had been raised and both were now considering separation. When asked about the cause of this situation, both parents were reticent but did say that Mr. Dillon's extensive work schedule and the stress of having a 2-year-old child were the core issues. The therapist suspected that other issues were also present but didn't press the Dillons further at this time.

Verbal fighting between Mr. and Mrs. Dillon was apparently substantial, occurring about twice per week, and Amber had even run out of the house on two occasions to escape it. However, none of the family members were reportedly victims of physical abuse. When asked if the marital problems were possibly tied to Amber's current elimination and academic problems, both parents said they didn't think so. Their reasoning was based on the fact that Amber had always had some problems with bed-wetting.

With Mr. and Mrs. Dillon's permission, the therapist also interviewed Amber's teachers. Mrs. Thelmisa said that Amber was a very good student "when she wanted to be" but confirmed that Amber's daily performance was slipping. The teacher said that Amber had no outward behavior problems, but noted that she often needed reminders to complete her assignments, to stay awake, and to listen to instructions. Mrs. Thelmisa and Mrs. Mayberry agreed, however, that Amber's most annoying behavior was her constant requests to use the bathroom. This had not been a problem earlier in the year, but Amber was now asking to go to the bathroom three or four times a day. Both thought that Amber was seeking attention because she would ask other, unnecessary questions as well. In addition, both speculated that family problems at home were related to Amber's current behaviors and offered to help the therapist in whatever way possible.

Based on her interviews, the therapist made a preliminary conclusion that Amber had an elimination disorder, specifically enuresis. In addition, she felt the enuresis was largely of the nocturnal type. However, she delayed her decision about whether Amber had primary or secondary enuresis.

Assessment

According to the *DSM-IV*, the essential feature of enuresis is "repeated voiding of urine during the day or at night into bed or clothes" (APA, 1994, p. 108). Voiding of urine may be involuntary or intentional, and a child must wet at least twice a week for 3 months *or* show substantial distress or impairment in academic, social, or other areas of performance because of wetting. In addition, the child must be at least 5 years old or of similar developmental level. Finally, enuresis must not be due to substances like medication or medical conditions like epilepsy or infection. Subtypes of enuresis include:

1. Nocturnal, when a child wets only during sleep at night
2. Diurnal, when a child wets only during daytime
3. Nocturnal and diurnal

Also, primary enuresis generally refers to cases in which a child has never completely achieved urinary continence, whereas secondary enuresis refers to cases in which a child becomes incontinent after a one-year period of dryness. Cases of secondary enuresis often follow some environ- mental stressor.

In Amber's case, she clearly met criteria for enuresis given her age, frequency of bed-wetting, and lack of medical problems. In addition, Amber's wetting was primarily nocturnal: She had had only one daytime accident. A tougher call, however, was whether Amber had primary or secondary enuresis. This was difficult because Amber never did completely end her bed-wetting, even during first grade. This would indicate primary enuresis. However, the behavior was rare that year and not considered problematic. Therefore, her increased wetting now would indicate secondary enuresis. The presence of stressful life events (e.g., marital conflict) that preceded Amber's increased bed-wetting would also suggest secondary, not primary, enuresis.

The assessment of youngsters with elimination disorder, which include those with encopresis or soiling, must focus first on possible medical explanations. This is particularly true for those with developmental disabilities, but it applies to children like Amber as well. Walsh and Menvielle (1997) have cited a number of competing medical explanations for enuresis, including these:

- Diabetes
- Urinary tract infection
- Seizure disorders
- Neurological damage affecting fluid intake and urinary control
- Renal problems
- Medication use
- Anatomical dysfunctions of the urinary system

Other possible factors include hormonal changes and central nervous system lesions. Urinalysis, urogram, cystourethrogram, sphincter electromyography, and cystoscopy are often used to identify these problems. In Amber's case, a new physical examination revealed no major medical problems. Her enuresis was therefore considered functional or psychogenic in nature.

A key method of assessing children with an elimination disorder is the interview. This is especially applicable to clients like the Dillons, where the child's disorder is highly influenced by family variables. Fielding and Doleys (1988) stated that the interview should cover a full description of the onset and development of enuretic symptoms, family history of enuresis or related problems, family circumstances, comorbid disorders, parental attitudes and reactions to the child's enuresis, and previous treatments. During the intake interview, the Dillons had described the onset and development of Amber's enuretic symptoms.

In subsequent interviews, the therapist investigated family variables that might be affecting Amber's wetting. No family history of enuresis was reported, although Mrs. Dillon did have a history of minor urinary tract infections. With respect to marital problems, both parents admitted that their conflict probably diminished their attention to Amber in recent months. The therapist then asked if Amber's behavior was possibly a way of diverting parental attention from their own problems to her life. Mrs. Dillon acknowledged that this may have been so. The therapist also asked if Amber was reacting to the stress of the family situation, and Mrs. Dillon conceded this was possible as well. Certainly the household atmosphere was tense, but neither parent was reportedly overanxious in their interactions with Amber. Both claimed instead to be supportive of their daughter during her wetting and academic problems, but they said their own ability to cope was becoming strained. Finally, no systematic treatments for Amber's wetting had been tried in the past, although Mrs. Dillon did try to restrict Amber's fluid intake prior to bedtime.

Separate interviews with Amber confirmed these statements and focused on her depressive symptoms and academic performance. Amber said she didn't like the fact that her parents fought and that it made her "feel bad." She said she had trouble concentrating on her work because she often worried about her parents and whether dinnertime would be calm or loud. Amber added that she often cried and wanted to go to the bathroom during the day to compose herself. She said as well that she had her own bedroom and sometimes felt lonely and sad at night. In addition, she often felt tired. When she wet the bed, she would usually ask her mother to come to her room. On most occasions, Mrs. Dillon did so, and helped her daughter change her pajamas and bedsheets before returning to sleep.

Amber accurately described how to use a toilet and said that she had no problem waiting to urinate during the day. In response to the therapist's request, Amber went to the bathroom during one of the sessions and was able to stop her urination midstream. Thus, good bladder control was evident. Interestingly, Amber was not overly concerned about her bed-wetting, but she did express a lot of fear about the possibility of having a daytime accident. The therapist also asked Amber if she wanted more attention from her parents. Amber said that she did, but mostly that she wished her parents would simply stop fighting.

The assessment of children with enuresis can also take the form of daily logbooks or diaries to obtain baseline information about the child's wetting frequency, bedtime, time of accident, degree of accident (e.g., large or small), appropriate use of the toilet, morning wake time and procedures, and unusual events (e.g., sleepovers; Fielding & Doleys, 1988). The therapist in this case asked Mrs. Dillon and Amber to record these events, and they did so. A 2-week baseline revealed that Amber wet the bed five times. On each occasion, she and her mother changed the bed together. Each accident was neither small nor large, and no unusual events were noted. However, Mrs. Dillon raised the point that it was difficult to wake Amber and get her out of bed in the morning. The family was asked to continue monitoring these events throughout treatment.

Causes and Maintaining Variables

As noted earlier, enuresis may be caused by various physiological conditions or medications. These problems can usually be treated medically and are excluded here. In other rare cases, enuresis is caused by a developmental lag in bladder functioning (MacKeith, 1972). With respect to functional enuresis, where no medical explanation is apparent, researchers have looked at child, family, genetic, and other variables to explain the cause of the disorder.

With respect to child factors, early enuresis has been linked to high motor activity, aggression, poor adaptability to new situations, low achievement motivation, overly dependent behavior, and lack of aversion to being wet (Kaffman & Elizur, 1977). The only one of these factors that truly applied to Amber was her attention-seeking, dependent, and immature behavior. For example, she often played with her food, pretended to be like her 2-year-old brother, and whined and cried when she wanted something. Children and adolescents with enuresis sometimes show these kinds of regressive behaviors, which can be manifested also in preferences for younger playmates.

Amber did not show any of the other characteristics mentioned by Kaffman and Elizur (1977). For example, she was not overactive or aggressive and did not like being wet at all. In addition, she was motivated to do well in school, although this applied more to past academic work than it did now. Mr. and Mrs. Dillon also reported that Amber adjusted relatively well to new situations, like meeting new people.

A traditional psychological view of enuresis links the problem to emotional disturbance, in that children with high levels of anxiety or depression also have enuresis or that children with enuresis also have high levels of anxiety or depression. In cases of the latter, the child's anxiety and depression may be closely associated with family dysfunction or stressful life events. At first glance, this view seems to fit Amber perfectly, as she said that she felt nervous and sad about her parent's fighting. Possibly, the 7-year-old was overwhelmed by physical symptoms of worry and tension. These physical symptoms may then have led to her increased need to urinate.

A closer look at Amber's problems, however, revealed a stronger pattern of attention-seeking behavior than emotional disturbance. In particular, Amber's behavior was often done to purposely divert parental attention from their fighting to her needs. In addition, there was no history of traumatic life events during Amber's earlier childhood, a phenomenon sometimes seen in children with emotional disturbance and functional enuresis (Douglas, 1973). Still, Amber was clearly upset by her parents' situation, and the therapist recognized that the successful treatment of her enuresis would have to involve a resolution of some family issues.

Other suspected causes of enuresis in children include failure to learn (1) to use the bathroom properly or (2) to control the urination reflex cognitively. With respect to the first point, some children with enuresis refuse to use the toilet or have a history of toilet training problems or toilet fears. This did not apply to Amber, however. With respect to cognitive control, most children learn to contract and relax certain muscles in the bladder to delay urination. Failure to control the bladder muscles may have explained Amber's enuresis as a preschooler, but no formal assessment was done at that time to know for sure. Currently, Amber had no problem waiting to go to the bathroom during the day, although the thought of waiting made her uncomfortable.

Some children with enuresis also have different sleep and arousal patterns from children without enuresis. For example, some studies indicate that children with enuresis are hard to wake, and this did seem to be the case with Amber. Enuresis can occur during any stage of sleep, but some researchers claim that children who wet the bed are very light or very deep sleepers. As such, children with enuresis may be more or less aroused than the general population (Fielding & Doleys, 1988). In this case, Mrs. Dillon reported that Amber slept fitfully and did have a short history of nightmares when she was 4 years old. However, she couldn't identify any common pattern to Amber's sleep or arousability levels as she wet the bed. Usually, it was Amber who woke her mother when an accident occurred during the night.

Twin studies indicate that genetic factors may also influence the etiology of enuresis. Enuresis is almost twice as common in identical than fraternal twins. In addition, parents with enuresis are likely to have children with enuresis (Bakwin, 1973). However, genetic transmission may not be specific to enuresis per se but rather to other factors like maturation of the urinary system, general learning ability, arousability, and responsiveness to cues related to urination (e.g., feeling pressure).

Enuresis is therefore caused by different variables, but parental reactions often determine whether the problem is maintained over time. This applies especially to critical attitudes that a parent has toward a child with enuresis. For example, some parents partly blame their child for wetting, citing characteristics like laziness, vindictiveness, and noncompliance to nighttime routines (Butler, Brewin, & Forsythe, 1986). In addition, some parents become intolerant of a child's wetting, going so far as to embarrass the child or apply severe punishment following accidents. These parental behaviors tend to aggravate enuresis, however.

The Dillons initially said they were very supportive of Amber when she wet the bed or did poorly in school. Subsequent interviews, however, revealed that Mr. Dillon was extremely irritated with his wife and daughter over the handling of these issues. Mrs. Dillon had adopted a supportive approach, helping Amber change her sheets and pajamas and telling her the problem was not her fault. In addition, operating on the advice of the pediatrician 2 years before, Mrs. Dillon had kept telling Amber that the problem would eventually go away. Mr. Dillon strongly disagreed with this approach, however, and told Amber that her behavior was "unacceptable." He often lectured Amber on the need to take more responsibility for her actions. In addition, he warned her that he would start spanking her if she didn't improve her nighttime behavior and academic performance. Not surprisingly, Mr. and Mrs. Dillon had several arguments over this issue and had agreed to seek therapy as a result.

Another factor that clearly maintained Amber's bed-wetting was the attention she received from (1) her mother during the night, (2) her father during his lectures, and (3) both parents now during therapy. The therapist noticed that Amber showed good affect when her parents were getting along and discussing her behaviors. For example, she smiled and listened attentively when they were calmly talking. Conversely, Amber was more uptight when her parents disagreed about something or when the therapist raised the issue of helping Amber become more self-reliant following her accidents.

🐾 Developmental Aspects 🐾

Most children, especially girls, develop relatively good bladder control by the age of 3 years, and data indicate that the prevalence of enuresis declines with age. Nocturnal enuresis is common to about 33% of 3-year-olds, 25% of 4-year-olds, 15% to 20% of 5-year-olds, 5% of 10-year-olds, 2% of young adolescents, and 1% to 2% of older adolescents and adults. Diurnal or daytime enuresis is much less common and seen in about 3% of youngsters after age 5 years. As a general rule, the percentage of total cases of enuresis that are primary in nature declines over the developmental period (Walker, Kenning, & Faust-Campanile, 1989). This means that older children and adolescents are more likely to have secondary enuresis than younger children, although Amber may have been an exception.

In this section, the important developmental milestone of toilet training is discussed. According to Brazelton (1962; Brazelton & Cramer, 1990), young children must be physically and psychologically ready to successfully engage in toilet training. Physical readiness, which includes the ability to control the sphincter, is often evident by the end of the first year. A child's abilities to sit and walk are also important signs that toilet training can begin. In addition, the child should be psychologically ready. This means the child should be responsive to caregivers and have basic receptive language skills, an ability to imitate others, and eagerness to learn to use the toilet. Other researchers have also indicated that children should be able to empty their bladder, stay dry for at least 2 to 3 hours, coordinate their muscle movements, and indicate in some way (e.g., pointing, facial expressions) a need to urinate or defecate (Azrin & Foxx, 1974). A typical child is ready for toilet training at 24 to 30 months of age.

Brazelton (1962) offered a step-by-step approach for toilet training that allows children to proceed at their own pace. The first step involves getting a child acclimated to the toilet or smaller toilet chair. This can be done by showing the chair to the child, asking the child to walk around and sit on the chair while dressed, and singing or doing other fun activities when on the chair. Second, the child should learn to sit without pants or a diaper on the toilet or toilet chair and adapt to this position over time. In the future when the child urinates or defecates in the diaper, a parent should remove the diaper, place it in the toilet or toilet chair, show this to the child, and have the child sit on the toilet/chair. At this time, the parent may give the child feedback as to why the diaper is in the toilet/chair as well as the purpose of the toilet/chair.

The next phase of toilet training involves taking the child to the toilet/chair several times during the day. During each trial, a parent should encourage the child to urinate or defecate in the container and give verbal praise for effort and success. Over time, the child should associate the need to urinate or defecate with the need to attend the bathroom and use the toilet. Occasional relapses are common, of course, and parents should handle these events in a matter-of-fact way and encourage the child to do better next time. In addition, other toileting skills may be taught. These skills include dressing and undressing, approaching the toilet, flushing, and washing, among others (Azrin & Besalel, 1979; Azrin & Foxx, 1974).

Most children with good verbal and motor skills can master toilet training within hours or days. Several obstacles could arise during this process, however. For example, youngsters with developmental disabilities or learning problems may require more detailed modeling and feedback. For those with severe cognitive difficulties, a longer and slower process may be necessary. In addition, parents may object to the amount of time and effort required for toilet training. Therefore, it might be best to start the process over a holiday or extended weekend period when a parent can afford to give extensive feedback. Finally, children may object to the procedure, especially if the process is going too fast. Parents should let children progress at their own pace, avoid harsh comments or unrealistic expectations, and monitor the child for possible fears of the toilet.

If a child refuses to use the toilet, parents may want to consider toilet training at a later time. In addition, according to Christophersen and Rapoff (1992), parents should check to see whether the child is constipated; typically, a preschooler has about one bowel movement per day. If the child is constipated, mineral oil and fiber can be added to the diet, and dairy products can be reduced. The use of suppositories may also be helpful. If the child is fearful of the toilet, steps leading to the toilet can be added so the child can better approach it. In addition, parents should give feedback to children to demonstrate that the toilet is not harmful during flushing. For example, they could place their hand in the toilet while flushing.

Most children will develop toilet training with no problem, as Amber did. However, there is no guarantee that successful toilet training will prevent future enuresis or soiling. In Amber's case, she did learn toilet training over a one-month period, but continued to wet at night. This wetting was then inadvertently reinforced by her parents, who initially let Amber sleep in their bed following an accident. This practice was ended 2 years before when Amber's brother was born, but Amber had already associated nighttime wetting with parental attention.

 **Treatment**

The treatment of children with enuresis may involve medical or psychological procedures and is typically marked by success. Medication for enuresis includes tricyclic antidepressants like imipramine, which may relax the muscles surrounding the bladder. Imipramine often works quickly, which makes the intervention useful for children who need their symptoms resolved fast (e.g., during upcoming summer camp). However, relapse is seen in about two-thirds of cases. In addition, desmopressin, an antidiuretic, may be administered in the form of a nasal spray. Effectiveness and relapse rates are similar to those for imipramine, however (Walsh & Menvielle, 1997).

In many cases of primary nocturnal enuresis, a moisture alarm is the most effective long-term intervention. The traditional method is a "bell-and-pad"; with this, the child sleeps on a special blanket attached to an alarm. The alarm may be in the child's room, parent's room, or both. When the child starts urinating during the course of the night, initially producing a few drops, the moisture completes a circuit that triggers the alarm. The child awakens to the feeling of a full bladder and goes to the bathroom appropriately. Over time, the child should associate the feeling of a full bladder with waking and using the toilet. This procedure is effective in up to 90% of cases. In addition, relapse rates are low if the procedure is used for one or two time blocks of 5 to 12 weeks each (Walker et al., 1989).

Amber's therapist asked Mr. and Mrs. Dillon if a urine alarm could be used, but Mr. Dillon vetoed the idea. Problems related to the urine alarm include its inconvenience, time requirement, and possible malfunction. The therapist suspected that Mr. Dillon did not want to be bothered during the night and preferred instead to let his wife continue to take care of Amber.

Another common intervention for children with enuresis is urine retention training, in which the child practices waiting to use the toilet (Houts & Liebert, 1984). This is done to help a child learn to control urination cognitively and physically. Once on the toilet, children may also be asked to practice stopping their urination midstream. This is done to help a child, in the future, prevent a small accident from getting worse. These procedures work very well for some children but not for others. In Amber's case, urine retention training was not used because Amber could already wait appropriately and stop her urine stream if necessary.

As mentioned earlier, Amber's case involved secondary enuresis triggered by parent and family factors. As a result, her therapist designed a treatment program that included the formation of nighttime and morning routines, family therapy, classroom behavior management, and modified dry bed training. Mr. and Mrs. Dillon were heavily involved in Amber's treatment. Both were also referred to a second therapist for marital therapy to address some of the more personal issues raised earlier.

The therapist first designed nighttime and morning routines that would become very predictable for Amber. Currently, no such routines were in place and both parents had become lax regarding bedtime and nighttime discipline. This was due primarily to their own fighting, increased attention to the 2-year-old, and a desire to give Amber more independence. Working with Amber and her parents, the therapist devised a "getting-ready-for-bed" routine. Specifically, Amber would be told at 8:00 P.M. that it was time to get ready for bed. This meant the end of television and play activities. At that time, Amber would get into her pajamas, have a small drink of water (this was purposely done), brush her teeth, and climb into bed. These activities were expected to take 15 to 20 minutes. At 8:20 P.M., Mr. or Mrs. Dillon would enter the room and read Amber a short story. This was designed to calm Amber down and ease her transition to sleep.

A morning routine was also established for waking, rising from bed, dressing, eating, brushing teeth, and preparing materials for school. In addition, the therapist and Mr. and Mrs. Dillon set up consequences for Amber's compliance or noncompliance to these routines. Specifically, any noncompliance would be met with a loss of privileges for one night. These privileges might include television, dessert, helping Mrs. Dillon with Daniel, or certain playthings, among others. On the other hand, compliance would be rewarded using verbal praise, later bedtime on weekends, and special activities with Amber's parents. Amber agreed to these conditions once it was pointed out to her that she could get a lot of appropriate attention for her compliance. The therapist found over the next few sessions that Amber's compliance was relatively good, although Mr. and Mrs. Dillon had occasional lapses in fulfilling their end of the bargain. In general, however, Amber was now on a regular routine at night and in the morning.

During this process, the therapist also concentrated on general family therapy. In particular, the therapist described the various family dynamics that seemed to maintain Amber's behaviors. The Dillons were shown, for example, how Amber would complain, cry, be noncompliant, or do poorly in school to get their attention. In addition, the therapist pointed out that Mr. and Mrs. Dillon got along best when discussing their daughter's behavior problems. Amber enjoyed this immensely, of course, and often misbehaved to maintain these positive parental discussions. Specific examples were given of how parental interactions were linked to Amber's behaviors, and the Dillons agreed to have more private discussions of family issues. They also agreed to attend more to Amber's positive behaviors like completing her homework, receiving good notes from the teacher, and achieving dry nights.

In conjunction with this, the therapist asked Amber's teachers, Mrs. Thelmisa and Mrs. Mayberry, to grant Amber only one trip to the bathroom each day. Subsequent requests would be granted only when there was an emergency, when the teachers were sure that Amber actually needed to go, or when Amber's on-task and general classroom behavior were good. Amber was informed of this plan and seemed content with it. Fortunately, the teachers were quite vigilant about enforcing the plan, and Amber's inappropriate requests to use the bathroom were reduced. Some improvements in Amber's general classroom behavior were also seen during therapy, especially more completed work. Frequent feedback was still necessary, however. Other procedures were also implemented to help Amber academically. For example, she received a daily report card regarding her work behaviors and Mr. Dillon started helping her at night with homework.

The other major treatment component for Amber involved modified dry bed training. Dry bed training can be done in different forms, but primarily it involves cleanliness training, practice, regular nighttime waking, and consequences for wetting and dryness. The general protocol involves several steps on the first night of training:

1. Giving the child something to drink prior to bedtime
2. Setting a urine alarm
3. Using 20 trials of having the child lie on the bed, count to 50, and try using the bathroom
4. Waking the child every hour to encourage toilet use and urine retention
5. Having the alarm wake the child and parents should an accident begin

On subsequent nights, the urine alarm is set and the child is given rewards for dry nights and mild punishments for wet nights. In addition, the child is taught to practice changing sheets and clothes before returning to a dry bed (Walker et al., 1989). Research indicates that dry bed training is effective but that parents find it inconvenient.

Amber was initially taught how to change all the blankets and sheets on her bed, place them in the hamper, and put on new bedsheets and clothes. The goal here was to make Amber expend a significant amount of effort for wetting. Mrs. Dillon was initially asked to wake Amber four times a night to see if she had to use the toilet (no urine alarm was used). If an accident occurred, Amber would have to practice the cleanliness skills taught earlier *without* her mother's help. In addition, Mrs. Dillon was asked not to talk with Amber at this time, only to give instructions. Thus, no extra verbal or physical attention was provided. Following a nighttime accident, Amber was also required to complete an extra chore the following day. If an accident did not occur, then Amber was rewarded by her parents. The therapist also asked the Dillons to eliminate any lectures about wetting and treat the problem with a more "matter-of-fact" attitude.

Amber initially balked at the cleanliness training following an accident, and Mrs. Dillon reported trouble getting up four times a night. The therapist and Mr. Dillon encouraged both parties to continue, however, and some success was evident soon after. Amber's nighttime wetting frequency dropped to about once a week within 4 weeks and once every 2 weeks within 8 weeks. As therapy progressed, a regular clock alarm was rigged to wake Amber twice a night, at which time she used the toilet or changed her sheets and bed.

Within 3 months, Amber's rate of wetting was similar to her low rate of the previous year. In addition, her work and incessant questioning at school had improved. At this time, however, Mr. and Mrs. Dillon decided to separate. Amber reacted badly to this event, alternately throwing tantrums and appearing sad and unmotivated. Fortunately, however, the Dillons remained in marital therapy and continued meeting with Amber's therapist to address these new concerns. In addition, Amber's bed-wetting did not increase. Therapy was ended 2 months later when Mr. and Mrs. Dillon were convinced that Amber was functioning well and had adjusted to the separation. Informal contact with the family 4 months later indicated little change.

Discussion Questions

1. Would you change the toilet-training program described in this chapter? How so? What might parents say to their child during this process?

2. In some cases of elimination disorder, a child will lie about the frequency of his or her wetting or soiling, either saying it happens more often or less often than it actually does. Why might a child falsify this information to someone? What could a therapist or parent do to prevent this? Discuss ways of confirming the child's report.

3. What psychological factors might explain why boys tend to display more enuresis than girls?

4. Most children seem eventually to outgrow functional elimination problems, but some do not. What factors might explain why older children or teenagers continue to have difficulties in this area?

5. Many children with elimination problems experience social problems at school as a result of their condition. What procedures might you recommend to school officials if a child was stigmatized or alienated because of accidents there? What should a child or teacher do if a child has an accident in the classroom? How might you change your recommendations if a child had soiling rather than wetting problems?

6. In Amber's case, much of her bed-wetting appeared to be involuntary. What treatment procedures might you propose for a child who deliberately wets or soils himself or herself? What if the person had a severe developmental disability?

7. What child, parent, or teacher behaviors would you most certainly want to *avoid* when treating someone with an elimination disorder?

8. Explore the advantages and disadvantages of using medication to control elimination problems.

CHAPTER SIX

Attention Deficit/ Hyperactivity Disorder

Symptoms

Ricky Smith was a 7-year-old African-American male referred by his school psychologist, principal, and mother (Mrs. Smith) to an outpatient community mental health clinic. At the time of his initial assessment, Ricky was in second grade. During her initial call to the clinic, Mrs. Smith indicated that her son was "out of control." When asked for specifics, Mrs. Smith simply said that Ricky "was all over the place" and "constantly getting into trouble." As a single mother, she was particularly overwhelmed by her son's behavior and scheduled an appointment for 7 days later. Following a postponement, Mrs. Smith and Ricky came into the clinic about 3 weeks after her initial call.

As part of the evaluation, Ricky and his mother were interviewed separately by a doctoral intern in clinical psychology. Ricky was interviewed first and was polite, reserved, and a little socially anxious. He reported having difficulty adjusting to his new school and especially to his new teacher. He said that his teacher, Mrs. Candler, was always yelling at him and sending notes home to his mother. When asked why the teacher was yelling at him, Ricky said first that he didn't know, but then he said it was mostly about not paying attention or following class rules. Ricky said he was often "on red"; the classroom had a discipline system in which students had to change their name card from green to yellow to orange to red for each infraction of the rules. A red card meant an automatic call to the child's parents. In the past month alone, Ricky had accumulated five red and seven orange cards.

When asked if he liked school, Ricky shrugged and said that he liked some of the classroom activities, especially those related to science (the class was currently studying the growth of tadpoles). He said he had a few friends, but often he had to keep to himself. This was because Mrs. Candler had him spend much of the school day in a corner of the classroom to complete his work. Unfortunately, little of the work was successfully finished. Ricky said he felt bored, sad, tired, and angry in the classroom. He wanted to leave school and stay home but knew this was not likely.

With respect to events outside school, Ricky said that his mother also yelled at him a lot. However, because his mother was often working, Ricky was usually taken care of by his 14-year-old sister. During this time, Ricky would watch television, play videogames, or ride his bicycle outdoors. He said he felt happiest when riding his bike because nobody yelled at him and he could "go wherever I want." Other questions revealed that Ricky had no problems with adaptive behaviors like dressing and eating but did have difficulty sleeping through the night. In addition, Ricky said he felt bad about "being a pain to my mom" and felt confused about why he was doing so poorly in school.

A subsequent interview with Mrs. Smith confirmed most of Ricky's report, with added detail. For example, Mrs. Smith revealed that Ricky was almost intolerable in the classroom, often throwing tantrums, crying when asked to do something, stomping his feet, and being disrespectful to the teacher. In particular, Ricky had a habit of saying "No" and "I don't care" to the teacher, who would make him change his card as a result. Mrs. Smith had already attended four conferences with the teacher at school, including one with the principal and school psychologist as well. The teacher wanted Ricky referred to special education classes, but Mrs. Smith opposed this. The school psychologist instead recommended that Ricky be evaluated by someone outside the school district. This suggestion prompted Mrs. Smith's call to the mental health clinic.

Mrs. Smith also reported that her son was generally "out of control" at home. He would not listen to her commands and often ran around the house until he got what he wanted. She and her son often argued about his homework, chores, misbehavior, extended absences from home, and her work schedule. Mrs. Smith complained that Ricky did not seem to understand what she said some of the time, and that he seemed depressed. More detailed questioning revealed that Ricky often fidgeted and tended to lose many of his school materials. He was quite disorganized and paid little attention to long-term consequences. In addition, the child was difficult to control in public places like a supermarket or church.

Mrs. Smith speculated that certain family factors contributed to Ricky's behavior. She and her husband had separated about 14 months earlier, and Ricky's contact with his father was only sporadic. Mrs. Smith described Ricky as a "fussy" child prior to the separation, but hinted that intense marital conflict may have triggered his more severe behavior. Following the separation, for example, Ricky had started first grade and seemed completely uninterested in school. He was sent home once for fighting and was disciplined several times for taunting other children. Mrs. Smith said Ricky's problems had grown worse over the past 14 months, especially since she was not able to supervise her son as much as before. Mrs. Smith described Ricky's relationship with his older sister as positive but said the teenager could do little to influence Ricky's behavior.

Permission was granted to speak with school officials about Ricky. Ricky's teacher, Mrs. Candler, reported that her student was becoming less manageable than he had been at the beginning of school 2 months before. Initially, Ricky was somewhat withdrawn, but as he became more familiar with the classroom, his behavior became more difficult. He averaged about three severe tantrums per week, each of which consisted of a 20- to 30-minute tirade about people picking on him, his inability to understand the classroom assignments, and wanting to die. On most occasions, Ricky was ignored and was able to compose himself. On other occasions, however, his acting-out behaviors were severe enough to have him sent to the principal's office for supervision the rest of the day.

Mrs. Candler added that Ricky's academic performance was below average but not failing. He appeared to understand and complete his reading and math assignments when motivated to do so, but his attention was sporadic and insufficient. Ricky seemed to pay closer attention when an assignment or method of teaching was relatively new, but he was easily distracted soon afterward. In recent weeks, Ricky was getting out of his seat more and more, requiring a constant response. Mrs. Candler was unsure whether this behavior was intentional and attention-seeking, or uncontrollable. She also indicated that Ricky responded best to individualized attention and structure but that the curriculum didn't allow for much one-on-one instruction. Mrs. Candler suggested that Ricky be evaluated for special education.

A discussion with the school psychologist, Mrs. Dee, revealed that Ricky's tested intelligence level was in the normal range. In addition, his overall level of tested achievement, while low, was not more than two standard deviations from his intelligence test score. A diagnosis of learning disorder was thus deferred. Ricky's greatest problem was paying attention to extended tasks. In addition, his interpersonal relationships with his classmates were somewhat distant, but he was not unpopular. In fact, he excelled during physical education class and was one of the more popular children there. Mrs. Dee felt that Ricky did not belong in special education but did require some behavior modification or medical program to control his disruptive behaviors. On a preliminary basis, the intern diagnosed Ricky with attention deficit/hyperactivity disorder (ADHD) of the predominantly inattentive type.

Assessment

According to the *DSM-IV*, the essential feature of attention deficit/hyperactivity disorder is a "persistent pattern of inattention and/or hyperactivity/impulsivity that is more frequent and severe than is typically observed in individuals at a comparable level of development" (APA, 1994, p. 78). Symptoms of ADHD may include the following:

- Inattention
- Not following through on instructions
- Avoiding tasks that require sustained mental effort
- Losing things
- Distractibility
- Forgetfulness
- Fidgeting
- Leaving one's seat
- Running or climbing about
- Excessive talking
- Difficulty waiting
- Interrupting others

These symptoms must be evident much more so than one would normally expect in a youngster. For a diagnosis to be given, some interfering symptoms must be present before the age of 7 years, the symptoms must be shown in two or more settings, and a significant impairment in functioning must be present. Subtypes include predominantly inattentive, predominantly hyperactive-impulsive, and combined. Although the latter two types appear to be valid, the inattentive type remains controversial (Barkley, 1996).

As mentioned, the clinical psychology intern who evaluated Ricky had arrived at a preliminary diagnosis of attention deficit/hyperactivity disorder, predominantly inattentive type. He based this on knowing that, over the past several months, Ricky had failed to pay close attention to his schoolwork, had difficulty sustaining attention to work tasks, was quite disorganized, often lost school items, and was typically distracted and forgetful. In addition, Ricky sometimes, though not often, failed to understand what others said to him. This latter symptom occurred mostly with his mother, however.

The clinical psychology intern also determined that Ricky's symptoms affected his test scores and grades, and that some of his symptoms (e.g., being distracted, failing to sustain attention) were present before the age of 7 years and before his parents separated. Also, impairment in three different settings was noted: school, home, and religious education classes at church. Each of these presenting problems supported the diagnosis of ADHD, inattentive type.

Ricky was *not* diagnosed with attention deficit/hyperactivity disorder of the hyperactive-impulsive or combined type because his other symptoms did not occur with sufficient frequency or severity. For example, Ricky did fidget and run about, but these behaviors were not considered outside the range of normal 7-year-old male behavior. In addition, Ricky often left his seat at school and home, but the presence of just one symptom does not warrant a diagnosis of ADHD, hyperactive-impulsive type.

In cases of possible ADHD, medical conditions should be ruled out first. The classic symptoms of ADHD—inattention, hyperactivity, and impulsivity—are sometimes caused by neurological, sensory, metabolic, skin, and/or tic disorders (Waslick & Greenhill, 1997). Knowledge of these, especially the latter, is important when deciding whether stimulant medication should be used. In Ricky's case, none of these conditions was present, although Ricky's mother later revealed a past history of moderate alcohol use. Mrs. Smith did drink alcohol during Ricky's prenatal period of development; therefore, signs of fetal alcohol syndrome may have been manifested. Possible signs in Ricky included agitation, moderate impulsivity, and failure to focus or sustain attention fully. However, as noted earlier, Ricky had no intellectual deficits, which are common to those with fetal alcohol syndrome. Thus, it was unclear as to whether fetal alcohol syndrome was relevant to this case.

Mrs. Smith's alcohol use had also helped trigger her marital separation, but an assessment indicated no impairments at this time in her occupational functioning or parental obligations. Still, during the course of Ricky's treatment, the intern suggested to Mrs. Smith that she pursue individual therapy for her alcohol use. However, these suggestions were rebuffed.

Following an inconclusive medical examination, the clinical intern focused his assessment on multiple sources regarding Ricky's behavior in different settings. This is a necessity for a complex disorder like ADHD and involves interviews, rating scales, and behavioral observations, among other techniques.

During parent interviews regarding a child with possible ADHD, interviewers should focus on marital problems, stressful life events, family functioning, and parent complaints, attitudes, and possible psychopathology. In addition, they should explore the child's developmental history and current problems at length, especially "motor, language, intellectual, thinking, academic, emotional, and social functioning" (Barkley, 1997a, p. 91). Finally, and perhaps most important, adult interviews should focus on parent-child and teacher-child interactions. In Ricky's case, significant family factors may have been exacerbating his behavior. The intern therefore concentrated on the possible negative effects of his parents' conflict, separation, and alcohol use.

Interviewing a child with possible ADHD is also important, but be aware that children with ADHD often don't show their symptoms in a novel environment. In Ricky's case, this was particularly true; he showed self-control and was even reserved during his initial interview. In addition, Ricky's teacher had reported that her student paid closer attention to new teaching methods or assignments. Over time, however, as habituation occurs, inattention and hyperactivity tend to resurface with these children. Indeed, in Ricky's case, his classroom behavior had gotten worse since September, and he became more difficult to interact with as therapy progressed.

Initial interviews with a child with possible ADHD should concentrate on the child's perceptions of his or her behavior, interpersonal relationships, and school performance. However, interviews with young children regarding these topics are sometimes unreliable. In Ricky's case, for example, he was quite confused about all the problems he was facing and was unsure about the quantity and quality of his interpersonal relationships at school.

Teacher interviews are critical for this population as well and should concentrate on the antecedents and consequences of the child's behavior. Such information is important for knowing why certain behaviors among these children are maintained over time. Mrs. Candler did not have a great deal of information as to what maintained Ricky's behavior, but she did say he responded best to one-on-one attention.

Rating scales may also be helpful for identifying ADHD problems. The Child Behavior Checklist (CBCL) and Teacher's Report Form (Achenbach, 1991a, 1991b), Conners Parent and Teacher Rating Scales (Conners, 1991), Home and School Situations Questionnaires (Barkley, 1990, 1997b), and Self-Control Rating Scale (Kendall & Wilcox, 1979) are particularly useful in this regard. In Ricky's case, Mrs. Smith completed the CBCL and gave her son high ratings for thought and attention problems. Key items included concentration difficulties, trouble sitting still, and confusion. Tests for inattention, such as a continuous performance test (e.g., Conners, 1995), are also useful for children with ADHD. However, these tests were not conducted in Ricky's case.

A direct behavioral observation is indispensable for assessing children with possible ADHD to (1) evaluate behavior in academic and natural settings, and (2) confirm that ADHD symptoms are present in two or more settings. The intern's observation of Ricky in class and at home largely confirmed previous teacher and parent reports. In addition, the intern found that Ricky initiated and received a lot of social contacts from his peers, more so than reported by anyone during the interviews.

Finally, in assessing a child with possible ADHD, one should certainly try to rule out other possible disorders. For example, ADHD may be misdiagnosed because other conditions like oppositional defiant or conduct disorder, learning or mild developmental disability, or general disruptive behavior are misinterpreted as ADHD. In addition, many of these disorders are comorbid with ADHD, further complicating assessment and diagnosis. To distinguish these disorders, close attention should be paid to general intellectual and adaptive behavior functioning, academic performance, aggression and hostility, quality of interpersonal relationships, social skills, judgment skills, and the classic symptoms of ADHD. In Ricky's case, ADHD was considered the best diagnosis given his normal intellectual functioning, passing grades, nonaggressive interpersonal functioning, and classic ADHD, inattentive-type symptoms.

🐾 Causes and Maintaining Variables 🐾

Several variables, especially biological ones, likely work in tandem to cause ADHD in children. Because this population was thought for several decades to have poor motor coordination and "minimal brain dysfunction," many have concentrated on possible neurological deficits in these children. For example, children with ADHD appear to have some asymmetry in certain areas of the brain. In particular, abnormalities of the frontal lobe have been implicated because this area is associated with inhibition, thinking, reasoning, concentration, attention, expressive language, and motor control. Indeed, some studies have found less blood flow and metabolic activity in the frontal lobe (Zametkin et al., 1993). Children with ADHD also tend to have a smaller left caudate nucleus (Hynd et al., 1993), which is partially responsible for voluntary movement. However, brain differences likely account for only a fraction of those with ADHD, and the causes of these differences remain unclear.

Other unusual neurological patterns have been noted in this population as well. Children with ADHD tend to have smaller amplitudes in evoked response patterns when responding to tasks that require vigilance and sustained attention (Klorman, Salzman, & Borgstedt, 1988). Electroencephalogram (EEG) studies also indicate that children with ADHD show less general arousal than children without ADHD. These data indicate, only on a preliminary basis however, that children with ADHD are underaroused or underresponsive to tasks commonly seen in school. An interesting observation is that the use of stimulant medications like Ritalin increases such arousal and serves to alleviate many ADHD symptoms (Werry & Aman, 1993).

No formal neurological testing was performed on Ricky but, as mentioned earlier, he did maintain his attention better in situations involving new and possibly more arousing stimuli (e.g., a new science assignment). The clinical psychology intern also speculated that prenatal problems created brain changes in Ricky. However, this was never confirmed.

Physical problems of early childhood have been linked to ADHD as well, including meningitis, thyroid problems, otitis media (chronic ear infections), and sensory impairments (especially hearing loss). Contrary to popular belief, however, diet, sugar, and allergies have little if anything to do with ADHD symptoms. Lead toxicity is more pertinent to the onset of ADHD and is especially problematic in urban areas with high concentrations of automobiles, lead in the drinking water, and industrial pollution. Although Ricky did live in a poor area, it was largely rural and these issues did not seem to be a factor in his case.

Evidence for a genetic component to ADHD includes findings that ADHD (1) runs in families, (2) is more prevalent in identical than fraternal twins, and (3) is more prevalent in biological than adoptive parents of children with ADHD (Stevenson, 1992). In addition, relatives of children with ADHD have higher rates of psychopathology compared to the general population. However, because many children with ADHD, like Ricky, have no relatives with ADHD, some have suggested that ADHD has familial and nonfamilial types (e.g., Sprich-Buckminster, Biederman, Milberger, Faraone, & Lehman, 1993). In other words, some types of ADHD may be influenced more by genetic factors, whereas other types may be influenced more by environmental factors.

In Ricky's case, the causes of his ADHD symptoms were never clearly established (as is the case for most children with ADHD). However, Mrs. Smith, as mentioned earlier, did drink significant amounts of alcohol during Ricky's prenatal period. Ingestion of alcohol and tobacco during pregnancy can lead to different symptoms that mirror ADHD, especially inattention (Ricky's predominant ADHD type). In addition, Mrs. Smith reported that Ricky's delivery was difficult. Although no further information was gathered about this, it is possible that Ricky's birth complications and later symptoms of ADHD were related. Complications at birth include anoxia and hemorrhaging, among others.

Overall, different biological factors likely account for most of the variance in explaining the cause of ADHD. Whatever the etiological pathway, however, the end result is a core deficit in response inhibition (Barkley, 1997c) or a person's ability to stop his or her own behavior. This deficit may then lead to other characteristics of children with ADHD, including poor self-regulation, memory, rule-governed behavior, problem solving, persistence, and motor and emotional control (Barkley, 1997c).

Biological factors are thus important in explaining the cause of ADHD. However, environmental variables likely play a substantial role in maintaining ADHD symptoms over time and influencing eventual outcome. The most significant of these environmental variables involve parent-child and teacher-child interactions.

Several parent behaviors are key to controlling, or failing to control, ADHD behavior. Many of these children, as noted, have difficulty paying attention to or comprehending parent commands. Some parents, including Mrs. Smith, consider this behavior to be deliberate noncompliance or vindictiveness. As a result, strong physical punishment is sometimes administered, but this often exacerbates the problem. On the other hand, some parents will acquiesce to their child and his or her ADHD behaviors, administer over-the-counter medication to control the behaviors, or placate the child by letting him or her watch television or play videogames for long periods of time. These strategies generally fail in the long run, however. Parents who provide structure, feedback, and consistent and appropriate discipline for misbehavior or poor schoolwork will achieve better control over their child's ADHD behaviors than those who do not. Treatment plans for children with ADHD must therefore include extensive parental education and involvement in therapy.

Similar conditions apply to teacher behaviors toward a child with ADHD. In general, teachers must pay close attention to children with ADHD or risk letting their classroom deteriorate into chaos. However, a teacher may overattend to a child with ADHD, possibly reinforcing the child's behavior or depriving the child of social interactions with peers. Conversely, teachers who provide structured education, frequent feedback on academic and social behavior, and consistent discipline tend to influence more positively a child with ADHD. Therefore, any treatment plan for children with ADHD must involve extensive consultation and cooperation with teachers and must include their input as to what can feasibly be done in the classroom.

Developmental Aspects

Many researchers have charted the developmental aspects of children with ADHD, and a general course of the disorder has been identified. Much of this developmental research has focused on five growth periods: infancy and toddlerhood, preschool, childhood, adolescence, and adulthood. Little information is available regarding the infancy and toddlerhood period (0–2 years), although many babies who eventually develop ADHD are retroactively described as temperamental. Sometimes, these babies show erratic eating and sleeping patterns, irritability, resistance to regular routines, mood swings, and unpredictability (Ross & Ross, 1982). In Ricky's case, Mrs. Smith initially said her son was "fussy" during his first few years of life. She also reported that Ricky sometimes resisted being held, crawled all over the house, and was overly curious about things potentially dangerous to him (e.g., poisonous cleaners). It remained unclear, however, whether Ricky's early behaviors were "hyperactive" or fairly normal for a 2-year-old.

In the preschool period (ages 3–5), children who eventually develop ADHD have symptoms more characteristic of the disorder. Usually, the most noticeable symptoms are those related to hyperactivity and impulsivity. Specifically, these children begin to "get into everything," become more difficult to control, and show erratic patterns of behavior. In addition, they leave their seats more often than their peers, become excessively vocal and verbal, and disrupt others' activities (Campbell, Schliefer, & Weiss, 1978). In Ricky's case, Mrs. Smith described her son as "rambunctious" but was unsure that his behavior was beyond that normally expected from a 3- to 4-year-old. She did report that Ricky was extremely curious about things, in particular things he'd never seen before. This seemed consistent with Ricky's current behavior; he tended to pay closest attention to stimuli that were newest to him.

Preschool children who eventually develop ADHD also tend to be more noncompliant and aggressive than most children their age. In fact, some symptoms characteristic of oppositional defiant and conduct disorder may begin to appear. These include excessive arguing, sharp and short temper, willfulness, verbal and physical aggression, and negative affect. Mrs. Smith reported that Ricky was not generally aggressive toward others and, in fact, was well liked by most kids in his neighborhood. However, she did say her son was often insistent about having things done his way. If Ricky didn't get his way, for example, he would often run around the house and scream. Still, none of Ricky's symptoms was severe enough to qualify him for a diagnosis of ADHD, hyperactive-impulsive type.

The preschool period for these youngsters is also marked by greater emotional reactivity to events surrounding the child. For example, these kids tend to get more upset than their peers about things that bother them. In addition, they tend to *stay* upset for longer periods of time. Although many ADHD symptoms characteristic of the preschool period did not apply to Ricky, he *was* emotionally reactive. Mrs. Smith said her son would get upset "at the drop of a hat" and that the family often felt they were "walking on eggshells around Ricky." Apparently, Ricky would throw a tantrum if something made him nervous or if he didn't get his way. This was true especially if he was deprived of something new. In addition, Ricky's tantrums would sometimes last up to 2 hours, even for something as minor as not being allowed to watch television. Mrs. Smith said that Ricky's behavior in this regard had not changed much since preschool.

Finally, the preschool period for a child who eventually develops ADHD is sometimes marked by intense parent-child conflict. Some of this conflict arises from the child's chronic inattention to parent commands, which the parent often construes as noncompliance. Although sometimes difficult to tease out, Ricky's behavior was more inattentive than noncompliant. His mother reported that, when she knew she had Ricky's undivided attention, he would listen to her and carry out his assigned task. However, Ricky fought a lot with his mother when he didn't understand what she was saying. As an aside, Mrs. Smith said she couldn't understand why her daughter had grown to be such a responsible and compliant person while at the same time her son was persistently irresponsible.

During the school-age period (6 to 12 years), ADHD symptoms become full-blown as school and social demands increase expectations for appropriate behavior and provide more opportunities for failure. In cases where inattention is the primary problem, as with Ricky, goal direction becomes especially problematic. In addition, problems are chronically evident in work completion, organization, concentration, memory, planning, and social commitments (Barkley, 1996). About half these children also remain defiant and hostile throughout childhood. Self-regulation deficits appear as well and may lead to problems in self-care, completion of chores, social skills, and timeliness (Barkley, 1996). Ricky himself showed many of these problems, although his social skills were not too disturbed.

In adolescence, less severe symptoms of inattention, hyperactivity, and impulsivity are seen. However, these symptoms are still more problematic than those found in the general population. In addition, adolescents with ADHD show more academic problems, antisocial behavior, immaturity, and lower self-esteem than their peers (Hechtman, 1996b). Up to 80% still qualify for a diagnosis of ADHD (Cantwell & Baker, 1989). According to Barkley (1996), the major predictors of ADHD that persist into adolescence include comorbid oppositional behavior or conduct disorder, poor social skills, parent-child conflict and family dysfunction, shorter treatment length, and depression in the child's mother (which presumably interferes with appropriate parenting). Because Ricky had fairly good social skills and was receiving treatment at an early age, his prognosis for adolescence was considered to be good compared to that of other children with ADHD.

Less is known regarding the persistence of ADHD into adulthood, but possibly 30% to 50% of this population continue to show characteristic symptoms as adults (Barkley, 1996). This may be especially so for inattention. In addition, adults who had ADHD in childhood are more likely to show current substance abuse and antisocial or criminal behavior (e.g., Farrington, 1990). Other adult consequences of ADHD include less education, low self-esteem, poor social skills, and suicide attempts (e.g., Weiss, Hechtman, Milroy, & Perlman, 1985). However, note that there is great variability in this population; not everyone with childhood ADHD necessarily develops problems in adulthood. Indeed, other factors like a supportive family environment may enhance positive long-term outcome (Herrero, Hechtman, & Weiss, 1994).

Treatment

Treatment for youngsters with ADHD often involves a multicomponent approach with an emphasis on medication and behavior modification. As mentioned earlier, children with ADHD may be biologically underaroused and lack behavioral inhibition. Stimulant medication is therefore useful in treating some of these children. The most popular stimulant medication, methylphenidate or Ritalin, is relatively short-acting and, in some cases, produces dramatic change in a child's behavior. This is particularly so for symptoms related to hyperactivity and impulsivity.

Ritalin may be given two to three times per day, usually in the morning, at lunch, and sometimes in the late afternoon. Dosage levels vary, but many children are started on a regimen of 5 milligrams (mg) per dose. Dosage levels are typically increased as needed over the next few days and weeks, but generally they do not exceed 60 mg per day (Waslick & Greenhill, 1997). Other psychostimulants commonly used for this population include dextroamphetamine (Dexedrine) and pemoline (Cylert). About three-quarters of children with ADHD who take stimulant medication improve to some degree. For children with ADHD with tic disorders or those who don't respond to stimulant medication, tricyclic or other antidepressants are sometimes used.

In Ricky's case, there was substantial debate as to whether medication should be used. In general, school officials were very much in favor of medication; however, Mrs. Smith was unsure and the clinical intern was initially unconvinced that medication would remediate Ricky's primary problem of inattention. Much of the debate surrounded possible side effects. With respect to stimulant medication, common side effects include loss of appetite and weight, insomnia, anxiety and irritability, crying, tics, and possible long-term suppression of growth (Werry & Aman, 1993). Other concerns about medication for this population include (1) overmedication from overdiagnosis, (2) use of drugs as a panacea (many children receive medication without concurrent behavior modification programs), (3) stigmatization and social ostracization (many children have to take one dose during the school day), and (4) mixed messages concerning drug use to control or modify behavior.

In Ricky's case, Mrs. Smith eventually decided to give medication a try. She also revealed that she sometimes gave over-the-counter cold medication or caffeine to control her son's behavior. She did this about two or three times per month, but the intern recommended that she stop this practice immediately. This recommendation was made to get a better reading of Ricky's "true" behavior, reduce possible harm from frequent use of the cold medication, and eliminate any confounds in the pediatrician's upcoming evaluation. Mrs. Smith complied at once, though no major change was seen in Ricky's behavior.

Ricky was referred to a pediatrician who specialized in ADHD, and she confirmed the original diagnosis. Ricky was initially given a 5 mg dose of Ritalin twice per day (10 mg total). The medication was to be taken in the morning and after lunch in the nurse's office at school, and Ricky complied with the regimen without complaint. The intern and Mrs. Smith explained to Ricky that the drug was given to help him pay closer attention to his mother and teachers. The regimen was begun 2 days later, but no effects were seen. The pediatrician then increased Ricky's dosage twice over the next 4 weeks to a final regimen of 30 mg per day.

Over this 4-week period, Ricky was watched closely at school and home. His teacher, Mrs. Candler, reported that Ricky was somewhat more manageable and did seem to pay greater attention and stay in his seat more. His level of daily academic performance, however, did not improve. Mrs. Smith reported a similar effect, though it was not clear whether her expectations of improvement clouded her perception. The clinical intern therefore conducted two observations of Ricky in the classroom. He noted that Ricky did sit in his seat more, but also that his attention had improved only slightly from pretreatment.

To complement the medication, Ricky was placed on a behavior modification program. This program was primarily designed to improve Ricky's attention, organizational and study skills, and completion of daily school assignments. Initially, it consisted of an extensive token economy system that supplemented the classroom card system mentioned earlier. At first, the token economy was applied only to Ricky's in-seat behavior. He could earn 20 points for every hour he sat appropriately. During this time, he was allowed to leave his seat when asked to do so by a teacher. In addition, Ricky was allowed one "mistake" or unexcused absence from his seat. The first unexcused absence resulted in a warning; subsequent absences during the one-hour period resulted in a "response cost" of two points. Therefore, no points would be given if Ricky left his seat unexcused more than nine times following the warning. In-seat behavior was chosen first because his teachers and the intern believed that Ricky could earn these points with relative ease. By earning points, he would be receiving positive reinforcement for good behavior and would become familiar with the token economy system.

If Ricky accumulated at least 100 points by the end of the 6-hour school day, he earned the right to participate in an interesting classroom activity. These activities included a new game, videotape, or one-on-one conversation with Mrs. Candler. Over a 4-week period, Ricky's in-seat behavior improved somewhat, but the change was not dramatic because the behavior was not overly problematic to start with. Subsequently, Ricky's in-seat behavior was linked only to the green-to-red card system, with rewards given for two consecutive "green" days.

The next token economy program targeted Ricky's attention and completion of school assignments. Ricky was instructed to listen to Mrs. Candler's instructions and repeat them quietly to himself. If Mrs. Candler felt that Ricky was not paying attention, she took away two points. In this case, not paying attention was defined broadly and included behaviors like talking to others or failing to make eye contact during instructions. In addition, Ricky lost points for any assignments he had not completed by the end of the school day. This token economy initially progressed slowly, as each adult had several questions about how to define certain behaviors and how to supervise Ricky during the day. Fortunately, everyone was motivated to help Ricky, and his attentive behavior and completion of assignments improved an estimated 50% over a 6-month period of treatment.

During this 6-month period, the token economy was expanded to include different study and organizational skills. With respect to study skills, for example, Ricky was rewarded for spending time studying, raising his hand appropriately when he had a question, and not distracting children around him. With respect to organizational skills, Ricky was rewarded for keeping his desk neat, telling time appropriately, handing in his homework on time, and telling his mother what supplies he needed at school. Although these skills were not formally measured, Mrs. Candler did report general improvement in both of these areas.

Parent training was also implemented to control Ricky's oppositional problems at home, educate Mrs. Smith and her daughter about Ricky's attention problems, and maintain each party's motivation and consistency regarding the token economy. In particular, Mrs. Smith was taught how to use time-out at home to control Ricky's tantrums and noncompliance. Ricky also received a daily report card from Mrs. Candler, who graded his behavior for that day. If he did well, Mrs. Smith gave him extra rewards at home. If he did not do well, he was sent to bed early. Other aspects of contingency management (e.g., appropriate parent commands) were employed as well.

Ricky progressed fairly well during 6 months of therapy, becoming less disruptive and showing general improvement in his attention. However, no changes were seen in his weekly test scores or grades. Unfortunately, Mrs. Smith ended Ricky's psychological treatment the following summer. She felt, despite the intern's skepticism, that Ricky had improved enough to be maintained only on drug treatment. This is a common occurrence in this population. Telephone contact with Mrs. Smith the following year revealed that Ricky's misbehavior was still manageable, but that his school performance remained mediocre to poor.

Discussion Questions

1. What is the difference, if any, between a child diagnosed with ADHD, hyperactive-impulsive type, and one who is overly rambunctious for his age? What about a child who is simply not motivated to pay attention?

2. ADHD, conduct disorder, mild mental retardation, and learning disability are sometimes difficult to distinguish. What signs and symp-

toms would lead you to conclude almost definitely that a child had one over another?

3. A substantial debate exists as to whether ADHD is overdiagnosed or simply very prevalent among children. What do you think? What biases about a child's behavior would you want to avoid when deciding on a diagnosis of ADHD?

4. ADHD is three to four times more common in boys than girls. Do you think this is a "real" difference or one more easily explained by the expectations we have for boys and girls as they grow up? What possible differences in socialization between boys and girls might explain why boys display symptoms of ADHD more often?

5. What is the best way to assess a child with ADHD? What questions would you like to have asked Ricky or others in his life? What would you look for if you were examining a child at school through a one-way mirror?

6. A substantial debate exists as to what role, if any, the medical establishment should play in the treatment of ADHD. What do you think of medication for this population? What are the pros and cons? Why do you think that so many children with ADHD are placed on medication for extended periods of time? Is this good policy? Be sure to consider the rights of other children to receive an undisturbed education.

7. Develop a treatment plan for a child with ADHD whose teacher does not wish to participate. How might you go about it? Who else would you involve?

CHAPTER SEVEN

Learning Disability

Symptoms

Gisela Garcia was an 8-year-old Hispanic female referred to a school psychologist for evaluation and recommendations for possible treatment. At the time of her referral, Gisela was in second grade. The referral was made late in the academic year and only after Gisela's parents, Mr. and Mrs. Garcia, dropped their initially strong objections to an evaluation. During the school year, Gisela had many difficulties with her reading assignments and spelling tests. These difficulties also affected Gisela's math and science performance because many of her assignments in these areas were based on story problems that required extensive reading and writing.

The school psychologist, Mrs. Dartil, had been aware of Gisela's academic problems for about 2 months. Gisela's second-grade teacher, Mrs. Martinez, informed the school psychologist that one of her students was having particular trouble in reading and spelling, but also that the girl's parents were resisting any form of additional assessment or intervention. Mrs. Martinez hoped the school psychologist could join her for a meeting with the parents to convince them of the need to evaluate Gisela. After several weeks of delay, Mr. and Mrs. Garcia reluctantly agreed to such a meeting.

At the meeting with Gisela's parents and the school psychologist, Mrs. Martinez outlined her student's academic problems. Foremost was Gisela's reading and spelling performance, which lagged severely behind the rest of the class. Gisela was currently in Mrs. Martinez's lowest-functioning reading group and had trouble paying attention to, and understanding, the covered material. For example, Mrs. Martinez would read a story to the group, after which questions about the story were presented. Most of the children readily answered simple questions about the story, although many struggled with more complex questions. Gisela, however, often had trouble answering even simpler questions (e.g., what animal was this story about?). Part of the problem stemmed from Gisela's inattention, as she sometimes sat on the floor and twirled herself around as

Mrs. Martinez read a story. She usually stopped after being reprimanded but would soon continue again.

Mrs. Martinez also reported that Gisela was having trouble identifying new and different words, even those that appeared in word groups (e.g., law, paw, saw). For example, each member of the reading group was asked to read a short passage from a particular book. Most of the time, Gisela was able to read the passage if it had been covered within the past month. For relatively new book passages, however, Gisela had trouble identifying almost every other word. Ironically, Gisela had no trouble identifying letters of the alphabet and, if given enough time, could eventually decipher the meaning of a word and resume her reading. Unfortunately, this often required a lot of time and was disruptive to the reading group.

Mrs. Martinez further explained that Gisela's reading problems were related to her spelling problems. Gisela had enormous trouble spelling words presented orally, as on a test. However, she had little trouble copying a word from a book or rewriting the word several times. For example, the teacher required her students to study new words given on a Monday by spending time rewriting the words during the week. On Friday, the oral test was given. Gisela had little problem with the studying process during the week, although she did write her words at a very slow pace. However, her performances on recent oral spelling tests averaged only about 30% correct. This supplemented other failures on rote reading and writing assignments.

Mrs. Martinez further explained that Gisela's reading and spelling problems were also affecting her progress in math and science. This was primarily because the teacher often taught math and science using story problems and creative lab projects (e.g., growing plants) that involved reports and other written work. These assignments would thus be difficult for someone struggling with reading and writing. During these projects, however, Gisela had little trouble with hands-on work or with tasks that captured her interest and attention.

Mrs. Martinez felt that Gisela was functioning at an early first-grade academic level. However, the teacher also said that Gisela seemed "bright" and did have several strengths in school. In particular, Gisela excelled in music and art class, taking a keen interest in activities there and showing strong motivation. Gisela's strengths also included her social skills. She was witty, highly interactive, and one of the best-liked children in the class. In addition, Gisela's verbal skills were normal. Overall, Mrs. Martinez said that Gisela seemed of normal intelligence but was certainly struggling with the schoolwork assigned this year.

Mrs. Martinez then commented on Gisela's classroom behavior. The teacher said that Gisela was somewhat fidgety and had trouble paying attention but had no disruptive behavior problems. For example, she was not aggressive, highly overactive, impulsive, or impolite. In addition, Gisela was generally compliant, but she needed constant reminders to stay on task. Mrs. Martinez also reported that Gisela was extremely disorganized with her classroom materials and in her study skills. Her desk, for example, was stuffed with irrelevant papers and writing instruments. She also had no systematic way of preparing for tests, completing her assignments, or telling time.

These reports were not well received by Gisela's parents, Mr. and Mrs. Garcia. They adamantly refused to believe their daughter had any internal problem, blaming the school instead (and, indirectly, Mrs. Martinez) for "bad teaching practices." They said Gisela performed well the previous year in another state but refused to release those educational records to the school psychologist. They also said Gisela concentrated well at home and finished her schoolwork whenever they supervised her. In addition, they claimed that Gisela had no trouble paying attention to them and that, overall, she seemed to be a normal 8-year-old child.

Mrs. Martinez responded by saying that Gisela may have been completing her homework with her parents, but very few of the assignments were being turned in (Gisela often claimed they were "lost"). The teacher recommended that, over the next month, Mr. and Mrs. Garcia observe their daughter in her reading group and closely review her tests and assignments completed in class. Gisela's parents agreed to do so.

Two months later, a second meeting was held. The school psychologist and teacher, Mrs. Dartil and Mrs. Martinez, reviewed Gisela's progress and repeated their recommendation for an evaluation. Gisela's school performance was essentially unchanged, and Mr. and Mrs. Garcia were now more aware of their daughter's daily academic problems. Both parents were still reluctant about testing, but following some private discussions over the next two weeks, they finally relented and gave their consent. Mrs. Dartil immediately scheduled a comprehensive testing session for Gisela with her initial intent to discover whether the child had a learning disorder or disability.

Assessment

According to the *DSM-IV*, a diagnosis of learning disorder is pertinent when one's "achievement on individually administered, standardized tests in reading, mathematics, or written expression is substantially below that expected for age, schooling, and level of intelligence" (APA, 1994, p. 46). With respect to the latter, "substantially below" means a discrepancy of more than two standard deviations between levels of achievement and intelligence. In addition, the learning problems must significantly interfere with academic or daily life functioning. In Gisela's case, her learning difficulties were certainly interfering with her academic functioning: She was receiving grades of "F" in reading, spelling, and math and a "D" in science (although she did receive "A's" in music and art). The *DSM-IV* divides learning disorders into those associated with reading, mathematics, and written expression. On a preliminary basis, Gisela seemed to qualify as having learning disorders in reading and written expression.

Learning disorders are *not* diagnosed if the child's academic problems are primarily due to "normal variations in academic attainment, . . . lack of opportunity, poor teaching, or cultural factors" (APA, 1994, p. 47). Malnutrition should also be ruled out. In addition, learning disorders are not generally diagnosed if the person has a sensory deficit (e.g., visual problems), but may be diagnosed if the learning problems are clearly in excess of that deficit. In Gisela's case, Mr. and Mrs. Garcia argued that their daughter's "problems" were the result of poor teaching in particular and a poorly funded school district in general. They didn't think Gisela had a learning disorder. This issue is obviously a delicate one when deciding if a diagnosis of learning disorder applies to a child who is failing classes.

According to Taylor (1988), those who evaluate children with possible learning disorders must consider some key points. First, the child's learning problems must be examined in detail because the problems can take many forms (e.g., poor organization, inability to stay on task, perceptual problems). For example, Mrs. Martinez had mentioned several problems that prevented Gisela from doing well in school. Second, one should keep in mind that even specific deficits like word decoding problems could have wide-ranging consequences for general reading or academic achievement. Third, an assessor should carefully consider the expectations and concerns of parents and teachers. This was especially pertinent to Gisela given her parents' reservations about her school.

Fourth, an assessor should remember that cognitive and behavioral characteristics may influence one another. Taylor (1988) stated, for example, that language deficits may predispose a child toward social withdrawal. In Gisela's case, her ongoing academic problems may negatively affect her self-esteem. Fifth, environmental variables like sociocultural factors must be taken into account. These factors, including socioeconomic status, could affect a child's school-based motivation, competitiveness, achievement orientation, or attitudes. Finally, the presence of biological factors should also be considered.

With these general points in mind, Mrs. Dartil began her assessment of Gisela using the Wechsler Intelligence Scale for Children (third edition; Wechsler, 1991). Cognitive functioning is a central focus when assessing a child with a possible learning disability. In particular, one should note any wide discrepancies between intelligence test scores and achievement test scores. Gisela received a full-scale IQ score of 104, which placed her in the normal or average range. Her performance IQ score was 98 and her verbal IQ score was 110.

Mrs. Dartil also administered the Wide Range Achievement Test (WRAT–third edition; Wilkinson, 1993) to identify any weaknesses in Gisela's academic math, reading, and spelling skills. As generally expected, Gisela's standard scores were only 88 for math, 68 for reading, and 60 for spelling. Gisela's intelligence level and achievement level were therefore quite different. In other words, she was not performing to her potential. Another common reading test often used for this population is the Test of Phonological Awareness (Torgeson & Bryant, 1994).

Discrepancies between intelligence test scores and achievement test scores are considered by some, however, to be invalid indicators of learning disabilities. Instead, some researchers suggest that reading and listening comprehension be the focus of assessment (Lyon, 1996). Tests for comprehension should center on the child's absorption of factual information from a particular passage, inferences made from the passage, and the child's use of information from his or her own background knowledge (Raphael, 1982).

Another problem with intelligence and achievement tests is that they don't identify a child's specific deficits or problems. Because of this, Mrs. Dartil reinterviewed Gisela's parents and teacher and examined Gisela's schoolwork and classroom behavior in more detail. According to Mr. and Mrs. Garcia, Gisela had always been a normal child, talking and walking at appropriate ages and being interested in others. They did finally admit that Gisela struggled somewhat in first grade but said that her teacher claimed nothing was seriously wrong. Indeed, no history of language problems was reported. These assertions from the first-grade teacher led Mr. and Mrs. Garcia to their current position that nothing was wrong with their daughter. Mrs. Garcia also conceded, however, that Gisela was a slow reader who had trouble identifying certain words. Both were surprised that Gisela could not read by the end of first grade, but just assumed she was a "late bloomer." Both reaffirmed that Gisela was a well-behaved child and both insisted they were highly motivated to help her academically.

Mrs. Dartil then collected copies of Gisela's written classroom work and watched her in the classroom. She noticed that Gisela often took a long time to finish reading and writing assignments and lost points as a result. However, when allowed enough time, her performance improved. In addition, Gisela was easily distracted and fidgety, and these behaviors interfered with her on-task behavior. However, when Gisela was isolated from the rest of the class, her work performance did improve. Finally, the school psychologist saw that Gisela's written work was marked by several problems. These problems included very slow, compressed, and unevenly drawn writing. In general, Gisela spent a lot of time copying and recopying her work, a practice that sometimes frustrated her.

The school psychologist then spoke with Gisela's teacher in more depth. Mrs. Martinez felt that Gisela had some type of "processing deficit," or trouble assimilating and integrating incoming information. She based her assumption on Gisela's struggles with words presented *visually*. For example, Gisela had problems remembering spelling words that she studied from a book. However, Gisela did better when the teacher emphasized learning through the *auditory* sense—for example, saying a word, spelling it out loud, and asking the children to write the word on paper. Because Gisela had no history of visual sensory deficits, perceptual or linguistic processing problems were thought to be responsible for her struggles.

Fortunately, the school psychologist also found that Gisela's motivation was good despite her academic setbacks. For example, Gisela said she was interested in extra help to improve her grades and especially her reading. When asked about her fidgeting and moving around, Gisela said she "felt nervous" and sometimes bored in class. She did feel she could control herself, however. Indeed, Mrs. Dartil saw that Gisela concentrated better and moved less when a task was new or particularly interesting. Mrs. Dartil concluded from her assessment that Gisela did have a moderate learning disorder for reading and written expression. However, she also conveyed to the teacher and to Mr. and Mrs. Garcia that the problems could likely be addressed with steps described later.

Causes and
Maintaining Variables

Traditionally, the cause of learning problems was thought to involve some unknown or diffuse brain damage (i.e., "minimal brain damage or dysfunction"). Today, many still believe that cognitive deficits in learning disorders are likely caused by different neurological problems. These cognitive deficits may include (1) perceptual problems, such as trouble distinguishing letters and words, and/or (2) linguistic processing problems, such as trouble organizing speech sounds to form words (Feinstein & Wiener, 1997).

In children with reading problems, general cognitive deficits or specific linguistic processing difficulties may be related to left hemisphere abnormalities (Feinstein & Wiener, 1997). These abnormalities may include perisylvian/left temporal region anomalies, asymmetrical development of the left hemisphere, or poor activation of the angular gyrus. However, disruptions in any number of interconnecting neural networks may also lead to a learning disability (Beitchman & Young, 1997).

Learning disabilities may be influenced as well by genetic factors. Twin studies indicate greater concordance for reading disability in identical than fraternal twins, and aspects of learning disabilities do tend to run in families (Lewis, 1990; Shepherd & Uhry, 1993; Wong, 1996). More specifically, data suggest that changes in chromosome six or fifteen may predispose children for problems in phonological awareness or single-word reading (Grigorenko et al., 1997).

Changes in the brain's left hemisphere may explain the core deficits that make up reading problems. These core deficits, which are independent of intelligence, often include trouble decoding and reading single words (Lyon, 1996). Good readers are able to recognize single words quickly as they read. However, children with reading disabilities identify words more slowly, and this lack of speed interferes with their integration and comprehension of the overall material (Stanovich, 1994). Because of this difficulty, whole-language learning, in which children figure out a word by looking at the context of the sentence, may be ineffective for this population.

Children with reading disabilities have trouble recognizing words as they read. This problem in recognition is, in turn, related to processing deficits. The deficits may spring from memory problems but are more likely manifested in language or phonological deficiencies. In essence, children with reading problems have trouble putting together the various phonemes, or basic sound units that make up a word (e.g., the phonemes "sp," "ee," and "ch" make up the word "speech"). This inability may affect their spelling as well.

Gisela's reading and spelling problems did seem to involve trouble with single word identification. Therefore, her academic problems might be due to changes in the left hemisphere, whereas her academic strengths in music and art might be due to a more dominant right hemisphere. Also, Gisela was left-handed, which suggests right-brain dominance. However, no medical or neurological tests were ever performed on her.

At a more specific level, Gisela's reading problems may have been due to memory and phonological processing deficits. She clearly had trouble remembering words she had supposedly learned before and often failed to connect sound units to make up a word. For example, whenever Mrs. Martinez asked the class to "sound out a word" like "poisonous," Gisela became frustrated with the task. Mrs. Martinez thought Gisela's troubles were simply due to inattention from fidgeting and twirling around. However, inattention and phonological awareness, or knowing how to use phonemes to recognize words and process information, are largely independent of one another (Lyon, 1996). Gisela clearly had learning problems above and beyond any minor behavior problems or symptoms of attention deficit/hyperactivity disorder.

What about Gisela's writing problems? Berninger's (1994) work in this area reveals that children with learning disabilities tend to (1) write less, (2) have less organized ideas and transitions in their writing, (3) show less goal orientation, and (4) inadequately monitor their work for appropriate spelling and grammar. Many children with writing and spelling difficulties also have trouble producing letters, organizing finger movements, mapping out written words phonologically, and integrating visual-motor stimuli.

Gisela certainly had trouble integrating the phonological structure of words. In addition, she often became frustrated and did not check her work properly for mistakes. Her ability to coordinate visual and motor movements was also questioned by her teacher. However, Gisela did show some characteristics of good readers and spellers. For example, she was goal-oriented, had no obvious trouble with finger movements, and produced letters without difficulty (albeit slowly and in a compressed manner). Patterns like this are not unusual in children with learning disabilities and attest to the enormous heterogeneity or variety of symptoms often seen in this population.

Gisela did not have many problems with math (dyscalculia), but a brief description of their etiology is presented here. Children with dyscalculia often have trouble enumerating; manipulating amounts; understanding mathematical concepts; doing computations; and reading, writing, or naming mathematical symbols (Kosc, 1974). These children may also have problems with visual-spatial and visual-perceptual functioning, intelligence, verbal ability, and anxiety. These problems could result from changes in the brain's right hemisphere, which accounts for spatial abilities, as well as changes in the frontal and temporal lobes (Rourke & Conway, 1997). In addition, some have linked dyscalculia to the structure of elementary textbooks in arithmetic. For example, these textbooks have been criticized for their lack of attention to the mastery of basic mathematical processes (Lyon, 1996).

Any proposed cause of learning disabilities (LD) should also account for their frequent comorbidity with attention deficit/hyperactivity disorder (ADHD). Wong (1996) reported that the prevalence of learning disabilities in children with ADHD ranges between 7% and 92%. In addition, those with ADHD *and* LD tend to have more severe problems with attention and cognition than those with either ADHD *or* LD. The causes of ADHD and LD may therefore overlap. Indeed, in Gisela's case, she was often distracted and sometimes overactive when she fidgeted and twirled. Children with learning disabilities may also have social, emotional-depressive, and conduct disorder–related problems. However, these problems are more variable—they didn't apply to Gisela—and are possibly related to the frustration and social rejection that sometimes comes with academic failure.

Developmental Aspects

As mentioned earlier, children with reading disabilities (dyslexia) often have language or phonological processing deficits. These deficits can occur as early as the first year of life. For example, delays may occur in vocalizations like babbling or cooing. In addition, toddlers may show delayed speech or developmentally inappropriate speech errors (Beitchman & Brownlie, 1996). Comprehension problems can also occur at this time and might be suspected in children who have trouble understanding what others say. Finally, behavior problems associated with language difficulties also become more apparent at this time. Common behavior problems include overactivity, impulsivity, inattention, aggression, and social withdrawal.

Mr. and Mrs. Garcia reported that Gisela had been fairly normal during her preschool years. This is not unusual and indicates that it is hard to identify children with learning disabilities before they have begun formal schooling. Mr. and Mrs. Garcia did say that Gisela was sometimes "scattered" and inattentive, but they assumed this was either part of her general personality or normal for a preschooler. In addition, they noticed Gisela's constant fidgeting, but they didn't see this or any of her other behaviors as seriously problematic.

During the initial school-age period, learning disabilities become more apparent as children try to meet academic requirements. In kindergarten, for example, children must listen to instructions, verbally express their desires, sit still, engage in basic writing, and identify letters, among other tasks. Children with learning disabilities sometimes have trouble with these areas and may, as a result, act out or withdraw from others. In many cases, extra practice and behavior modification programs can help curtail these problems. However, if the problems go undetected or if the child "gets by," then learning disabilities will worsen during first and second grade. This applies especially to speech and language impairments, which are one of the best predictors of later learning disabilities (Beitchman & Brownlie, 1996).

Kindergarten was largely unremarkable for Gisela. Her teacher at the time said Gisela took longer than most children to start a task and was easily distracted. However, she had no language problems or trouble identifying letters. In addition, Gisela's behavior was socially appropriate and she was generally well behaved, though she sought a lot of the teacher's attention regarding class projects. Gisela's learning disabilities came into full bloom during first and second grades, however, as she grappled with formal reading, writing, spelling, and mathematical tasks. Phonological processing problems also became more evident at this point as Gisela had trouble decoding various words.

Reading problems appear to be fairly stable over time, reaching even into adulthood. However, there is controversy as to whether these problems are truly stable or simply a function of other factors. According to Lyon (1996), for example, reading problems may be stable because many children with learning disabilities are not identified until third grade, when discrepancies between intelligence and reading achievement become more apparent. A delay in finding a learning disability may therefore delay treatment and add to the intransigence of the disorder. In addition, the stability of learning disabilities may partially result from the use of various and uncoordinated interventions by educators and others. This practice is quite harmful to those with severe learning problems, so their troubles remain stable. Finally, Lyon (1996) pointed out, as many children with learning disabilities continue to experience academic failure, their motivation for completing schoolwork declines. This decreased motivation would obviously harm their chances for achieving normal academic performance in the future.

Gisela had a mixture of good and bad prognostic signs. In one respect, she was fortunate that her assessment and treatment took place near the end of second grade. However, earlier detection and better parental cooperation might have led to faster treatment. Gisela was also fortunate that Mrs. Rankin, the school's special resource teacher, was highly experienced in treating children with learning disabilities. What remained of most concern, however, was Gisela's motivation. Mrs. Martinez, the second-grade teacher, said Gisela was getting increasingly frustrated with her assignments. Her frustration may have been related to the difficulty of her assignments, which were now more complex as the end of the year approached. In addition, Gisela may have been disappointed in having so few passing grades despite several months of effort.

The stability of learning disabilities, especially those in reading, has been documented several times. Lyon (1996), for example, reported from longitudinal studies that 74% of children with reading disabilities in third grade continue to show these problems in ninth grade. In addition, Frauenheim (1978) followed 40 students with dyslexia from ages 11.5 to 22 years. The sample was functioning at a third-grade level in reading, spelling, and math at the beginning of the study, but had advanced only one grade level by the end of the follow-up period. Prognosis often varies, however, as many children with learning disabilities end up doing well in school (Bruck, 1985).

The prognosis for a child with learning disabilities depends largely, as is does for those with pervasive developmental disabilities, on the severity of his or her speech and language impairments. These impairments involve delays in expressive language, auditory language comprehension, visual motor skills, and overall cognitive functioning. Fortunately for Gisela, her skills in these areas were relatively good. In addition, Beitchman and Brownlie (1996) reported that an excellent predictor of learning disability in a child over time was a mother with an incomplete high school education. In Gisela's case, her father had completed high school, but her mother had dropped out of school in tenth grade.

The severity of learning disabilities over time may also be linked to comorbid disorders. Children with learning disabilities and ADHD, conduct disorder, or depression usually have a less favorable prognosis than children with learning disabilities alone. In addition, children with learning disabilities may develop other problems because of their early academic failure. Possible long-term consequences include antisocial behavior, poor impulse control, negative attitudes toward academic achievement, social withdrawal, and interpersonal difficulties (Taylor, 1988). Those who experience these long-term consequences earlier in life, as in adolescence, often have a poorer prognosis than those who experience them later.

Gisela's long-term prognosis is probably good because her intelligence is normal, her learning difficulties were addressed in second grade, and significant others in her life were motivated to improve her condition. Good outcomes may not always be the case, however, in districts whose school psychologists are overwhelmed by the number of children with learning disabilities. Many youngsters in these schools continue to struggle academically without help and drop out of school prematurely. Long-term prognosis can therefore depend heavily on whether extracurricular resources are available.

 Treatment

Treatment for children with learning disabilities usually involves several elements:

1. Placement in academic remedial programs (sometimes in a part-time, segregated classroom setting)
2. Improving metacognitive skills
3. Controlling associated behavior problems that interfere with learning
4. Increasing student motivation

In most cases, these treatments require a coordinated effort among teachers, parents, and the student.

Taylor (1989) issued several recommendations regarding academic remedial programs. First, remedial programs should emphasize ample opportunities for success and devote extensive time to presenting information to students. In addition, these programs must allow students to demonstrate their abilities in different areas and practice various skills. Teachers must also provide frequent feedback and closely follow a child's progress in deficient academic areas.

Second, remedial programs must be highly structured and directed. They should emphasize concrete concepts, eliminate distractions, and progress step-by-step. For example, programs that offer directed instruction for word decoding and recognition skills work well for those with reading problems. According to Taylor (1989), remedial programs should also emphasize one-on-one teaching, mastery learning, generalization of learned material, and incentives for academic performance. These programs should also target all a child's learning deficiencies.

After substantial discussion, Mr. and Mrs. Garcia allowed Gisela to attend a special instruction class for one hour each school day. In addition, they agreed to help their daughter practice what she learned during this class for 30 minutes each night. Mrs. Rankin, the special resource teacher, began working with Gisela immediately because little time remained in the school year. Mrs. Rankin decided to concentrate heavily on Gisela's reading and decoding problems. At first, this involved a review of basic concepts, such as knowledge of different vowel and consonant phonemes, phoneme combinations (e.g., "ou" and "sp"), and the blending of phonics into words. For Gisela, only the latter seemed particularly difficult.

Following this basic review, which took about 2 weeks, Mrs. Rankin decided to move quickly to mastery of reading material. In doing so, she adopted an approach similar to one recommended by Wong (1996). In this approach, a teacher reviews a particular passage from a book and writes down any words that he or she believes a student will find troublesome. These words are written on index cards, which are then presented to the student for decoding. The student practices identifying the phonemes of each word, blending the phonemes, and learning the definition of the word. When the student has practiced each word twice without error, the teacher reads the assigned passage twice as the child follows along with a finger or pencil. Then, the child reads the passage once aloud to the teacher and once to himself or herself. Each page of the book is repeated until the child eventually commits no more than two errors per page (Wong, 1996).

As part of this process, spelling can also be addressed, as it was for Gisela. Because a number of vocabulary words are generated from the reading exercises, the child can take a certain number home to study. Wong (1996) recommended that children in grades one and two take home three words, and those in grades three and four take home four words. The child studies the assigned words and takes a spelling and vocabulary test on the words the next day. Specifically, the child must spell the word presented orally and write out its definition. Words the child has mastered, both in spelling and meaning, are prominently displayed to enhance the student's self-esteem and to give feedback on his or her academic progress.

The extra attention spent on reading and spelling, especially word decoding and recognition, was helpful to Gisela. In addition, Mrs. Rankin's rapport with Gisela was very good, and this helped improve Gisela's mood in the classroom. At first, Gisela averaged about 11 errors per page read, but this quickly diminished to two errors per page by the end of the school year. Unfortunately, the books chosen for Gisela to read were at a late first-grade or early second-grade level. However, Mrs. Rankin felt that continued work over the summer might boost Gisela to a mid-second-grade level by the time she entered third grade.

Another goal of treatment for children with learning disabilities is enhancing their general metacognition. Metacognition essentially refers to an awareness of one's own thinking or problem-solving processes. Metacognition is particularly applicable to children with dyscalculia, who have trouble conceptualizing and solving arithmetic problems abstractly (e.g., Montague, Applegate, & Marquard, 1993). To enhance metacognition in this case, children may be taught to state a math problem in words of their choosing, visualize the problem, predict an answer, and self-monitor their computations.

With respect to reading, Wong (1996) outlined several metacognitive targets for children with dyslexia:

1. Increase the child's awareness of the purpose of reading (i.e., for meaning, not simple decoding)
2. Improve knowledge of reading strategies (e.g., reading differently for pleasure and for mastery of material)
3. Develop sensitivity to important parts of a text (i.e., emphasis on relevant information)
4. Learn to detect inconsistencies in sentences
5. Develop the ability to resolve a comprehension problem (e.g., by using "lookback" strategies)

In similar fashion, metacognitive skills for reading involve an understanding of the reading process and why the process is important. Mrs. Rankin focused primarily on teaching Gisela to monitor her own comprehension and refer back to the reading material as quickly and frequently as possible to enhance her retention.

Another important goal of treatment for this population is to control excess behavior problems that interfere with learning. This was not too pertinent to Gisela, whose behaviors were fairly limited to fidgeting and minor distraction. To counteract these behaviors, Mrs. Martinez gave feedback to Gisela whenever she was overactive or distracted and gave praise for her appropriate on-task behavior. For other children, however, more extensive procedures may be needed. A subset of children with learning disabilities also show symptoms of hyperactivity, so stimulant medication is sometimes used to focus their attention and curtail excess motor activity. Token economies with response cost may also be useful for reducing acting-out and disruptive behaviors.

Finally, a key challenge when addressing children with learning disabilities is to maintain their motivation to complete homework and other assignments. Part of this involves teaching children to attribute failure to a lack of effort, not a lack of ability (Borkowski, Weyhing, & Can, 1988). Children may be taught to think that "Failure means you have to try harder." Other, more tangible reward systems can also be used to increase motivation. In Gisela's case, for example, her parents placed her on a reward system that included weekend privileges for completing and turning in a certain number of homework assignments (recall that many of Gisela's earlier assignments were "lost"). In the following year, this reward system was extended to include studying appropriately, organizing materials, and developing typing skills so Gisela did not have to write so much.

Gisela's progress through the following summer was good, but she attained a reading level equivalent only to early second grade. As a result, Mrs. Rankin, Mrs. Martinez, and Mrs. Dartil discussed the possibility of retaining Gisela in second grade. Mr. and Mrs. Garcia were strongly opposed to this, however, and agreed instead to increase Gisela's reading instruction time with a resource teacher to 90 minutes per day. In addition, both parents promised to remain active in helping their daughter practice her academic skills at home. This was largely successful, and Gisela did reach a mid-third grade reading level by the end of the next school year.

Discussion Questions

1. One of the thorniest issues in deciding on a diagnosis of learning disorder is discovering whether the problem is internal to the child or a function of external factors like poor teaching or inadequate schools. What information would you use to make this distinction? What criteria would you use to conclude that a child does not have a learning disorder or that the surrounding environment is to blame for his or her academic problems? How would you address a case involving this latter situation?

2. Some have claimed that boys, who often have trouble with reading, are given many tutorial and special resource programs at school. Girls, however, who often have trouble with arithmetic, are not always given the same type of resources. Do you think this is true? If so why?

3. On average, boys receive more attention from classroom teachers than girls. Do you think this is related to the gender difference seen in learning disorders? If so, how can it be remedied? Explore the possible benefits and disadvantages of gender-specific classrooms.

4. Are tests for intelligence culturally or racially biased? What evaluation process could you use to eliminate all bias? Is this possible?

5. Assume that Gisela's family was new to the United States. How would the evaluation and treatment process mentioned here change, if at all?

6. How might the use of new technology in computers and computer software affect future education in general and the prevalence and treatment of learning disorders in particular?

7. In the case described here, Gisela's parents were quite resistant to having their daughter evaluated. How might you address parents like these in the case of a child with a possible learning disorder?

8. How might you increase a child's self-confidence about his or her schoolwork?

CHAPTER EIGHT

Conduct Disorder/Aggression

Symptoms

Derek Pratt was a 15-year-old Caucasian male referred by his school guidance counselor, juvenile detention officer, and father to an outpatient mental health clinic for youngsters with disruptive behavior problems. At the time of his initial assessment, Derek was in tenth grade. Mr. Pratt, Derek's father, contacted the clinic and insisted on an immediate appointment given his son's recent lawbreaking activities, school absences, and contact with the juvenile criminal justice system. An initial evaluation appointment was scheduled for 5 days later.

As part of the evaluation, Derek and his father were interviewed separately by a clinical psychologist who treated adolescents with externalizing behavior disorders. At the outset of the interview, Derek was belligerent and confrontational, insisting that the interviewer address him by his street name ("Tree") and making it clear that he would not answer any questions "I don't feel like answering." When informed in greater detail about his right to confidentiality, Derek was dismissive and said to the therapist, "You'll say anything you want to anyway, so just get this over with so I can get out of here."

Questioning revealed that Derek was getting into more serious trouble of late, having been arrested for shoplifting 4 weeks before. Derek was caught with one other youth when he and a dozen friends swarmed a convenience store and took everything they could before leaving in cars. This event followed similar others at a compact disc store and a retail clothing store. Derek blamed his friends for getting caught because they apparently left him behind as he straggled out of the store. He was charged only with shoplifting, however, after police found him holding just three candy bars and a bag of potato chips. Derek expressed no remorse for the theft or any care for the store clerk who was injured when one of the teens pushed her into a glass case. When informed of the clerk's injury, for example, Derek replied, "I didn't do it, so what do I care?"

The psychologist decided to question Derek further about other legal violations in the past. He discovered a rather extended history of trouble.

Ten months earlier, Derek had been arrested for vandalism—breaking windows and damaging cars—on school property. He was placed on probation for 6 months because this was his first offense. In addition, Derek boasted of other exploits for which he was not caught, including several shoplifting attempts, heavy marijuana use on the weekends, joyriding, and missing school. With respect to the latter, Derek had missed 23 days (50%) of school since the beginning of the academic year (as an aside, he said his father was well aware of this particular violation but not the others). In addition, Derek described break-in attempts of his neighbors' apartments and his precocious sexual activity, the latter of which seemed overly boastful to the psychologist. In fact, only rarely during the interview did Derek stray from his bravado. Toward the end, for example, he indicated he didn't like himself much, saying, "I really don't care what happens to me."

Derek was asked about his current situation and about his goals for the future. He said he didn't expect to receive serious consequences from the judge for the shoplifting charge and didn't care about going back to school. He was indifferent or hostile to suggestions made by the interviewer about attending part-time school programs, stating cryptically instead that he and his friends would "take care of ourselves." In addition, Derek said his father often worked and didn't spend much time with him. Derek didn't mind this, however, seeming content and even insistent about maintaining the status quo.

A subsequent interview with Mr. Pratt confirmed some of Derek's report, although it was clear that Mr. Pratt was not well informed about his son's behavior. He said the school counselor and juvenile detention officer strongly recommended that he and Derek pursue therapy given the upcoming consequences that were expected. With respect to school, for example, Derek was about to be expelled for extended absences. With respect to criminal charges, Derek's recent shoplifting arrest marked his second charged offense, so it was expected that some jail or a community service sentence would be given. However, the counselor believed that family counseling could mediate punishments from both the school and court.

Mr. Pratt was not uncooperative during the interview, but he was careful to justify his actions as a parent and not assume too much blame. He complained that being a single parent was difficult, that he often worked, that school officials waited too long before telling him of Derek's absenteeism, and that the police officers had deliberately chosen his son instead of the gang leaders for arrest. Mr. Pratt said he wanted to help his son "get on the right track" and was hopeful the psychologist would "do what's needed to get through to Derek." This latter statement implied that Mr. Pratt didn't want to expend a lot of personal effort in Derek's treatment.

Mr. Pratt also said Derek was usually compliant when home, but that his son was often with his friends during the day and night. He was unsure of what Derek did when his son was away from home, but he speculated that his son probably stayed with friends and played videogames. He said he had a good relationship with his son and that they had talked at length about Derek's recent school and legal problems. Mr. Pratt indicated, in fact, that Derek was willing to change his behaviors and return to school. However, he also said that Derek usually lied about such things and generally could not be trusted. Mr. Pratt stated as well, rather bluntly, that he planned to leave Derek and the area as soon as his son was 18 years old.

With permission, the psychologist also contacted Derek's school counselor and juvenile detention officer. Derek's school counselor said she was unfamiliar with Derek because of his many absences, but that she had spoken with several of his teachers. In general, the teachers reported that Derek withdrew in class, contributed little to in-class projects, and completed few homework assignments. He was failing each class, and his prospects of passing the academic year were slim. No overt behavior problems were reported, however. The counselor speculated that the presence of several strong male authority figures at school prevented any antisocial behavior on Derek's part.

The juvenile detention officer said Derek was scheduled to appear before a judge in the near future, at which time the teenager might receive a sentence of some kind. The officer believed that Derek was at risk of receiving a strong punishment because this was his second arrest in less than a year and because Derek had a disrespectful attitude. He was confident the judge would take family counseling into account and mediate the sentence but was skeptical that Derek and his father would continue to attend counseling sessions. The officer based his remark on their history: In the past 3 weeks, Mr. Pratt and Derek had kept only one of three appointments with him.

With permission, the psychologist also called Derek's mother, Mrs. Lander, who was remarried and living out of state. She said she had little contact with Mr. Pratt but did talk to Derek about once a month. She also voiced her concern that Derek was not properly supervised. Mrs. Lander added that she had no plans to visit her son nor did she think it was possible for him to live with her. She apparently made this decision based on Derek's behavior within the past 2 years. On the basis of all of these reports, the psychologist made a preliminary conclusion that Derek met *DSM-IV* criteria for conduct disorder.

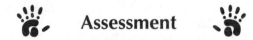

Assessment

According to the *DSM-IV*, the essential feature of conduct disorder is a "repetitive and persistent pattern of behavior in which the basic rights of others or major age-appropriate societal norms or rules are violated" (APA, 1994, p. 85). To meet criteria for the disorder, a youngster must show three specific symptoms for at least 12 months and at least one symptom over the past 6 months. These symptoms include the following behaviors:

- Intimidating others
- Starting fights
- Using a weapon
- Being physically cruel to people or animals
- Stealing
- Committing sexual assault
- Destroying property
- Setting fires
- Breaking into another's property
- Lying
- Staying out at night
- Running away from home
- School refusal behavior

Disruptive child behaviors are sometimes grouped into four main types: property violations, aggression, status violations, and oppositional behavior (Frick et al., 1993). These symptoms must be significant enough to cause impairment in the person's functioning. In addition, childhood onset of the disorder is determined if a symptom was present before the age of 10 years; adolescent onset is determined if no symptom was present before age 10 years. Severity of the disorder may be specified as mild, moderate, or severe.

The psychologist arrived at a preliminary diagnosis of conduct disorder for Derek based on knowledge that, over the past year, Derek engaged in shoplifting, school refusal behavior, acts of vandalism, and curfew-breaking. His troubles with the legal system and his poor school performance also indicated general impairment in functioning. Because Derek had not physically harmed anyone in recent months, however, the psychologist initially rated his conduct disorder as moderate.

When clinicians assess youngsters with possible conduct disorder, it is important that they obtain information from multiple sources. This is because conduct disorder often involves a negative impact on others or negative interactions with others. In addition, assessment should focus on the behaviors (e.g., aggression, noncompliance) that are most problematic, whether the behaviors are overt or covert in nature, the severity and scope of the behaviors, variables that maintain them, parental responses to the behaviors, onset of the behaviors, and comorbid conditions like attention deficit/hyperactivity disorder (McMahon & Estes, 1997).

During preliminary assessment, interviews were held with Derek and his parents, school counselor, and juvenile detention officer. In later sessions, the psychologist also spoke with three of Derek's teachers as well as two of his friends and one of his neighbors (all with Derek's and Mr. Pratt's permission). These interviews revealed that Derek was very peer focused and considered his fellow gang members to be his surrogate family. This attachment explained his earlier remark that he and his friends would "take care of ourselves." In addition, it became clear that Derek had a quick temper, seemed frustrated by recent life events, and was a threat to others. With respect to the latter, for example, a neighbor reported that several residents of the apartment complex were aware of Derek's behavior and took extra precautions to protect themselves and their belongings when he was around. This was especially true if Derek wanted something specific (e.g., money) or was under the influence of drugs.

In addition to relying on multiple sources of information, it is important for therapists to use multiple methods to assess youngsters with possible conduct disorder. Such methods include child self-report measures, parent and teacher rating scales, reviews of academic and legal records, and, if possible, direct observation. With respect to child self-report measures, two commonly used for assessing youngsters with conduct disorder include the (1) Youth Self-Report (Achenbach, 1991c), which solicits ratings from adolescents (age 11 to 18 years) of their own internalizing and externalizing behaviors, and (2) Children's Depression Inventory (Kovacs, 1992), which solicits youngsters' ratings of recent depressive symptoms and acting-out behaviors (e.g., fighting).

Derek's scores on these measures revealed clinical levels of externalizing behavior, as one might expect, but also near-clinical levels of internalizing behavior. On the Youth Self-Report, for example, Derek rated certain items as particularly relevant to himself, including feelings of sadness, worthlessness, self-consciousness, and suspiciousness. On the Children's Depression Inventory, Derek scored just below the clinical range (17). He endorsed items indicating worries about the future, doubts he was as good as other kids, and depressed mood. Based on Derek's self-report, the psychologist believed that his client did have some level of subclinical depression.

Because ratings from adolescents with conduct disorder are not always reliable, it is important to corroborate them with ratings from knowledgeable others. Parent rating scales commonly used for this population include the Child Behavior Checklist (Achenbach, 1991a), Revised Behavior Problem Checklist (Quay & Peterson, 1982), Conners Parent Rating Scale (Conners, 1991), Eyberg Child Behavior Inventory (Eyberg, 1992), and Family Environment Scale (Moos & Moos, 1986). Measures of parent attitudes or expectancies can also be useful (e.g., Parental Expectancies Scale; Eisen, Spasaro, Kearney, Albano, & Barlow, 1996) because negative parent attitudes or unrealistic expectancies sometimes predict whether a child with behavior problems will be referred for treatment. Teacher rating scales commonly used for this population include the Teacher's Report Form (Achenbach, 1991b) and Conners Teacher Rating Scale (Conners, 1991).

In Derek's case, ratings from his father were gathered from the Child Behavior Checklist (CBCL) and Family Environment Scale (FES). On the CBCL, very high levels of externalizing behavior and very low levels of internalizing behavior were reported. This may have been due to Mr. Pratt's overemphasis on Derek's recent, lawbreaking events and the father's general ignorance of his son's depressive symptoms. FES data were more illuminating and revealed high levels of independence and surprisingly low levels of conflict in the two-person family.

Teacher's Report Form data were not very helpful because school officials didn't know Derek well. However, a review of Derek's school records indicated a gradual decline in school performance over the past 3 years. In elementary school, Derek tended to be an "A" and "B" student; in junior high school, a "C" and "D" student; in high school now, he had no passing grades. Such a decline is not unusual in this population, but enhancing academic competence should be a top priority in treatment because good school performance is generally predictive of fewer behavioral problems.

Finally, direct behavioral observations are useful for assessing a youngster's interactions with his or her family. In this case, the psychologist watched Derek and his father interact in his office. Overall, their interactions were cordial but distant. Neither seemed too interested in the conversation of the other and, contrary to what one might expect, no arguing or major disagreements took place. Instead, each seemed content to let the other live his own life with the implicit assumption that the separate arrangement would eventually be permanent. As a result, neither party was particularly willing to make an effort to change the current situation. In fact, Derek's disruptive behavior was simply a source of irritation for Mr. Pratt, who was concerned with having to devote time to appointments with school officials, a juvenile detention officer, and a psychologist.

Outside the therapist's office, direct behavioral observations of a child in his or her natural environment can yield more information about family and peer interactions, antecedents and consequences of disruptive behavior and opportunities for reinforcement. In addition, direct observation may help a therapist (1) decide whether a child's behavior is severe enough to warrant residential treatment or (2) discover any parental abuse that may be taking place. Finally, direct observation may help a therapist dispel any bias regarding a family's willingness and ability to pursue behavior change (Hendren & Mullen, 1997). For example, a therapist might be assigned a court-referred adolescent with conduct disorder and develop erroneous expectations about the family's motivation to resolve their problems.

Causes and Maintaining Variables

Conduct disorder, like many of the childhood behavior problems discussed in this casebook, has a complex and intertwined etiology. Indeed, many biological and psychological variables have been implicated in the disorder. Although these causal variables are difficult to pinpoint in any particular case, a combination of biological predispositions and problematic environmental factors is often inferred. In many cases, for example, this likely involves an interaction of genetic or neurological factors with a highly dysfunctional family environment.

With respect to biological predispositions, no consistent evidence has linked a particular genotype to conduct disorder or aggression. Instead, family factors are probably better predictors of whether someone with a particular genotype will become antisocial. Genetic factors may instead be influential in conduct disorder by altering an individual's temperament, novelty-seeking, or levels of the neurotransmitter serotonin. Indeed, fussy temperament in young children has been associated with general behavior problems over time (Bates, Bayles, Bennett, Ridge, & Brown, 1991; Loeber, 1996). In addition, serotonin levels tend to be lower in those who commit violent offenses and in those with poor impulse control (Lewis, 1997). Lower serotonin levels are also common to people with depression, and many adolescents with conduct disorder have depressive symptoms. In Derek's case, these symptoms included low self-esteem, feelings of worthlessness, and social withdrawal during school.

Other biological factors may be related to conduct disorder as well, especially for boys. These factors include dopamine and endocrinergic changes (i.e., higher levels of testosterone and androstenedione), unusual brain wave patterns, minor central nervous system dysfunction affecting cognitive abilities, increased physiological responsiveness, and lower than normal levels of autonomic arousal (Lewis, 1997). With respect to the latter, it may be that adolescents with conduct disorder engage in risk-taking and thrill-seeking activities to increase their level of biological arousal. Indeed, in Derek's case, he said many of his illegal activities (e.g., drug use, shoplifting) made him "feel good." Thus, sensory reinforcement may be a key reason why some delinquent acts are maintained despite severe or ongoing punishment.

Although biological factors likely play some causal role in conduct disorder, familial or psychological variables are probably more dominant. Indeed, marital discord, family dysfunction, and parental psychopathology are present in many if not most cases of delinquency (Kazdin, 1996). With respect to the latter, for example, parents of children with conduct disorder sometimes have antisocial behavior, alcoholism, or other problems themselves. These behaviors, which may also have a hereditary component, can be modeled by a child or produce conditions that lead to acting-out behaviors. In Derek's case, for example, Mr. Pratt's lack of supervision for his son bordered on neglect. This led to more opportunities for Derek to engage in antisocial behavior.

Marital discord and divorce are also intimately tied to conduct disorder, as evidenced in Derek's case. The mechanisms of this relationship might at first seem obvious—the stress of a parental breakup may be difficult on children. Boys in particular often react to parental fighting and divorce with aggressive and rebellious behavior, although the increased involvement of noncustodial fathers in recent years may soften this finding (Hetherington, Bridges, & Insabella, 1998). Conversely, however, it is possible that acting-out behaviors in children develop first and then lead to marital disagreements about discipline and other issues. Either way, there remains a strong association between family problems and conduct disorder.

In Derek's case, his parents had been divorced for 4 years. During their marriage, Mr. and Mrs. Pratt often disagreed about alleged affairs, finances, and division of labor in the home. Their fights, while never physically violent, were marked by rather venomous verbal exchanges. Following their divorce after 12 years of marriage, Mrs. Pratt retained custody of Derek's two younger sisters and remarried within 18 months. Mr. Pratt retained custody of Derek and immediately moved out of state. Derek said these stressful events (divorce, school withdrawal, move) and the loss of contact with much of his family were difficult to handle, but he felt he'd adjusted well after one year. The psychologist disagreed, however.

Although not present in Derek's case, severe parental abuse is also related to the development of conduct disorder. The various short- and long-term effects of abuse sometimes include acting-out behaviors. For example, Widom (1989) found that twice as many abused children than nonabused children were later arrested for violent crimes in adulthood. The mechanism for how abuse leads to conduct disorder is unclear, but possibilities include modeling, displaced rage, and changes in the child's brain physiology from the abuse (Lewis, 1997).

Finally, child-based psychological factors may contribute to conduct disorder as well. Youngsters who are more aggressive, compared to those less aggressive, tend to be more egocentric and have less well-developed problem-solving and moral reasoning abilities (Hendren & Mullen, 1997). In addition, these youngsters tend to be impulsive, view the actions of others as hostile, get caught for negative behaviors, and show little responsiveness to rewards. The development of psychotic symptoms in adolescence may also be related to antisocial behavior.

What about variables that maintain conduct disorder across time? As mentioned earlier, sensory reinforcement may play a role for youngsters whose biological arousal is lower than normal. In these cases, certain behaviors may be designed to increase arousal, including drug use, speeding, sexual assault, fighting, and overactivity. In addition, some adolescents may engage in antisocial behaviors to escape aversive situations. Examples of such behaviors include school refusal, noncompliance, running away from home, and social withdrawal.

Achenbach (1991a), in his empirical classification system for childhood behavior problems, found that two major factors comprised externalizing behavior: aggressive and delinquent. Aggressive behaviors include arguing, bragging, being disobedient, fighting, attacking, screaming, showing off, talking too much, teasing, having temper tantrums, and issuing threats. These behaviors imply that social attention can maintain conduct disorder because most require interactions with, or negative attention from, other people (e.g., parents, teachers, peers).

In Achenbach's other externalizing factor, delinquent, antisocial behaviors include lying, cheating, setting fires, stealing, using alcohol and drugs, and vandalizing. These behaviors imply that tangible rewards can maintain conduct disorder. For example, a teenager may engage in shoplifting, vandalism, and lying to obtain clothes, food, or other items. This was certainly true in Derek's case.

Knowing what maintains conduct disorder can help a therapist choose the best treatment option. If an aggressive teenager is primarily motivated by social attention or escape, for example, treatment may need to focus on the adolescent, parents, and relevant others. However, if an aggressive teenager is motivated primarily by sensory reinforcement or tangible rewards, treatment could focus more specifically on the adolescent. Of course, many adolescents engage in conduct-disordered behavior for a variety of reasons, which would naturally make treatment more complex.

Developmental Aspects

A key aspect of conduct disorder is its stability over time. This may be due to characteristic patterns that begin in childhood and lead to long-term effects in adolescence and adulthood. For example, difficult temperament and social information-processing deficits may damage attachment with parents, conditions of poverty may limit intellectual stimulation or nutrition, family dysfunction may escalate a child's attention-seeking and aggressive behaviors, stressful life events and peer rejection may trigger depressive symptoms, and poor educational opportunities may blunt problem-solving abilities (McMahon & Estes, 1997). These childhood patterns may not necessarily lead to conduct disorder but, if they do, the disorder will tend to be quite severe and persistent.

Another childhood behavior pattern that might lead to conduct disorder in adolescence is oppositional defiant disorder. The essential feature of oppositional defiant disorder is a "recurrent pattern of negativistic, defiant, disobedient, and hostile behavior toward authority figures that persists for at least six months" (APA, 1994, p. 91). In addition to displaying the basic symptom of noncompliance, these children tend to lose their temper easily, become angry, argue, annoy others, and blame others for their mistakes. They may also be spiteful and oversensitive. These behaviors often worsen over time, and if combined with aggression and family dysfunction, become excellent predictors of adolescent delinquency.

How might parent/family variables and noncompliance/aggression interact in the development of conduct disorder? Patterson (1982) theorized that some youngsters are inadvertently rewarded by their parents for their aggression and noncompliance. Two scenarios may explain how this happens. In a positive reinforcement trap, a child is initially aggressive or noncompliant, and parents give rewards or try to bribe the child to stop. Alternatively, parents may blame others (e.g., school officials) for their child's behavior problems. In a negative reinforcement trap, a child is initially aggressive or noncompliant (1) to get something he or she wants, or (2) to get out of something he or she doesn't want to do. After a lot of arguing, the parents eventually give in to the child's misbehavior. In both traps, the child successfully learns to "coerce" family members into giving something that he or she wants by being aggressive or noncompliant. This coercion becomes more severe as the child ages.

In Derek's case, a formal negative reinforcement trap was not present during his younger years. However, as Mr. and Mrs. Pratt experienced more serious marital difficulties, a permissive family environment evolved. In essence, Derek's parents became more concerned with their own problems and less consistent in their parenting. As a result, Derek's moral reasoning and social skills may not have been well developed. In addition, Derek engaged in more problematic behaviors to get his parents' attention, including fights at school and stealing. These attempts to get attention largely failed, but Derek did get attention from his peers as well as tangible rewards from his criminal behaviors (e.g., shoplifting). As he became more popular with his delinquent peers, Derek felt his true "home" to be his association with them. Following Mr. Pratt's divorce and increased withdrawal from his son, Derek associated with these peers even more.

As adolescents with conduct disorder grow into adulthood, many no longer show aggressive or criminal behavior. However, almost 50% of those with severe conduct disorder will later display symptoms of antisocial personality disorder (APD). APD is sometimes marked by extreme sociopathy, failure to conform, deception, impulsivity, aggression, irresponsibility, and lack of remorse (APA, 1994). This is a serious personality disorder that may remit somewhat during middle age but which often leads to incarceration or death.

Prospective studies indicate that childhood and adolescent aggression are good predictors of antisocial personality disorder in adulthood. For example, in Robins's (1966) classic follow-up study of boys with delinquency, childhood antisocial behavior was found to be the best predictor of adult antisocial behavior and poor psychosocial functioning. In addition, Farrington (1991) found that children rated aggressive by their teachers at 8 years of age, compared to those rated less aggressive, were likely (1) to report being aggressive at age 32 years, and (2) to have committed a violent crime. Long-term and chronic problems like substance abuse and unemployment were also associated with childhood and adolescent aggression. A lack of support services following juvenile detention may also help maintain aggression and criminal behavior (Lewis, Yeager, Lovely, Stein, & Cobham-Portorreal, 1994).

In Derek's case, childhood aggression did seem to be a good predictor of his later delinquent behavior, although many other variables certainly contributed to his problems. Indeed, the mere presence of aggression does not guarantee the development of delinquency (Loeber & Stouthamer-Loeber, 1998). Authoritative parenting styles, appropriate punishment of aggression, reinforcement of prosocial behavior, and social and academic competence may help prevent adolescent conduct disorder. In Derek's case, it's possible that some of his behaviors could have been prevented by more careful parenting.

Most developmental studies in this area have involved boys, not girls. However, evidence regarding girls with conduct disorder has become more available. Findings indicate that girls generally become delinquent later than boys. This could be due, however, to the fact that girls are generally less expected to show disruptive behavior problems than boys. Furthermore, childhood aggression is a good predictor of adolescent conduct disorder in boys but not necessarily girls. Instead, girls in this population may show more nonaggressive conduct problems and experience better long-term outcome than boys (Zocolillo, 1993). Indeed, conduct disorder symptoms in girls are more likely to lead to anxiety and depression than antisocial behavior in adulthood (Robins & Rutter, 1990). In Derek's case, however, his two younger sisters had no maladaptive behavior problems.

Given the data presented here, Derek's long-term prognosis could only be described as fair. His childhood aggression, problem-solving difficulties, school failure, depressive symptoms, and extensive family dysfunction were all poor prognostic signs. However, there were some bright spots. Derek's intelligence was above average, he was largely self-sufficient, and he did have some insight into the futility of his current behavior. Although he didn't have any long-term plans, he wanted a more mainstream life like the one he had during childhood.

Treatment

Prevention of delinquency is desirable because treating adolescents with conduct disorder is often difficult and unsuccessful. This is due to the complex nature of the problem, its severity and duration, and frequently extensive family dysfunction. If treatment is administered, however, it often consists of one or more of the following types: parent-familial, social-cognitive, peer- and school-based, and community-oriented (e.g., residential) treatment (Offord & Bennett, 1994). Derek's treatment included elements of the first three types. Other common therapies include medication and group interventions, but these were not used in Derek's case.

Parent-familial interventions typically focus on contingency management or other ways to train parents to change a child's behavior at home (Kazdin, 1996). Parents are taught to shift social and tangible reinforcers away from inappropriate and antisocial behaviors and toward appropriate and prosocial behaviors. Techniques in this regard include contracting, restructuring parent commands, setting daily routines, and monitoring a child more closely. Communication skills training among family members is also commonly used as an adjunct treatment.

In Derek's case, much of therapy was spent to (1) improve communication between Derek and his father, and (2) increase Mr. Pratt's monitoring of his son. Both goals proved quite difficult to achieve, as Derek and his father missed several appointments and were generally unwilling to talk to one another. As a result, more time was spent discussing Mr. Pratt's personal issues that led to his emotional distance from Derek. For example, the psychologist discovered that Mr. Pratt's divorce was harder on him than first thought and that he actively tried to forget about his failed marriage. Derek was a constant reminder of this, however, and his problems seemed to reinforce Mr. Pratt's sense of personal failure. Although some progress was made in improving Mr. Pratt's mood, his ability to monitor his son's behavior and his motivation to change the current situation remained inadequate.

Communication skills training between Derek and his father was only partially effective because neither had much interest in talking to the other. The psychologist was able to get both to paraphrase the other's statements accurately, but poor motivation was the main problem in developing more extended conversations. In addition, the psychologist had to be wary of conducting therapy that was perceived by Derek and his father as too challenging or threatening lest they leave treatment altogether. As a result, a lot of therapy time was spent exploring general family issues that seemed to inhibit communication.

Contracts were also formed to try to reduce Derek's drug use and school refusal behavior. Although Derek and Mr. Pratt did put effort into designing these contracts, little effort was made to apply them at home. As such, poor motivation sabotaged this treatment technique as well, and no change was seen in Derek's drug use. The one bright spot was that Derek did agree to attend an after-school program that allowed him to earn partial credits toward his high school diploma. Although his attendance was spotty, Derek completed the necessary work over a 3-month period.

Treatment also involved social-cognitive techniques with Derek. Much of this treatment focused on Derek's negative self-statements and depressive symptoms, and he responded best to this approach. Initially, he was shown the link between his mood and his behavior, especially how his negative thoughts sometimes led to reckless and impulsive behavior. The psychologist then described different types of cognitive distortions, especially minimization; Derek had a tendency to undervalue himself and his interactions with others. Finally, Derek was taught to examine both sides of a thought he might have and to think about alternative and more realistic thoughts. Over the course of therapy, Derek's level of depression did improve to some extent.

Derek was also instructed in ways to manage his anger and control his impulses. Here, emphasis was placed on improving Derek's problem-solving skills. The teenager was presented with different problem scenarios and asked to develop potential solutions with the psychologist, who modeled various self-statements that Derek could use in the process. Both assigned a grade to each solution and Derek implemented the one with the best grade. He was then taught to evaluate the usefulness and effectiveness of the solution. For example, the psychologist gave Derek a hypothetical problem such as a dare from his friends to shoplift a compact disc. Various solutions to this problem were generated, including avoidance of these peers, declining the challenge on the basis of prior arrests, and walking away. The psychologist covered dozens of problem scenarios and potential solutions with Derek, who grasped the concept but never bothered to apply the skills to real-life situations.

Treatment also involved, to a lesser extent, management of Derek's wide range of behaviors in his new classroom. Derek often shifted between acting disruptively, appropriately, or withdrawn in the classroom. The psychologist identified the cues that led Derek to act in such different ways. For example, Derek was most disruptive when he was unexpectedly asked to answer a question in class, was most appropriate when social interactions in the classroom were under his control, and was most withdrawn when left alone. With Derek's permission, a meeting with the teacher was held to illustrate these patterns and prevent future misbehavior. For example, the teacher started giving Derek a short list of questions that might be asked in class the next day. He was then allowed to prepare answers for the questions the night before and answer them the next day in class. The teacher also made sure Derek had ample opportunity to interact with her and his classmates during breaks. Over several weeks, the teacher reported that Derek's attendance remained uneven but that his classroom behavior did improve.

Derek and his father remained in therapy for almost 4 months, but missed about 40% of the sessions during this time. Therefore, the continuity of therapy and rapport with the psychologist were constantly interrupted. Because Derek was involved in some level of family therapy, however, the judge decided to sentence Derek to only 50 hours of community service, which he completed. Following the completion of his sentence, however, Derek refused to attend therapy any further. After 3 weeks of meeting with the psychologist alone, Mr. Pratt also ended therapy despite recommendations from the psychologist that they continue.

Perhaps not surprisingly, Derek was arrested for a third time one year later. This time, the charges were shoplifting and assault, as Derek had punched a security guard following an attempted theft at a department store. As a result, he was assigned to a juvenile detention facility. He had dropped out of school in the interim and resumed many of his previous antisocial behaviors. In speaking with the psychologist originally assigned to his case, Derek said he was less depressed but had no interest in returning to school or therapy. In addition, his parents decided to transfer custody of Derek to the state and sever all contact with their son. As mentioned earlier, the recidivism rate for this population tends to be high, and prognosis tends to be poor. Recidivism and poor prognosis are aggravated by a lack of family contacts, as was now true in Derek's case, and so he was certainly at high risk for future delinquent behavior.

Discussion Questions

1. What is the difference, if any, between a teenager diagnosed with conduct disorder and a teenager going through a stressful and stormy adolescence? What about a teenager who is rebelling against abusive parents or runs away to avoid marital conflict?

2. Critique the *DSM-IV* diagnosis for conduct disorder. For example, are three symptoms too few to justify assigning a diagnosis? Which symptoms overlap? Is the diagnosis sexist or biased in any way? Are the subtypes or timeline valid? What symptoms might you add, subtract, or combine? Why would you do so?

3. Conduct disorder is about four times more common in boys than girls, and the rate of serious criminal behavior is about nine times more

common in boys than girls. What biological, psychological, familial, societal, or other factors do you think account most for these differences?

4. The issue of juvenile crime has become a topic of intense political and social debate in the United States. Do you think the problem is serious or overblown? What would be the best way to deal with a 14-year-old who has committed a rape and murder? What are the societal advantages and individual disadvantages of incarcerating a teenager in an adult prison?

5. How would you assess a child or adolescent with symptoms of conduct disorder? What would you want to emphasize during your assessment and why? With whom would you want to spend the most time talking?

6. Would you add anything to Derek's treatment? If an adolescent's parents were uninvolved in treatment, like Derek's, what would be the best way to proceed?

7. Conduct disorder is often comorbid with other problems like depression and substance abuse. How might these other problems complicate the treatment of an adolescent with delinquent behavior?

CHAPTER NINE

Substance Abuse

Symptoms

Jennifer McAllister was a 16-year-old multiracial (Caucasian and His-panic) female referred to an outpatient mental health clinic. The referral was made following Jennifer's second arrest in a 2-year period for drug possession. Jennifer was in tenth grade at an alternative high school that was designed for youngsters with a history of school attendance problems. School officials there actively promoted a "zero tolerance" policy regarding drug possession and use, and therefore they had Jennifer arrested when a random check revealed several ounces of marijuana in her locker. Jennifer was charged with drug possession and later sentenced to perform community service. She and her mother were also required to obtain counseling. The juvenile detention officer to whom Jennifer was assigned had made the referral to this clinic.

During the initial screening interview, Jennifer made it clear that she enjoyed her drug use and had no intention of stopping. She considered the interview and the counseling process to be a waste of time and fully planned to continue her life as before. She was remarkably cooperative and open about her life, but she provided details only after assurances that her information would be kept confidential from her mother, Ms. Ruiz. Jennifer felt it was important to shield her mother from many of the issues that pertained to Jennifer's life because of the family's substantial up-heaval in the past 2 years.

Jennifer explained that her mother had divorced her father 2 years before after a 15-year marriage marked by ongoing physical, verbal, and sexual abuse. The divorce process had apparently not been easy, as Mr. McAllister repeatedly threatened his wife with financial and physical ruin if she left. After various interventions by the police and social service agencies, Ms. Ruiz was finally able to divorce her husband and obtain a restraining order against him. Fortunately, Mr. McAllister soon moved out of state and severed all contact with Ms. Ruiz (her maiden name), Jen-nifer, and Samuel, Jennifer's older brother. However, he first deprived the family of all resources in the bank accounts. Therefore, Ms. Ruiz had to start from scratch to support the family and currently worked two jobs to do so.

Prior to the divorce, violence in the family had been going on since Jennifer was in elementary school. When the fighting was at its worst, Jennifer would surreptitiously leave the house and stay with her friends. As she entered junior high school, Jennifer's time with her friends relative to her family increased, and she started missing more school as a result. Her parents, who were entangled in their own problems, initially neglected Jennifer and allowed her to go as she pleased. However, when Jennifer entered seventh grade, her father insisted that she stay home more often. After complying with her father's request, Jennifer reported that he began to sexually assault her. He initially did so by coming into her room and fondling her, then kissing and caressing her. Jennifer said she felt confused, angry, and uncomfortable at the advances, but complied out of fear for her own and for her mother's safety. No vaginal penetration ensued, however, and her parents divorced shortly thereafter. Jennifer never told her mother of her father's advances, but she was reportedly depressed and anxious following these episodes.

Jennifer said it was at this time, in seventh grade at age 12 years, that she began using drugs. This first involved alcohol, which Jennifer often drank with her friends following a sexually abusive episode with her father. Apparently, the drinking was part of a general "counseling" session with her friends, who listened to her problems and provided support and alcohol. The group consisted of six to eight girls, some of whom had been sexually abused themselves. The alcohol use continued over a one-year period, gradually becoming more frequent and moving from beer to hard liquor. Despite this, Jennifer was able to hide her drinking from her parents and brother.

Jennifer's situation changed dramatically the following year as her father left, her mother began working two jobs to support the family, and her brother withdrew. Jennifer began to stay with her friends more, smoke cigarettes and marijuana, and expand her social group to include boys. On many occasions, the group would skip school and have day parties at one of the youngsters' homes. On one occasion, however, a neighbor called police, who arrested Jennifer and five other members of the group for drug possession. Because it was her first offense, Jennifer was sentenced to one year probation. Interestingly, her mother showed little interest in her daughter's situation. Jennifer reported that her mother was still recovering from the trauma of her own abuse and divorce.

Following her arrest, Jennifer's behavior improved somewhat, as she attended school and helped her mother tend the house. This lasted only about 6 months, however, during which time Ms. Ruiz became more distant from her daughter. Jennifer then began to hang out with her old group of friends, and used alcohol and marijuana to a greater extent than before. Jennifer usually became drunk about once or twice a week and used marijuana at least once a week, usually on the weekends. Her school attendance dropped badly, and she was placed in an alternative high school so that she could receive academic credits at a more moderate pace.

Jennifer also reported that, in the past few months, she had become sexually active with one of the boys in her social group. This was an anxiety-provoking experience for her, as the event reminded her of an earlier sexual encounter with her father. As a result, she drank alcohol to reduce her anxiety about engaging in sexual intercourse. Amazingly, despite having used no prophylactic measures, she was not pregnant and did not have a sexually transmitted disease. Jennifer reported that, in recent weeks, she had also decided to experiment with other drugs, most notably cocaine and methamphetamine. She tried the former only three times, but began using methamphetamine about four times a month (usually preceding or following sexual intercourse). At this point, Jennifer was missing school most of the time but had foolishly left some marijuana in her locker and was subsequently arrested.

The interviewer also spoke briefly to Ms. Ruiz, who provided little information. She was primarily interested in her own legal culpability, wondering aloud if she would be arrested for Jennifer's exploits. When assured that she would not be arrested, Ms. Ruiz said she had little knowledge of her daughter's behavior, but that Jennifer was probably doing what most kids in the neighborhood did. In fact, Ms. Ruiz also said she sometimes used marijuana herself to unwind and forget about past events involving her husband. Overall, Ms. Ruiz did not feel that Jennifer's situation was a serious one and expressed little interest in changing her own or her daughter's behavior.

The interviewer felt, however, that Jennifer's situation was serious and potentially life-threatening. After a further review of Jennifer's legal records, the interviewer thought on a preliminary basis that Jennifer met *DSM-IV* criteria for substance *abuse* regarding alcohol, marijuana, and methamphetamine. He did not think that a diagnosis of substance *dependence* was called for at this time, however, because no clear signs of tolerance or withdrawal were evident.

Assessment

According to the *DSM-IV*, the essential feature of substance abuse is a "maladaptive pattern of substance use manifested by recurrent and significant adverse consequences related to the repeated use of substances" (APA, 1994, p. 182). Four criteria over a 12-month period must be met for the diagnosis to be given:

1. "Recurrent substance use resulting in a failure to fulfill major role obligations at work, school, or home"
2. "Recurrent substance use in situations in which it is physically hazardous"
3. "Recurrent substance-related legal problems"
4. "Continued substance use despite having persistent or recurrent social or interpersonal problems caused or exacerbated by the effects of the substance"

In addition, the person must not currently meet criteria for substance dependence, which is partially marked by tolerance, withdrawal symptoms, and persistent drug-seeking behaviors.

Jennifer did not meet criteria for substance dependence, but she did meet criteria for substance abuse. Her substance use, in particular alcohol, marijuana, and methamphetamine, was recurrent and certainly interfered with her ability to attend school and complete her schoolwork. In addition, her ongoing use of drugs was done in settings that placed her at risk for physical harm. For example, she regularly rode with friends who were intoxicated and engaged in sexual intercourse without protection from disease. Furthermore, Jennifer now had a history of legal problems stemming from her drug use and was continuing to use drugs at the expense of family relationships and a long-term plan for her future.

As part of the court-mandated assessment, a mental health professional with an advanced degree in counseling psychology was assigned to Jennifer's case. The assessment of substance abuse can take many forms but should certainly concentrate first on any dangerous or life-threatening behaviors. A brief mental status examination for orientation, in which a person is asked to identify names, places, times, and current events, may be done to learn whether a person is intoxicated or in a state of delirium from substance use. In addition, a more detailed assessment should be conducted to determine the individual's risk of inflicting self-harm or harming others. This possibility did not apply to Jennifer, however.

More pertinent to Jennifer's case were events that were *potentially* life threatening in nature. This included riding with friends who were intoxicated and engaging in sexual intercourse without protection. Jennifer estimated that each of these events had occurred four to five times a month in the past year. However, none had occurred within the past month. This was primarily because Jennifer had been arrested and her mother was now closely supervising her.

Assessment in this area may also include a toxicology examination, in which a youngster is screened for past drug use by having samples of his or her urine, blood, or hair tested. Urine and blood analyses are useful for detecting a variety of drug metabolites and include tests such as the Breathalyzer to determine alcohol content of a breath sample. Alcohol use may also be detected by examining the cell volume of red blood cells and levels of gamma-glutamyl transpeptidase. Urine tests for the recent use of opiates (e.g., heroin), cocaine, amphetamines, anti-anxiety drugs, and marijuana are also available. These tests include thin layer chromatography, gas-liquid chromatography, high-pressure liquid chromatography, and enzyme-multiplied immunoassay techniques (Farrell & Strang, 1991). In addition, hair analysis is useful for checking drug use within the past several months. In Jennifer's case, a blood test was conducted because drug use within the past 2 weeks was of most concern. Some traces of cannabis (marijuana) were evident, but this may have been a residual reading from Jennifer's last reported drug use 3 weeks earlier. Jennifer was informed that blood tests would be a regular routine during her court-mandated treatment program.

Initial screening methods for adolescents suspected of substance abuse also include questionnaires or interviews. Common examples for alcohol use include the Adolescent Drinking Index (Harrell & Wirtz, 1990), Rutgers Alcohol Problem Index (White & Labouvie, 1989), Adolescent Alcohol Involvement Scale (Mayer & Filstead, 1979), Alcohol Problems Questionnaire (Drummond, 1990), Alcohol Use Disorders Identification Test (Babor, Ritson, & Hodgson, 1986), and the CAGE (Ewing, 1984; Mayfield, McLeod, & Hall, 1974). The latter concentrates on four basic questions about alcohol use:

1. Have you ever felt the need to *cut* down on your drinking?
2. Have other people *annoyed* you by criticizing your drinking?
3. Have you ever felt bad or *guilty* about your drinking?
4. Have you ever had a drink first thing in the morning (i.e., an *eye-opener*)?

Screening tests and interviews are also available for general drug use; they include the Adolescent Drug Involvement Scale (Moberg, 1991), Problem Oriented Screening Instrument for Teenagers (Rahdert, 1991), Addiction Severity Index for Teenagers (Kaminer, Bukstein, & Tartar, 1991), Personal Experience Inventory and Personal Experience Screening Questionnaire (Chatlos, 1991; Winters, 1992), and Adolescent Drug Abuse Diagnosis (Friedman & Utada, 1989).

As part of her interview, Jennifer was asked questions resembling those from the CAGE. Jennifer reported that she occasionally thought she was drinking too much and had even broached the subject with her friends a couple of times. She was especially concerned about her use of methamphetamine, which made her feel out of control. However, she was rebuked by her friends for these doubts and never brought them up again. Jennifer said that no one annoyed her about her drinking or other drug use, but this may have been because no one was paying much attention. Jennifer indicated as well that she didn't feel guilty about her drug use but was concerned that her mother would discover the full extent of it and suffer further mental strain. Finally, Jennifer reported that she rarely used alcohol or other drugs in the morning, usually preferring to do so in the late afternoon, evenings, and weekends, especially when having sex with her boyfriend.

Farrell and Strang (1991) recommended that, when interviewing an adolescent suspected of substance abuse, a clinician should concentrate on the adolescent's reasons for initial and continued drug use. In addition, the interviewer should note whether the youngster is motivated to move away from drug use. Jennifer's reasons for *starting* drug use were varied and complex but generally fell into one of these groups:

1. To escape thoughts about her family's fighting and her father's sexual advances
2. To conform to a peer group that made her feel welcome and that gave her support
3. To satisfy her curiosity about drugs
4. To experience a sense of rebellion against authority

She said her reasons for *continuing* drug use were more specific, however, and included (1) anxiety reduction during sexual intercourse and (2) sensory reinforcement ("feeling good") from the drugs themselves. These reasons were quite potent, so Jennifer had little interest in moving away from her current pattern of drug use.

Interviews with significant others can also be helpful in answering questions about an adolescent's substance use. Unfortunately, with respect to Jennifer, this was not the case. Ms. Ruiz had little knowledge of her daughter's activities, although it was not clear that she was telling the truth. She did express a desire to help Jennifer move away from drugs and toward regular school attendance and new friends. However, Ms. Ruiz's motivation to do so seemed questionable. In addition, contact with Jennifer's friends and school officials did not prove fruitful. Her friends did not want to give any information, possibly out of fear of self-incrimination, and her teachers and guidance counselor simply did not have enough information about Jennifer to provide a useful opinion. Jennifer's brother, Samuel, had moved away from home and had purposely distanced himself from the family. He was not available for interview.

Causes and Maintaining Variables

Multiple causes of substance abuse have been identified. Many researchers contend, for example, that substance-related disorders are influenced by genetic and biochemical variables, environmental and psychosocial stressors, cultural/societal factors, comorbid disorders, and individual personality characteristics. With respect to genetic factors, there seems to be clear evidence that alcoholism has a strong hereditary component (Cloninger, Dinwiddie, & Reich, 1989), especially for males. In addition, concordance rates for general substance abuse are twice as high in identical than in fraternal twins (Houston & Wiener, 1997). Heredity may thus be a strong predispositional factor in the development of substance-related disorders.

Other biochemical variables linked to substance abuse include changes in dopamine, serotonin, monoamine oxidase, and endogenous opioids (Goodwin, 1985). In addition, teens with a family history of alcoholism tend to have more neuropsychological problems and more brain wave and selective attention disturbances than those without a family history of alcoholism (Brown, Mott, & Stewart, 1992). However, each of these biological variables can be mediated to a large extent by environmental factors.

Jennifer's family history regarding substance abuse was unclear. Her father, for example, was reportedly more violent and sexually inappropriate after becoming drunk, but it was uncertain that he actually had alcoholism. Jennifer's mother, Ms. Ruiz, reported some drug use herself, but this was relatively new, infrequent, and in reaction to life events of the past few years. A diagnosis of substance abuse or dependence did not seem to apply to her. In addition, Jennifer's brother, Samuel, reportedly had no difficulties with alcohol or other drug use. Therefore, it wasn't clear that Jennifer had a genetic predisposition to drug use. An interesting observation, however, is that all family members did show various symptoms of depression, which is sometimes marked by changes in serotonin and which may lead to self-medication by substance use.

If a person does have a biological predisposition to substance abuse, it must be triggered, of course, by environmental events that are often stressful or aversive. This was clearly the case with Jennifer, whose stressful life events included an abusive father, neglectful mother, poor school achievement, sexual anxiety, feelings of isolation when not with her friends, legal problems, and low socioeconomic status. Environmental risk factors for substance abuse also include modeling or instruction about drug use from others, social reinforcement from drug use, and availability of drugs. In Jennifer's case, she modeled the use of alcohol for years from her father and, more recently, her friends. In addition, her social group, in particular her older boyfriend, taught her how to use different drugs and gave her a lot of attention when she did so. Jennifer felt as well that she needed to continue taking drugs to be accepted by the group. The group also had a steady supply of drugs, which were provided at no financial cost to Jennifer by her boyfriend.

Family and parental factors may also trigger biological predispositions toward substance abuse, and many of these were highly pertinent to

Jennifer. Family factors include detachment, conflict, lack of affection, inconsistent discipline, and nontraditional values. Parental factors include antisocial behavior, use of drugs, permissive attitudes toward drug use, and disinterest in their children's lives (Sadava, 1987). Other, more general environmental factors may have enhanced Jennifer's drug use as well, including local norms favoring drug use and neighborhood disorganization (Newcomb & Richardson, 1995).

Comorbid psychiatric disorders also exacerbate substance-related problems in youngsters. These include depression and bipolar, anxiety, eating, conduct, oppositional defiant, attention deficit/hyperactivity, and borderline personality disorders (Houston & Wiener, 1997). In Jennifer's case, she technically met diagnostic criteria for conduct disorder and was also somewhat impulsive, depressed, and anxious. The latter appeared as symptoms of posttraumatic stress disorder resulting from Jennifer's earlier sexual abuse.

Finally, individual personality characteristics, such as the following, may predispose a youngster to drug use:

- A desire for independence
- Curiosity
- Rejection of traditional social norms and values
- Rebelliousness
- Novelty- and high-sensation seeking
- Poor academic achievement
- Male gender
- Delinquent or criminal activity
- Anger
- Low self-esteem
- An expectation that drug use will lead to positive social and sensory consequences

Related characteristics include social alienation, decreased religiosity, tolerance of drug use in others, and difficult temperament (Houston & Wiener, 1997).

Some of these personality characteristics applied to Jennifer; others did not. This finding supports the notion that no one drug personality or profile marks this population. In fact, for many of these youngsters, a lot of "gray areas" are present. With respect to desire for independence, for example, Jennifer said she felt torn between wanting to have a normal family life and wanting to be completely autonomous with her boyfriend and other friends. She remarked that she hoped her mother would remarry and that her brother would rejoin the family, but she realized this was not likely to happen. Even if it did, however, Jennifer said her first loyalty was to her friends and that they were now her "family."

Some of the personality characteristics mentioned earlier clearly applied to Jennifer. For example, she was very curious and often pursued new and sensational experiences. As a result, she was not shy about experimenting with different drugs. In fact, she liked trying new drugs, and enjoyed the natural and physical "high" she got from doing so. Other characteristics that applied to Jennifer included her poor school performance (which was mostly a function of her absenteeism), internalizing symptoms, moderate self-esteem, and alienation from those not in her immediate social group.

On the other hand, some of the personality characteristics mentioned earlier clearly did not apply to Jennifer. She was female, not highly rebellious, did not steal or engage in any major criminal activity, and did not have a difficult temperament. Indeed, Jennifer had good verbal and social skills, was still somewhat compliant to her mother's requests, and was generally cooperative with clinic personnel. Jennifer thus had some but not other characteristics commonly ascribed to those with substance-related problems. This again reflects the high degree of variability in this population.

Various "protective" factors may also reduce the chances of substance abuse in youngsters. These factors include high self-acceptance, introversion, maternal affection, intelligence, and warm social interactions, among others (Newcomb & Richardson, 1995). In addition, many children show strong resilience, or good functioning in a challenging or maladaptive environment (Masten & Coatsworth, 1998). Protective factors do not lower drug use per se, but they reduce the risk of initial drug use and slow the progression of drug use to abuse. In Jennifer's case, these factors were present to some extent. For example, she was more introverted than extroverted. However, any protective factors in Jennifer's life were greatly outweighed by her family, sociocultural environment, and thrill-seeking behaviors. Her drug use was therefore problematic.

Developmental Aspects

The developmental progression of drug use in children and adolescents has been a subject of intense scrutiny and controversy, largely because adolescent drug use is so common, especially regarding alcohol. The lifetime prevalence rate of alcohol in high school seniors has been reported to be 80.7%. In addition, many seniors have used alcohol in the past year (73.7%), the past month (51.3%), and on a daily basis (3.5%; Johnston, O'Malley, & Bachman, 1995). Substantial rates of other drug use during the past month are evident as well. This includes tobacco (33.5%), marijuana or hashish (21.2%), hallucinogens (4.4%), stimulants (4.0%), inhalants

(3.2%), barbiturates (2.2%), and cocaine (1.8%; Johnston, O'Malley, & Bachman, 1995).

A popular model for understanding the developmental progression of drug use involves viewing the behavior along a continuum (National Institute on Drug Abuse, 1982). This continuum may involve stages of nonuse of drugs as well as experimental, casual, habitual, and compulsive drug use. For example, a "nonuser" might be one who has never used drugs inappropriately. An "experimental" user might be one who has used drugs a few times out of curiosity, peer pressure, or a desire for increased stimulation. Typically, however, the person is not caught and experiences no major problems from the drug use. In addition, the person's emotional state can be described as excited.

A "casual" or "social/situational" user might be one who engages in drug use on a regular basis (e.g., 2 to 4 times per week) and who makes an ongoing effort to maintain control. An example would be an adolescent who drinks alcohol on a regular basis and struggles to hide the behavior from parents and school officials. Common consequences include decreased school performance, atypical behaviors for that adolescent (e.g., increased lying), and loss of interest in previously enjoyable activities. The adolescent's emotional state at this stage can also be described as excited.

A "habitual" user might be one who engages in drug use on a daily basis, usually with a particular group of friends. The person has not necessarily "lost control" but experiences major problems with school and family. In this case, the adolescent's emotional state can be described as impulsive, erratic, guilt-ridden, and depressed. Finally, a "compulsive" or "obsessive-dependent" user might be one who has lost control over his or her drug use, which occurs multiple times per day. Here, the person's behavior largely surrounds the procurement, maintenance, and use of a regular drug supply. Life-threatening behaviors are not uncommon, and the adolescent's emotional state can be described as disorganized. People who fall into the last three categories of user—casual, habitual, and compulsive—are most likely to qualify for a diagnosis of substance abuse or dependence.

Jennifer was certainly more than an experimental drug user, but it is difficult to say whether she was a casual, habitual, or compulsive user. A key issue here is whether a person is able to maintain control of surrounding events, and Jennifer was usually able to do so. There were times, however, especially after taking methamphetamine, that Jennifer reportedly felt out of control. Her engagement in potentially life-threatening behaviors was also evidence of some lack of control. Still, Jennifer was able to go days and weeks at a time without using drugs, as she did in the past month. Also, her life did not completely surround the acquisition and use of drugs. Therefore, Jennifer might be described as a "moderate" user, or someone between a casual and a habitual user.

Another popular way of viewing substance use from a developmental perspective is with a stage model. Several researchers, most notably Kandel (1982), have proposed that certain "gateway" drugs lead to use of more serious drugs later. There are several stages in this process:

1. No use of any drug
2. Moderate drinking of beer and wine
3. Smoking cigarettes and moderate drinking of hard liquor
4. Heavier drinking of alcohol
5. Smoking marijuana
6. Using pill drugs like amphetamines and barbiturates
7. Using harder drugs like cocaine, hallucinogens, and opiates

(Donovan & Jessor, 1983; Kandel, 1982)

In particular, marijuana appears to be the major "gateway" to harder drug use, especially if the harder drug is cocaine (Newcomb & Bentler, 1986). However, not everyone who begins drug use necessarily progresses through each of these stages, and not everyone does so in this exact order (Yamaguchi & Kandel, 1984).

In Jennifer's case, a stage model of drug use could be loosely applied. Jennifer did start drinking beer first, moving to hard liquor the following year. Her use of alcohol did not dramatically increase, however, when she began smoking cigarettes and marijuana simultaneously. In addition, her use of cigarettes and marijuana overlapped with her experimentation with cocaine and methamphetamine. This demonstrates that adolescents with substance-related disorders may show similar patterns of drug use but that unique individual differences must always be considered.

Other developmental theories of substance abuse in adolescents focus on the behavior as part of a general lifestyle that depends on biological predispositions, temperament, peer influences, parental/familial factors, school-related problems, distorted cognitions, and stress (Sadava, 1987; Vik, Brown, & Myers, 1997). As a result, an adolescent can go down any number of different causal paths leading to different forms of drug use or nonuse. For example, a conforming adolescent whose friends occasionally engage in drug use to relax will likely go that route, whereas an adventurous teenager who is experiencing family stress and whose friends have a ready supply of drugs may become a heavier substance user. This model may apply well to Jennifer, whose novelty-seeking personality and acute family stress interacted with a supportive peer group that relied on frequent drug use to cope with problems.

What about the long-term prognosis for adolescents who engage in substance use and abuse? Not surprisingly, results vary, but some report that adolescents who experiment *lightly* with drugs like alcohol and tobacco are relatively well-adjusted later in life, even more than teenagers who completely abstain from such substances (Shedler & Block, 1990). As a general rule, most adolescents who drink alcohol or occasionally use other substances do not abuse such drugs or suffer major problems later in life. Keep in mind, however, that some adolescents are particularly sensitive even to small amounts of alcohol and other drugs and may eventually become addicted as a result.

More clearly, however, youngsters who engage in *heavy* use of substances are at increased risk for various problems in adulthood. Newcomb and Richardson (1995) stated, for example, that the more an adolescent engages in drug use, the higher will be the likelihood of later problems in "educational pursuits, work and job conditions, emotional health, social integration, criminal activities, and family establishment and stability" (p. 420). This applies especially to adolescents who use multiple substances (polydrug use) and/or use substances in highly excessive amounts.

What about Jennifer's prognosis? Quite frankly, her long-term outcome is probably poor given her family and socioeconomic background, frequent drug use at an early age, and lack of treatment responsiveness (see below). In addition, consequences of drug use will themselves place Jennifer at risk for poor outcome. These consequences include social isolation, refusal to attend school, unprotected sexual activity, and failure to seek appropriate medical care, among others.

 # Treatment

The treatment of adolescents with substance abuse or dependence is often marked by two essential goals: (1) maintaining abstinence, and (2) changing family and other factors that instigate or prolong the substance-related problem (Houston & Wiener, 1997). Many treatment programs share the view that abstinence is the best policy when addressing this population, and this philosophy underlies inpatient therapy as well as self-help groups like Alcoholics Anonymous or Alateen.

Inpatient therapy is often used in severe cases of substance abuse where the person (1) has not responded to outpatient therapy, (2) presents an imminent danger to himself, herself, or others, (3) is at risk for experiencing withdrawal symptoms that cause physical and emotional damage, and/or (4) has other problems (e.g., depression) that seriously exacerbate the drug abuse. Many inpatient settings are based on the so-called Minnesota model that emphasizes an abstinence-based and structured approach, education and support for the adolescent and family, short-term stay (usually less than 2 months), and adoption of the medical or disease model to conceptualize substance abuse. A referral to outpatient treatment after discharge is also recommended, sometimes in the form of a day treatment program. Inpatient therapy tends to be effective in the short term, but not the long term. Factors associated with greater success include female gender, use of one drug, fewer delinquent activities, and higher intelligence (Newcomb & Richardson, 1995).

In Jennifer's case, her substance use was obviously a problem that placed her at risk for serious consequences. However, she was in no immediate danger, had no withdrawal symptoms, and had relatively good social and verbal skills. In addition, because inpatient programs tend to emphasize the person's powerlessness over the substance problem as well as complete abstinence, the psychologist whom Jennifer met at the outpatient clinic did not feel that inpatient therapy would be well suited to her personality or current mood. Increasing Jennifer's isolation on an inpatient psychiatric ward would not have been helpful, either. Therefore, an outpatient therapy program was established for her and she was referred to Alateen.

Outpatient therapy for adolescents with substance abuse or dependence typically focuses on increasing a number of client attributes:

1. Insight into his or her problem
2. Motivation for change
3. Rapport with the therapist
4. Association with certain peer groups
5. Problem-solving ability

In addition, there is a focus on family therapy, contracting, contingency management, peer refusal skills training, socially appropriate leisure skills, and treating comorbid problems like depression (Bukstein & Van Hasselt, 1995).

Perhaps the foremost goal of treatment is getting the adolescent to see that a problem exists or to eliminate denial. In Jennifer's case, the therapist was able to take advantage of some of Jennifer's doubts about her lifestyle and get her to admit that she likely had a problem. Part of this "insight" process is heavily dependent on the client's past experiences, current functioning, and rapport with the therapist. In this case, rapport was good, and Jennifer responded well to the therapist's initial suggestions.

Another crucial aspect of outpatient treatment for this population is family therapy. This is necessary to change dysfunctional communication patterns, increase parental monitoring of the adolescent's behavior, address unresolved issues, provide support, educate family members about the child's substance-related problem, and set up activities to divert the adolescent away from drug use. Unfortunately, in Jennifer's case, this was only partially effective. Ms. Ruiz, who earlier indicated little desire to participate in Jennifer's treatment program, did attend the first few sessions but gradually became distant and uninterested. For example, when asked to discuss some of the sexual abuse issues that Jennifer had finally raised, Ms. Ruiz was dismissive and refused to accept Jennifer's accounts of what had happened. In addition, Ms. Ruiz constantly targeted her daughter as "the one with the problem" and downplayed her own ability to influence the treatment process. However, Ms. Ruiz was willing to support her daughter financially, bring her to treatment, and supervise her school attendance more closely.

The therapist also focused on Jennifer's connection with her peer group, which was a main trigger of her drug use. Specifically, he tried to get Jennifer to distance herself from the group by having her re-enroll in school, participate in extracurricular activities that took up a lot of her time, develop new friendships, and speak with her original peer group only over the telephone. Jennifer showed some initial enthusiasm for these ideas and did begin to attend school on a more regular basis. However, her boyfriend effectively sabotaged the treatment by encouraging Jennifer to resume her drug use and sexual activity. Attempts to get Jennifer's boyfriend to join the therapy process, or at least support the early initiatives of therapy, failed. A major reason why many people with substance-related problems suffer relapse is their re-exposure to cues that triggered substance use in the first place. In Jennifer's case, renewed contact with her boyfriend seriously damaged the progress made in treatment to that point. She also stopped attending Alateen meetings.

As treatment seemed to deteriorate, the therapist tried to bolster Jennifer's self-esteem, peer refusal skills, and problem-solving ability. Jennifer had several cognitive distortions regarding herself and her drug use, including her perceived need to use drugs to cope with stressful events and to keep her boyfriend. This is a form of "psychological addiction" to drugs. The therapist pointed to various skills and positive characteristics that Jennifer had and suggested ways of dealing with her boyfriend to avoid drug use. Unfortunately, Jennifer felt she had to choose sides between the therapist and her boyfriend, and ultimately she went with the latter. Over a period of several weeks, Jennifer's attendance at therapy became more erratic, and she and her mother stopped coming to appointments after 5 months. A telephone conversation 2 months later with Ms. Ruiz indicated that Jennifer had moved out of the house to live with her boyfriend, and that their current whereabouts were unknown.

Because therapy for adolescents with substance-related problems is fraught with so many possible obstacles, like the ones in Jennifer's case, prevention may be the best "treatment." Prevention programs in this area take different forms, including (1) media and law enforcement presentations and other interventions to promote abstinence and antidrug attitudes, and (2) specific early interventions for children and adolescents at risk for substance abuse. The latter consist of programs to teach youngsters the skills they need to refuse offers of drugs, bolster their social skills, establish appropriate recreational options for them, provide information about the harmful effects of drugs, and reduce risk factors in individuals, parents, families, and communities (Botvin, Baker, Renick, Filazzola, & Botvin, 1984; Hawkins, Kosterman, Maguin, Catalano, & Arthur, 1997).

Prevention programs can modify youngsters' attitudes toward drugs and increase their knowledge about drugs, especially programs that are peer based and focus on building skills and providing appropriate recreational activities (Tobler, 1986). However, positive changes in actual drug use have not been consistently demonstrated among most adolescents. Instead, prevention programs are more effective for adolescents *at risk* for substance-related problems. One can only wonder what effect such a program might have had on Jennifer if it had been available.

Discussion Questions

1. How would you make a distinction, if any, between occasional drug use that does not interfere with one's daily life functioning and substance abuse? Would you make a distinction between legal substances versus illegal substances? Why or why not?

2. Many sets of factors appear to explain why youngsters begin drug use and possibly progress later to drug abuse. Which factors (e.g., individual, family, sociocultural) do you think are most important and why?

3. The assessment of adolescent substance use/abuse is now being extended to home-based tests, which let parents submit samples of their child's hair, for example, to a laboratory for analysis. Do you think this is a good idea, and what are the familial, ethical, and clinical ramifications of this technology?

4. The notion that substance abuse is a disease has drawn a lot of controversy in recent years. What are the advantages and disadvantages of adopting the medical model to address substance abuse? Explore the issues of using drugs to treat substance abuse and the effect on recovery of absolving a person of blame and responsibility.

5. Some believe that for people with alcoholism, any use of alcohol is a relapse and will lead to dire consequences. Do you think this is true? Can or should a person with alcoholism be taught to use alcohol in moderation? How might you go about doing so?

6. Tobacco and alcohol companies have been accused in the past of directly marketing their products to youngsters. Do you think this is true and, if so, how do you think this is being done? What steps can or should be taken to prevent such exposure to children and adolescents?

7. How would you design an effective prevention program for substance abuse?

CHAPTER TEN

Family Conflict/ Noncompliance

Symptoms

Jeremy and Joshua Simington were two Caucasian males, aged 9 and 11 years, respectively, who had been referred to a marriage and family therapist. The referral had been made by the children's mother, Mrs. Simington, who was reportedly having a lot of trouble controlling the boys' behavior. During the telephone screening conversation, Mrs. Simington said that both boys were constantly getting into trouble and were increasingly defying her commands. In addition, the family was in turmoil over recent events, including the birth of a new baby daughter and Mr. Simington's extensive work schedule. The level of fighting in the household was becoming intolerable, and Mrs. Simington felt that therapy might be a good way of "reestablishing family harmony."

At the initial assessment session, only Mrs. Simington and her two boys were present. Mrs. Simington was interviewed first and quickly explained that her husband was working and would not be able to attend that day. She expressed hope, however, that he would be able to attend future sessions and that he was willing to do so. Mrs. Simington then reiterated, nearly in tears, that her boys were "out of control." The therapist felt it best at this point to obtain information about each boy separately and began with Joshua. Mrs. Simington said that Joshua had been getting into more trouble at school. Specifically, she said that Joshua, who is in sixth grade, had been suspended from school for 2 days one month ago for talking back to his teacher, showing a "poor attitude," and throwing a temper tantrum. The suspension required a meeting with the school principal and Joshua's teacher.

During her meeting with the principal and the teacher, Mrs. Simington discovered that her son had a pattern of misbehavior in the classroom. This included arguing with his teacher and teasing his classmates. The misbehaviors had been going on for most of the school year (it was now February) but had become more intense since Christmas. In addition, Joshua was refusing to do much of his work at school, and the principal asked Mrs. Simington directly if anything was happening at home to cause these problems.

Mrs. Simington told the therapist that she and her husband were under a lot of stress, and that her ability to deal with the boys was probably impaired. Specifically, their newest child, now about 1 year old, had been unexpected and had caused some financial strain on the family. As a result, Mrs. Simington went from working part time to full time, and time and money typically spent on the boys was reduced. Joshua's behavior had been particularly bad, as he began to argue more with his mother and withdraw from his father. Mrs. Simington explained as well that she and her husband were recently disagreeing about how to discipline the children, and this had led to inconsistent punishment. Mr. Simington preferred corporal punishment whereas Mrs. Simington preferred negotiation and positive rewards.

The therapist also asked about Jeremy, the younger child who was in fourth grade. Mrs. Simington noted that Jeremy had no problems in school, although he did have a history of minor reading difficulties. His behavior at home, however, had worsened as Joshua's had. Mrs. Simington suspected that Jeremy was largely copying his older brother's behavior, especially when he failed to clean his room, sulked, and occasionally refused to go to school. However, Jeremy did show some behaviors that his brother did not, such as running away from the house for extended periods of time, screaming as loud as possible to wake the baby and cause general mayhem, and running around the house. Mrs. Simington said that, between her job, caring for the baby, her husband's absence, and the boys' misbehaviors, her ability to maintain control of the household was now seriously compromised.

The therapist then asked Mrs. Simington to comment on how each family member (except the baby) got along with the others. Mrs. Simington reported that, despite their recent misbehaviors, her relationship with her boys was generally positive. Both, for example, sought her advice on problems and homework, and both showed better behavior when they saw that their mother was upset. In general, Mrs. Simington's relationship with the younger Jeremy was better than her relationship with Joshua, whom she believed was seeking more independence as he neared adolescence. Conversely, Mr. Simington had a better relationship with the older Joshua, with whom he shared interests in sports and other activities. His relationship with Jeremy was more distant and seemed to be getting worse during the recent family problems.

Jeremy and Joshua's relationship with one another was apparently more complicated. At some level, the boys were friends—they got along most times and helped each other with chores and homework. However, both had separate sets of friends, never interacted on the school bus or at school, and argued vehemently over who was getting "more of something" (e.g., food, videogame time, playthings). Mrs. Simington reported as well that the boys rarely worked in tandem to get something they wanted from her or her husband. Furthermore, the boys were sometimes aggressive with one another. On these occasions, Jeremy would usually pick a fight with Joshua, who was about his same size. On two such occasions, one the previous summer and one on New Year's Day, the fights were severe enough to warrant minor medical attention. Over the past 3 weeks, no physical aggression had taken place, but the boys were arguing and screaming at one another almost every day.

To Mrs. Simington's considerable surprise, the therapist also asked about her relationship with her husband. Mrs. Simington seemed guarded about this issue and explained tentatively that she had a good relationship with her spouse. She was quite apologetic about her husband's absence and needlessly explained further about his work schedule. She said she missed him, though the therapist wondered whether she missed more her husband's ability to deal with the boys or his affection and attention. Mrs. Simington also said, after gentle prodding by the therapist, that she and her husband did have heated arguments about whether to abort the third pregnancy (she was adamantly opposed) and how to handle the boys' misbehavior. She did not feel her marriage was in trouble but admitted this was the first time the relationship had been this strained.

Mrs. Simington agreed to encourage her husband to attend the next session, and he did so. Mr. Simington was more withdrawn about the family situation than his wife, but he said he felt the "problems" indicated by his wife were not as bad as she believed. He did acknowledge some financial strain, which added to his skepticism about the need for therapy. He described his relationships with his boys as good and with his wife as fair. When asked about the arrival of the baby and his feelings about the family since then, Mr. Simington acknowledged that he felt pressure to support the family and provide quality time to his children. His manner, however, indicated that he was aware of his wife's discomfort with the family situation and that he wanted to avoid blame from her and the therapist.

The therapist also spoke with school officials—with parental permission. The teachers and principal confirmed Mrs. Simington's account and reported that each child was developing serious behavior problems. The principal, in particular, added that she felt "something was going on with Mr. and Mrs. Simington" that helped produce the boys' classroom problems. The therapist preliminarily concluded that the Simington family had extensive conflict, perhaps more so than reported in the sessions, and that the boys, especially Joshua, met *DSM-IV* criteria for oppositional defiant disorder.

Assessment

According to the *DSM-IV*, the essential feature of oppositional defiant disorder is a "recurrent pattern of negativistic, defiant, disobedient, and hostile behavior toward authority figures" that lasts for at least 6 months

(APA, 1994, p. 91). The child must show four of eight symptoms to meet criteria for the diagnosis. These symptoms include frequent loss of temper, anger, vindictiveness, arguing with adults, noncompliance, annoying others, blaming others for mistakes or misbehavior, and oversensitivity to the behavior of others. "Frequent" means that the behavior occurs much more than in most children that age. In addition, the behaviors must cause some impairment in areas of functioning like interpersonal relationships or schoolwork.

In Jeremy and Joshua's case, these criteria seemed to apply. Mrs. Simington reported that both boys were constantly arguing with her and were noncompliant. In addition, the boys, especially Jeremy, often lost their temper. Conversations with school officials confirmed the boys' tendency to blame others for troublesome events they were involved in, and noted that Joshua in particular was vengeful. The therapist's interview with both boys also revealed a pattern of anger toward their parents as well as beliefs that others were out to do them harm. For example, Joshua insisted that two of his classmates wanted to get him into trouble, and both boys expressed anger toward their parents regarding recent events at home.

When assessing a family with conflict and children with oppositional defiant disorder, it is important to interview the family members about (1) the *content* of problems within the home and (2) the *process* by which family members communicate, solve problems, and try to get what they want (content is often thought of as the "what;" process is often thought of as the "how"). Foster and Robin (1988, 1997) stated that content-related questions should focus on likes and dislikes of different family members, the subjects of most arguments, methods of coercing other family members to agree to something, what comes before and after an argument or noncompliant act, and each member's perception of the current family problems.

In the Simington family, it seemed clear that different members were trying to coerce one another into giving what little there was of the family's resources (i.e., money, attention, time). In the case of the boys, for example, attention from their parents had sharply declined after the arrival of the baby and after changes in their parent's work schedule. However, following more troublesome behavior in school and noncompliance at home, Mr. and Mrs. Simington's attention toward the boys, though negative, increased. The boys were thus actively coercing their parents into giving them more family resources.

This coercion process was not limited to the boys, however. Mrs. Simington complained about her husband's lack of attention to the family because he was not home as much as in the past to discipline the children. She therefore drew her husband more into the family structure by nagging him and by bringing him to therapy sessions. Because of these coercive family processes however, few problems were being solved and little cooperation was evident.

According to Foster and Robin (1988, 1997), family interviewers should also concentrate on process questions, which involve actual methods of arguing, effects of communications on others, and hypothetical scenarios. Examples include describing a typical family argument, methods of communicating anger, reactions to the anger of others, feelings about family member behaviors, methods of problem-solving, possible targets of change, ideal situations, prevention of arguments, family dynamics, family rules, and parental discussions about the children.

In the Simington household, very few family rules and routines had survived the arrival of the baby. For example, the family rarely ate dinner together, chores were more haphazardly done, it was more difficult to get the boys to go to school in the morning and to sleep at night, curfew was regularly broken, and homework was not always completed. In general, because of Mrs. Simington's exhaustion and Mr. Simington's withdrawal, problems were not solved with the same efficiency or cordiality as they were before the baby came. Instead, both parents were now letting problems slide until they were serious and then administering strong punishment. However, this practice was becoming less effective over time.

Various rating scales are also available for assessing family style and dynamics. Examples include the Conflict Behavior Questionnaire (Prinz, Foster, Kent, & O'Leary, 1979), Parent-Adolescent Communication Scale (Barnes & Olson, 1985), and Family Adaptability and Cohesion Evaluation Scales (Olson, Portner, & Lavee, 1985). One of the most commonly used family scales is the Family Environment Scale (FES), a 90-item true-false measure with 10 subscales: cohesion, expressiveness, conflict, independence, achievement-orientation, intellectual-cultural orientation, active-recreational orientation, moral-religious emphasis, organization, and control (Moos & Moos, 1986). Mr. and Mrs. Simington completed the FES, which revealed very low scores on cohesion, independence, all three orientation subscales, and organization. In addition, a very high score was evident for conflict. Together, these scores indicated that the family did not interact much until problems became severe or until someone wanted something.

Direct observation is also an excellent way of assessing family dynamics and communication patterns, especially those patterns that seem to contradict one another. For example, dysfunctional families sometimes engage in "double-bind communications" in which verbal and nonverbal messages conflict. Direct observation may be done using formal coding systems, in which case the therapist audiotapes or videotapes a family interaction and later dissects the communications into parts (e.g., hostile, neutral, positive). Examples include the Marital Interaction Coding System and Parent-Adolescent Coding System (Robin & Canter, 1984).

More commonly, though, therapists informally observe family members in their office. In this case, the therapist looked for nonverbal behaviors that contradicted positive family interactions. She saw several, including Joshua's eye-rolling when his mother talked about the "family situation," Jeremy's folded arms and angry looks, and Mr. Simington's sighing. These behaviors indicated that it was Mrs. Simington alone who felt that a "family problem" existed, and indeed she was the one who initiated therapy and insisted that everyone attend. None of the other family members, however, wanted to be in therapy. This gave the therapist some insight into the family's interactions with one another and supported the view that the family was largely disengaged, with sporadic episodes of conflict.

The therapist also asked the boys and the parents to keep a logbook of arguments, broken rules, and other problems that occurred at home. Not unexpectedly, Mrs. Simington kept her logbook with rigor, but the males preferred to rely on memory when giving their reports to the therapist. Still, the logbooks and stories indicated an interesting and ongoing pattern: (1) initial confusion about who was responsible for a certain task, (2) subsequent fighting about it, and (3) eventual completion of the task by Mrs. Simington. Given this pattern, it was not surprising that Mrs. Simington was the one who most wanted therapy and a change in the status quo.

Causes and Maintaining Variables

Therapists have identified various family patterns that are dysfunctional and often lead to childhood behavior problems (e.g., Minuchin, 1974). One is an enmeshed family, in which the boundaries between family members are diffuse and every member seems overly involved with every other member's life. Often, this family type is marked by separation anxiety, tension, overcontrol, and hostility. In addition, an isolated family is one that eschews contact with those outside the family. As a result, children tend to spend most of their time with their parents and engage in few extracurricular activities.

In the case of the Simingtons, detachment and conflict seemed to be the primary family patterns. Detachment is marked by rigid boundaries, as each family member keeps to himself or herself until necessary or until he or she wants something from someone else. Communication in this type of family is poor, and members interact only when the situation absolutely demands it (e.g., a severe behavior problem). Conflictive families, of course, are marked by ongoing fighting and animosity. Typically, communication and problem-solving strategies are impaired, and cognitive distortions among family members (e.g., perceived harmful intent) are common. Families with children with behavior problems may also show multiple dysfunctional patterns, as was evident in the Simingtons' detachment and conflict.

Problems in communication can take many forms and are sometimes caused by family members who contradict their own statements as they say them (Hansen & L'Abate, 1982). For example, Mr. Simington had a habit of stating his desire for positive family change; at the same time, he would sigh and look quite unenthusiastic. No one in the family therefore believed his statements, and all appeared frustrated as a result. In addition, communication problems may result because of family members, like Jeremy, who are passive and rarely initiate conversations. Problems may also result from family members who are overly concerned, almost paranoid, about coalitions among other family members (i.e., people "ganging up" on him or her). This did not appear to be the case with the Simingtons, however.

Communication problems may result from a refusal to understand or appreciate another's point of view. For example, one family member may say something to another, but the second family member will disavow the statement, ignore it, or think the person meant something else. The last behavior illustrates differences in communication and metacommunication, or differences between the actual message and what "underlies" the message (i.e., what the person is *really* trying to say). When communications and metacommunications greatly differ, problems develop quickly. This seemed to be the case for Mr. and Mrs. Simington, whose level of sarcasm when talking to one another had increased dramatically over the past year. Essentially, they had moved away from direct communication and were instead using snide remarks to coerce or punish one another.

Other family communication problems are more specific. These problems include accusations, interruptions, communications through a third person, lectures or commands that substitute for simple communications, going off on tangents, dwelling on the past, intellectualizing, making threats, joking around, monopolizing a conversation, and, of course, silence (Foster & Robin, 1989).

Problem-solving strategies also tend to break down in dysfunctional families. Problems may relate to everyday family situations (e.g., the garbage is not being taken out) as well as family member feelings of isolation or persecution. The Simington family presented with both sets of problems, and these were likely caused by poor communication patterns. Families with problem-solving difficulties tend to define problems poorly, disagree about solutions, fail to negotiate solutions, and implement faulty solutions. In the Simington's case, the family had drifted toward a problem-solving strategy of letting Mrs. Simington carry most of the disciplinary and child-rearing load. This strategy was falling apart, however, as Mrs. Simington experienced more stress and could not adequately address all the family's responsibilities.

Dysfunctional families also tend to focus on past, unsolvable, or overly complicated problems that are not easily fixed. For example, old "hurts," like a past affair or an incident at school, might be constantly raised not to solve problems but to punish the offending party. In addition, problem-solving strategies may falter because family members (1) coerce one another to accept their own particular solution, (2) offer solutions that are too vague or self-serving, (3) show inflexibility, or (4) become frustrated with the process and give up.

Foster and Robin (1988, 1997) indicated that dysfunctional family patterns are also caused or exacerbated by cognitive distortions held by parents and youngsters. With respect to parents, these distortions include ruination, obedience, perfectionism, self-blame, and malicious intent. Ruination involves the belief that any freedom given to a child will result in disastrous consequences. Obedience involves the belief that youngsters should obey every command given by the parent (the norm is closer to 75% to 80% of commands). Perfectionism involves the belief that youngsters should always know and make the right decisions about everyday events. Self-blame involves the belief that it is the parent's fault if a child makes a mistake. Malicious intent involves the belief that the youngster is acting badly only to annoy and anger the parents. In the Simington's case, this latter cognitive distortion did seem to apply. On several occasions, Mrs. Simington broke into tears when saying she believed the boys were deliberately trying to upset her. It was unclear, however, whether her statements were also designed to elicit guilt from the boys and her husband.

Cognitive distortions may also be found in youngsters; these include fairness, ruination, autonomy, and approval (Foster & Robin, 1989). Fairness involves the belief that parents are unfair in enforcing rules. Ruination involves the belief that family rules will ruin the youngster's status with his or her friends or overall life. Autonomy involves the belief that the youngster should be allowed to do as he or she pleases. Approval involves the belief that the youngster should do nothing that would upset his or her parents. In the Simington's case, all these distortions except approval applied to Joshua, the older child. He believed that he should have been allowed more independence and that his parents, especially his mother, were purposely trying to interfere with the time he spent with friends. These statements supported Mrs. Simington's earlier assertion that Joshua was entering adolescence and demanding more freedom.

Developmental Aspects

Although dysfunctional family patterns are often caused or exacerbated by difficulties in communication, problem-solving, and cognition, these difficulties do not develop overnight. Indeed, in families with defiant children or extensive conflict, a long-term pattern of inadequate parenting, coercion, or other dysfunction is usually present. Unfortunately, some families in therapy are reluctant to admit this or to offer information that might cause a family member to "look bad." In the case of the Simingtons, for example, family members tended to blame their current problems on the recent arrival of the baby. However, it became clear as therapy progressed that many of the issues raised had been active for years.

According to Patterson's (1982) coercion model, child defiance and family conflict develop gradually through a process of misdirected positive and negative reinforcement. For example, a parent may issue a command (e.g., "Go to school") to a child, who says "no." The parent may then excuse the child's behavior, blame his or her noncompliance on someone else (e.g., a school official), bribe the child to carry out the command, or complete the task for the child (e.g., clean the child's bedroom). Here, the child is positively rewarded for his or her noncompliance, and the defiant pattern continues and worsens over time.

In a second case, a parent may again issue a command that is met by child refusal. In this case, however, the child and parent escalate their yelling as the parent tries to force the child to comply. In some situations, the parent may use physical punishment to force compliance, but this is often ineffective. In other situations, the parent may finally give up trying to get the child to comply. Here, the child has been negatively reinforced for noncompliant behavior because the parent has given in and relieved the child of a task (e.g., cleaning one's room). Over time, the child learns that noncompliance or throwing a tantrum is all that is needed to force parental acquiescence. In both cases presented here, family members are coercing one another to get what they want.

In the Simington household, part of Patterson's model seemed to apply. For example, the boys had learned to take advantage of their father's absence and their mother's exhausted state by badgering her about something until she gave in. Mrs. Simington herself knew that she was often too overwhelmed to give the boys much of a challenge, which was why she insisted on getting more help from her husband. Interestingly, this negative reinforcement "strategy" was also used by Mrs. Simington, who sometimes nagged her husband until his behavior improved. In addition, Mrs. Simington used veiled threats of divorce to get her husband to attend therapy.

Family systems therapists also postulate a developmental model of dysfunction. Instead of focusing on behavioral contingencies, however, family systems therapists view families as progressing through a series of developmental stages (Brown & Christensen, 1986). In general, these stages include the following:

1. Marriage
2. Birth of the initial children (beginning family)

3. Children's entry into school and parent's renegotiation of work-load and household labor (school-age family)
4. Children's entry into adolescence and changing parental roles (adolescent family)
5. Children leaving home and entering college (launching family)
6. Parental retirement and interactions with grandchildren (postparental family)

Most families progress through these stages with some turmoil, but problems are usually solved and the family moves forward. In some cases, however, a family may become "stuck" at one or more stages and fail to resolve key issues. The role of the family systems therapist is partly to help the family resolve the issues that restrict growth.

In the Simingtons' case, three developmental sequences were most problematic. First, Mrs. Simington complained that she had children before she had fully developed her career. This led to simmering resentment over the years, and was intensified by recent events. A second developmental problem was the unexpected arrival of the new baby. This event diminished Mrs. Simington's social life and her ability to raise her sons effectively. A third developmental problem was the boys' growth in general and Joshua's entry into adolescence in particular. Such an entry is usually marked by the adolescent's desire for autonomy from parents, stronger peer influence, better reasoning skills, increased ability to experience wider and deeper emotions, and more intimate heterosexual relationships. By itself, entry into adolescence can be a turbulent time. However, this is more likely if the teenager's family is in conflict or if stressful life events are occurring. Such a situation obviously was true for Joshua.

Developmental sequences can also be found in divorced and remarried families. For example, Brown and Christensen (1986) described four stages and associated tasks that must be addressed in these families:

1. Separation and divorce, which are marked by the need to address grief, loss of friends, family reactions, and issues of self-esteem
2. Single parenthood, which is marked by the need to reorganize the family, develop new social support networks, and resolve guilt and anger
3. Courtship, which is marked by the need to accept new intimacies and conflicts from outsiders
4. Remarriage, which is marked by the need to develop a new family history and boundary system

Family systems therapists also propose that various alliances within families develop over time to cause conflict and childhood behavior problems (Minuchin, 1974). One of these, triangulation, occurs when two family members consistently disagree about an issue and then ask a third party member to intervene and choose sides. An example would be a mother and daughter whose relationship was strained and who constantly asked the father to decide their arguments. In a case of triangulation, the father would likely vacillate, moving his support from one party to another to "even things out" and to avoid suffering rejection himself.

Another problematic alliance is a coalition, in which two or more family members align themselves against another. This might involve two children who "gang up" on another, or in the case of an extended family, a grandparent and grandchild who assert themselves against a parent (i.e., a cross-generational coalition). Children might also align themselves to change their parents' behavior. For example, some children act out in school to force their parents to stop fighting and focus instead on the child's immediate problem.

Some family coalitions are appropriate, of course, as when two parents effectively unite to raise their children. In the Simingtons' case, however, a primary problem was a weak parental coalition. In such a coalition, parents disagree about discipline, or each disciplines the children alone or without support. The result may be children who effectively manipulate their parents, set up their own rules, and/or ignore their parents. Jeremy and Joshua Simington were good examples of this, as they had clearly increased their ability to get what they wanted in a family marked by parental disarray. In this case, the therapist must recognize that a shift in power toward the parents is necessary to restore balance and help the family progress through their next developmental sequences.

Treatment

Some of the primary treatment techniques of family therapists, including some used for the Simingtons, involve (1) parent training in contingency management, (2) family communication and problem-solving training, and (3) contracting, reframing, and paradoxical interventions. In some cases, family therapy also involves separate marital therapy. This was recommended to Mr. and Mrs. Simington, but they declined the suggestion.

Contingency management is a process whereby parents are taught to provide a united, consistent, and effective front when addressing misbehavior in their children. Contingency management was highly pertinent to Mr. and Mrs. Simington, who needed to agree on house rules, joint enforcement of those rules, and administration of consequences. As a result, the therapist initially outlined all relevant house rules with the family members. Specific rules were set, for example, for curfew, homework, and chores. In addition, consequences were established for noncompliance. All family members agreed to the rules, and a copy was displayed on the door of the refrigerator.

Contingency management also involves changing parent behaviors, including commands given to the children. In this case, the therapist aimed for parent commands that were succinct, clear, and repeated only once. In addition, Mr. and Mrs. Simington were instructed to refrain from lecturing, criticizing, or questioning during commands. The therapist also discussed ways in which Mr. Simington could help his wife in dealing with the children. Mr. Simington agreed to alter his work schedule to leave home earlier in the morning and get home earlier at night. In addition, he agreed to issue more commands to the boys, increase his time with them in recreational activities, and administer more consequences himself. Over time, however, Mrs. Simington had to keep reminding her husband to maintain his level of effort in these areas.

The therapist periodically reviewed the house rules with the family and any problems that subsequently arose. For example, there was some initial confusion about who would take out the garbage and when, so the therapist assigned different days to the males in the household. In addition, the therapist found it necessary to help Mr. and Mrs. Simington set up a regular routine for the morning and evening. This was done to smooth the transition to school and bed and was carried out with moderate success. The therapist found, however, that the family was becoming increasingly dependent on her to set up rules and resolve disputes. Therefore, a focus was also made on communication skills and problem-solving training.

Communication skills training is used to improve the ways family members talk to one another and listen appropriately. Initially, the therapist may set ground rules for the family, such as no name calling or interrupting in his or her office. One family member then makes a statement while other family members listen and, in turn, paraphrase what the first person said. This process helps increase attention and listening skills, allows one person's message to be heard by everyone, and gives the family practice in absorbing everyone's point of view. Problems in listening and paraphrasing are handled by the therapist, who may intervene and temporarily halt the process to give corrective feedback.

With respect to the Simingtons, the therapist explained the ground rules and allowed Joshua to speak first. Joshua then gave a litany of complaints, at which time the therapist interrupted (only the therapist is allowed to do so) and asked if Joshua could make a one-sentence statement about one issue. Joshua then said he wanted to do more things with his friends outside the home. Jeremy was asked to paraphrase this statement, but instead made the mistake of starting his own statement. After being told that he could make his statement later, Jeremy correctly paraphrased what his brother had said. Mr. and Mrs. Simington were also tempted to respond to Joshua's statement rather than to paraphrase it, but they did so at the therapist's urging.

Communication skills training may focus later on developing short conversations, in which one person makes two or three statements and the second person listens, paraphrases what was said, and responds in kind as the first speaker listens. During this process, a therapist supervises what is being said and provides feedback about how it is said. In cases where two people do not wish to speak to one another, a therapist may play the role of one and talk to the second as the first one watches. Advanced communication skills training can then focus on more extensive conversations, positive statements like compliments, and expressions of appreciation for another's point of view.

For the Simingtons, communication skills training progressed well in the therapist's office but not at home. The family reported that too much chaos there prevented the kind of relaxed atmosphere found in the clinic. As a result, the therapist told the family to schedule "meeting times" during which everyone would sit down and practice the communications skills they had learned. The family agreed to do so during dinner, and this was met with moderate success.

In conjunction with communication skills training, problem-solving training was deemed highly pertinent for the Simingtons. Here, a specific problem is raised and all family members take turns writing down as many solutions as possible (brainstorming). Solutions are written even if preposterous (e.g., hiring a maid to make the beds). Initially, a small problem is addressed so the family can practice the procedure with success. For the Simingtons, an initial problem was curfew—the boys wanted to be in by 10:00 P.M. and the parents wanted them in by 8:00 P.M. All possible solutions were described, and family members then gave a grade to each (i.e., A, B, C, etc.). The solution with the highest grade was then chosen for implementation. This involved a curfew of 8:30 P.M. on school nights and 10:00 P.M. on weekend nights if all relevant chores had been completed. More intricate problems were addressed later in therapy.

Family therapists also use other techniques to improve family dynamics and solve problems (Griffin, 1993). These techniques include contingency contracting, reframing, and paradoxical interventions. Contracting is often used to address parent-adolescent conflict and requires both parties to agree to a written contract drawn by a therapist. The contract contains responsibilities for each party as well as positive and negative consequences for adhering or not adhering to its conditions. An advantage of this method is that it gives the adolescent a say in negotiations, and all viewpoints are considered.

Reframing is a process whereby the therapist helps family members transform a seemingly negative statement or problem into a more positive one. For example, saying that a child is missing a lot of school could be reframed as saying he or she desires more time with his or her parents. Finally, paradoxical interventions are sometimes used to demonstrate family dynamics to family members (Weeks & L'Abate, 1982). For example, a therapist could encourage a child to tantrum as much as possible to show the parents that he or she is doing so for their attention.

The Simingtons remained in therapy for 7 months, after which the family ended treatment. Overall, each family member reported good progress, although it was unclear as to whether therapy had simply prevented things from getting worse over time. Telephone contact with the family 6 months later did reveal some regression to the family's previous level of functioning, but nothing severe enough to warrant a return to formal therapy. A particular bright spot was Mrs. Simington's statement that her husband was taking a much greater role in caring for and disciplining Jeremy and Joshua.

Discussion Questions

1. What do you think is the major difference between children who are regularly noncompliant and children with oppositional defiant disorder? What about the difference between a family that is functional and one that is dysfunctional? Is it possible that a family can have elements of both? Give an example.

2. What might happen during socialization to explain that boys are generally more defiant than girls? Do you think parents and teachers have different expectations for boys and girls? If so, what are they?

3. Would you describe your own family as healthy, enmeshed, isolated, detached, or conflictive? Did different patterns emerge among different subsystems (e.g., parent-parent, parent-child, child-child) in your family?

4. What is the best way to assess a family that has a lot of secrets and is afraid to tell you what is "really" going on? What types of issues do you think families are most reluctant to talk about?

5. A common problem in family therapy overall, and the Simington's case in particular, is the transfer of skills from the therapist's office to home. What would you recommend or do as a therapist to help a family communicate or solve problems better in a chaotic home environment?

6. Do you think family dynamics are substantially different across cultures? What major differences do you think exist, if any, among Hispanic, African-American, Asian-American, Native American, and Anglo-American families? How might ethnic status influence family therapy?

7. How is the family structure changing in the United States? How might a family therapist modify treatment to meet the needs of a single-parent family, a divorced family, one headed by inexperienced teenagers, or one in which the parents are unable to spend a lot of time with their children?

CHAPTER ELEVEN

Autism/Mental Retardation

 Symptoms

Jennie Hobson was a 7-year-old Caucasian female who lived with her parents but attended a school for youngsters with severe disabilities during the day. A special education teacher, Ms. D'Angelo, was recently hired by the school to supervise the education and training of a small group of children that included Jennie. Ms. D'Angelo's immediate task was to evaluate the five children in her designated group and decide whether their previously assigned diagnoses were still accurate. In addition, she was to design and implement for each child an individualized education program that reflected the child's current needs.

Ms. D'Angelo first observed Jennie in a small classroom over a 5-day period. Jennie was often nonresponsive to others, especially her classmates, and rarely made eye contact with anyone. When left alone, Jennie would usually stand, put her hands over her throat, stick out her tongue, and make strange but soft noises. This would last for hours if she was left alone to play. When seated, Jennie would rock back and forth in her chair, although she never fell. Indeed, her motor skills seemed excellent, and she was able to use crayons and manipulate paper when asked to do so. However, her dexterity was also evident in her aggression. For example, Jennie had a tendency to grab people's jewelry and eyeglasses and fling them across the room. She could move quickly enough to accomplish this in less than 2 seconds.

Ms. D'Angelo noticed that Jennie was most aggressive when introduced to something or someone new. For example, a new intern entered the room one day to work with Jennie but was promptly met with a slap across his face and a look of consternation on Jennie's face (Ms. D'Angelo took note not to lean into Jennie when talking to her for the first time). Jennie then sat in a corner of the room facing the wall and pulled at her own hair. The intern ignored the behavior and began to work with the other students in the room. After an hour, Jennie returned to her seat at the request of the intern but refused to work on her educational tasks. Her next day with the intern was less problematic, however, as she seemed to adjust to the new situation.

Ms. D'Angelo noticed as well that Jennie did not speak and vocalized only when making her soft sounds. Although the volume of her sounds rarely changed, she appeared to make the sounds when she was bored or anxious. Jennie made no effort to communicate with others and, in fact, was often oblivious to the presence of other people in the room. For example, she was sometimes startled when asked to do something. Despite her lack of expressiveness, however, Jennie did understand and did adhere to simple requests from others. For example, she complied readily when told to get her lunch, use the bathroom, or retrieve an item in the classroom. These commands were apparently part of her regular routine and therefore worthy of adherence.

Jennie also had a "picture book" with photographs of items she might want or need. Although Jennie never picked up the book on her own or presented it to anyone, she did follow directions to use the book to make requests. For example, when shown the book and asked to point, Jennie would either (1) push the book onto the desk if she didn't want anything, or (2) point to one of five photographs (i.e., a lunchbox, cookie, glass of water, favorite toy, or toilet) if she did want something. However, Ms. D'Angelo saw that no one currently implemented any *expressive* language programs for Jennie.

Jennie's cognitive skills were generally poor and had developed at an excruciatingly slow pace. Currently, she was unable (or unwilling) to make simple discriminations between colors, understand the concept of "yes/no," or follow commands that had more than one step (e.g., clap your hands and touch your nose). Jennie's former teachers, Mr. Evan and Mrs. Taylor, revealed that Jennie could learn basic discriminations, but often didn't retain or generalize the information. For example, Jennie would learn the difference between "red" and "blue" in the classroom but was then confused by the same distinction in a more natural setting.

Despite her arrested cognitive skills, Jennie's adaptive behaviors were only moderately impaired. Jennie fed herself, although she never used a knife or fork. This latter skill may have been left undeveloped because of her aggression. Jennie did require some help in dressing; Ms. D'Angelo noted that Jennie needed assistance putting on a winter jacket. In addition, Jennie used the toilet without difficulty, but had to be reminded to redress and wash afterward. Ms. D'Angelo later discovered from Jennie's parents, Mr. and Mrs. Hobson, that Jennie also needed help when bathing. However, it was unclear whether she lacked the skill to wash or was simply being non-compliant. Finally, Jennie needed to be supervised in all public places and most of the time at school and home. She had no history of running away, but she often touched things that were potentially harmful (e.g., the stove).

Following her classroom observations of Jennie, Ms. D'Angelo had an extensive conversation with Mr. and Mrs. Hobson. They said that Jennie "had always been like this" and then gave examples of her early impairment. Both noticed that Jennie was "different" as a baby when she resisted being held and when she failed to talk by the age of 3 years. Mr. and Mrs. Hobson initially thought their daughter was deaf, but all medical tests indicated normal physical functioning and slightly better than normal motor skills. Over time, Jennie did acquire some basic daily living skills, but her behavior problems often prevented full instruction. For example, Mr. and Mrs. Hobson said that Jennie would throw tantrums, become aggressive, and stand in the corner for hours when physically prompted to do something (e.g., hold a spoon).

Mr. and Mrs. Hobson enrolled their daughter in her current school when she was 4 years old. They reported that Jennie's behavior problems had improved tremendously over the past 3 years, a fact that was critical to their decision to keep her in their home. The reduced behavior problems allowed others to teach Jennie more adaptive skills, but Mr. and Mrs. Hobson stated sadly that their daughter "still has a long way to go."

Ms. D'Angelo reviewed Jennie's school file last so as not to bias her initial observations and interviews. Limited psychological testing but extensive observations over the past 3 years largely confirmed Jennie's persistent problems in cognitive and social functioning. However, her behavior problems had improved to a point that she could be integrated with other children at the special school. Language remained severely deficient, a fact that distressed Ms. D'Angelo the most. Based on her initial observations, interviews, and review of previous information, Ms. D'Angelo tentatively concluded that Jennie still met criteria for autistic disorder and mental retardation, severity unspecified. The latter indicates the suspected presence of mental retardation in someone who (1) cannot be successfully tested using standardized tests or (2) is unwilling to comply with such tests.

Assessment

According to the *DSM-IV*, the essential feature of autistic disorder is "markedly abnormal or impaired development in social interaction and communication and a markedly restricted repertoire of activity and interests" (APA, 1994, p. 66). Children with autism must show delays in normal functioning or show abnormal functioning prior to age 3 years. However, the extent of these delays can vary considerably. Social, communicative, and behavioral areas of functioning are most greatly impaired in those with the disorder. Social interaction deficits are the hallmark of autism ("auto-" meaning "self"), as the child is uninterested in reciprocity, play with others, peer relationships, sharing, or even eye contact. In fact, for many children with autism, social and physical contacts are quite aversive (note Jennie's early response to being held and recent response to one who got too close to her).

A majority of children with autism are also mute, like Jennie, or have great difficulty initiating or maintaining a conversation with others. If language *is* used, it is often odd or difficult to understand. For example, echolalia, or repeating words one has heard, and pronoun reversal (e.g., using the word *you* instead of *I*) are common. Also, children with autism sometimes show behavioral problems, including self-injury, aggression, self-stimulation like Jennie's sounds and rocking, adherence to routines, and preoccupation with parts of inanimate objects (e.g., shoes on a doll). In Jennie's case, her social and language deficits were clear. Her level of problematic behavior, however, fluctuated. For example, she would stop pulling her hair if she was offered certain foods. This indicated that Jennie was somewhat responsive to external contingencies placed on her behavior.

The essential feature of mental retardation, according to the *DSM-IV*, is "significantly subaverage general intellectual functioning that is accompanied by significant limitations in adaptive functioning in at least two of the following skill areas: communication, self-care, home living, social/interpersonal skills, use of community resources, self-direction, functional academic skills, work, leisure, health, and safety" (APA, 1994, p. 39). Onset of the disorder must be prior to age 18 years. Mental retardation generally involves deficits in many if not most areas of functioning, whereas autism involves deficits in some areas (e.g., social, communicative) but not others (e.g., physical development, motor skills). At least 75% of children with autism also meet criteria for mental retardation (Bryson, Clark, & Smith, 1988). These disorders may be collectively referred to as pervasive developmental disabilities.

In Jennie's case, her intellectual functioning had not been formally tested because of her unwillingness to participate (hence the proposed diagnosis of mental retardation, unspecified type). Still, deficits in communication, self-care, social skills, self-direction, academics, and leisure were clearly evident. Despite these pervasive, almost psychotic-like deficits, however, most children with autism do not show symptoms of schizophrenia. In Jennie's case, for example, there was no history or evidence of delusions, hallucinations, or catatonia.

The assessment of a child with autism or mental retardation must concentrate on different areas of possibly impaired functioning. Most centrally, this involves an assessment of the child's intellectual functioning when possible. Standardized intelligence tests for evaluating typical youngsters include the Stanford-Binet Intelligence Scale (fourth edition; Thorndike, Hagen, & Sattler, 1986), Wechsler Primary and Preschool Scale of Intelligence-Revised (Wechsler, 1989), and the Wechsler Intelligence Scale for Children (third edition; Wechsler, 1991). However, these tests are not applicable to many children with autism or mental retardation because of the tests' heavy reliance on verbal content and language comprehension. Thus, an accurate picture of intellectual functioning in this population is often not possible.

Instead, cognitive functioning may be better assessed using tests that do not require verbal instructions. A good example is the Leiter International Performance Scale (Leiter, 1969). For higher functioning children, the Halstead-Reitan Neuropsychological Test Battery (Jarvis & Barth, 1994), Raven's Progressive Matrices (RPM; Raven, 1995), and Peabody Picture Vocabulary Test-Revised (PPVT-R; Dunn, 1981) are useful. The Halstead-Reitan is an excellent measure of sensorimotor ability, the RPM is useful for examining perceptual ability, and the PPVT-R is a good screening device for receptive language problems. Scores from each test correlate well with scores from traditional intelligence tests. Checklists that are more specific to autism have also been designed, including the Autism Behavior Checklist (Krug, Arick, & Almond, 1981) and the Childhood Autism Rating Scale (Schopler, Reichler, & Renner, 1988).

For children suspected of very low functioning or who are difficult to test, developmental scales may be more pertinent. Examples include the Gesell Developmental Schedules (third edition; Knobloch & Pasamanick, 1974) and the Denver Developmental Screening Tests (see Aiken, 1996). In Jennie's case, she was evaluated when she was 3 years old with the Bayley Scales of Infant Development (BSID, second edition; Bayley, 1993). The BSID is a measure of mental, motor, and behavioral functioning that requires a child to perform various tasks and provides a rating scale for emotional and social behavior. From the BSID, Jennie was found to have average to above average motor abilities (e.g., coordination, fine motor skills) but low mental abilities (e.g., discriminations, problem solving, memory). Such a pattern is often indicative of children who are deaf or who have autism. In addition, several behavior problems were noted, including resistance to touch and frequent temper tantrums.

Adaptive behavior is also a key aspect that must be assessed in this population, particularly for children with mental retardation and impaired physical and motor development. Too often, diagnoses of mental retardation are based solely on cognitive ability without regard to adaptive behavior. Several adaptive behavior scales are used for persons with mental retardation, the most common being the AAMD Adaptive Behavior Scales (second edition) and the Vineland Adaptive Behavior Scales (VABS; Nihira, Leland, & Lambert, 1992; Lambert, Leland, & Nihira, 1992; Sparrow, Balla, & Cicchetti, 1984).

The VABS, for example, involve caregiver interviews and provide norm-referenced scales for communication, daily living skills, socialization, and motor skills. A maladaptive behavior subscale is also included. In Jennie's case, Ms. D'Angelo used the VABS to interview Mr. and Mrs. Hobson, Jennie's baby-sitter, and Jennie's previous teachers at the school. As expected, they rated the child's communication and socialization skills very low, but rated her motor skills appropriate for her age. Primary maladaptive behaviors included withdrawal and unawareness of immediate surroundings.

Direct behavioral observation is also useful for identifying socialization problems and the functions of maladaptive behavior. With respect to socialization, for example, Ms. D'Angelo's observations over several days revealed that Jennie was most responsive to others when she (1) was in situations she considered routine, (2) was not anxious or bored, and (3) did not find her work to be excessive or overly demanding. Ms. D'Angelo noted that Jennie's social responsiveness improved significantly after a break or lunch, and the teacher made a note to schedule frequent breaks for Jennie during the course of the day. In conjunction with this, Ms. D'Angelo noted that Jennie's misbehavior occurred primarily to escape aversive situations. These situations included the introduction of new stimuli into her environment, tiring tasks, and physical contact. In addition, as noted before, Ms. D'Angelo found that certain foods attenuated Jennie's misbehavior.

Causes and Maintaining Variables

The causes of autism are not completely known but, because of the pervasiveness of the disorder and because it occurs at such an early age, biological variables are likely suspects. In fact, very few researchers now believe that environmental factors have much to do with causing autism. Initial attention in this area was paid to genetic causes, with some data indicating that autism is much more frequent in identical than fraternal twins (Steffenburg et al., 1989). In addition, autism is sometimes associated with aberrations that occur on chromosomes 1, 7, 11, 15, 18, 21, and X and Y (Tsai & Ghaziuddin, 1997). However, autism itself does not run in families, and parents of children with autism do not show much psychopathology themselves. Some data indicate that relatives of children with autism are at slightly higher risk for schizoaffective or Asperger's disorder (Gillberg, Gillberg, & Steffenburg, 1992), but whether and how these disorders are related to the development of autism in children is not known.

In Jennie's case, no immediate relatives displayed any overt psychopathology, although Mrs. Hobson said that her mother had once had a "nervous breakdown." Jennie did have two older siblings, a brother age 13 years and a sister age 9 years, but neither had a history of social, cognitive, or adaptive functioning problems. Mr. and Mrs. Hobson had once considered the possibility of having a fourth child, but they were now discouraged, given their experience with Jennie and the time needed to take care of her.

Other biological factors have been linked to autism as well, including brain conditions like cerebral palsy, meningitis, encephalitis, infections, and, of course, accidental injuries. Neurological problems likely account for a majority of cases of autism, however (Volkmar, Klin, Marans, & McDougle, 1996). Such problems may involve brain areas that are most responsible for motor and cognitive functioning, such as the basal ganglia, general limbic system, and frontal lobe. Assessment of these problems may involve brain imaging techniques like magnetic resonance imaging (MRI). For obvious reasons, however, this is very difficult to do with children with autism. In Jennie's case, no such evaluation had ever been done.

Causes of autism might also include biochemical changes. Some children with autism have high levels of the neurotransmitter serotonin, which is involved in mood and motor behavior (Volkmar et al., 1996). As a result, drugs that lower serotonin, like fenfluramine, have been used with some success to control excess motor activity (e.g., self-stimulation) in this population. In Jennie's case, no formal test was done to measure serotonin levels. Given her good motor skills and strange motor behaviors, however, an increased level of serotonin seemed plausible.

Many biological causes of autism have thus been implicated, but a variety of these causes likely conspire to produce the disorder. This is known as the "final common pathway" hypothesis—that different factors (e.g., genetics, poor brain development, high serotonin) interact in different ways for different children with autism. However, these factors all create the same end result, or type of brain dysfunction, that leads to autism. Unfortunately, as in Jennie's case, the factors are often not identified.

In contrast to autism, the causes of mental retardation involve a greater mixture of biological and environmental variables. In particular, biological variables during the prenatal period often serve to affect brain development. According to Szymanski and Kaplan (1997), prenatal changes that often lead to mental retardation include (1) malformations, especially problems of neural tube formation, (2) deformations, or abnormal growths of the head or organs, and/or (3) disruptions, or general damage from teratogens like prenatal alcohol use.

Malformations include genetic disorders or chromosomal aberrations like fragile X syndrome, Prader-Willi syndrome, and Down syndrome. The last, for example, is typically associated with three number 21 chromosomes, characteristic physical defects, and moderate mental retardation. Metabolic problems may also produce mental retardation, including phenylketonuria and Niemann-Pick disease. In Jennie's case, however, none of these conditions was present.

According to Szymanski and Kaplan (1997), unusual extrinsic factors may also lead to mental retardation. These factors include extensive lack of oxygen (e.g., from near drowning), brain trauma (e.g., from head injury), and poisoning (e.g., from excessive lead). Accidents are a leading cause of harm to infants and children, and their consequences regarding cognitive development can be quite catastrophic.

In Jennie's case, Mrs. Hobson did report that her daughter's birth was "a very trying experience." Although she had little trouble with her first two children, Jennie's birth was marked by prematurity (3 weeks), long labor (23 hours), and a complicated delivery. Apparently, Jennie had moved immediately before birth, which made her extraction difficult. Jennie also spent a longer period than usual in the birth canal, which placed her at risk for oxygen loss. Following birth, however, Jennie's Apgar test score was normal and she did not appear to have any ill effects from the birth process. Thus, it was not known whether the natal experience caused her cognitive problems.

Environmental effects also influence mental retardation and may have been prominent in Jennie's case. This involves what is known as "familial" retardation and may include factors like minor neurological impairment, natural placement at a lower intelligence level, and environmental deprivation (Hodapp & Dykens, 1996). Those with familial retardation tend to have mild cognitive deficits, poor educational experiences, low socioeconomic parents who are inconsistent in their child-rearing practices.

In Jennie's case, status, and/or early environmental deprivation was not severe but did occur to some extent. According to Mr. and Mrs. Hobson, Jennie's early withdrawal often led them to leave Jennie alone for fear of upsetting her. As a result, Jennie did not receive a lot of verbal or physical attention from her parents or siblings. In addition, Mr. and Mrs. Hobson made the "mistake" (as they put it) of waiting to evaluate Jennie until she was 3 years old. They were instead hoping that Jennie's behaviors were a "phase" or that she was simply developing at a slower rate than most children. Only when Jennie had not yet said a word by age 3 years did Mr. and Mrs. Hobson consent to an evaluation. Even then, both waited another year before enrolling Jennie in her current placement. The loss of educational time during this period, while perhaps not the cause of Jennie's problems, may have contributed to their severity. With respect to language, for example, the "window of opportunity" for teaching verbal skills had not been fully exploited.

Developmental Aspects

The developmental course of autism is not marked by much variation but does depend on the child's level of functioning and whether some type of intensive, early intervention was given. According to Klinger and Dawson (1996), the two best indicators of whether a child with autism will experience a favorable outcome over the long run are (1) average intelligence, and (2) the presence of some language before the age of 5 years. Unfortunately, in Jennie's case, neither of these conditions applied. However, Klinger and Dawson (1996) also reported that early special education services are associated with a better prognosis for autism. This is especially true if language and interpersonal skills are emphasized. In Jennie's case, her enrollment at age 4 years in a school that stressed these skills is a hopeful sign.

Werry (1996) summarized the major long-term follow-up studies regarding children with pervasive developmental disorders. Three patterns of development over time were identified. The first pattern, which accounts for 90% of cases, is marked by moderate to severe impairment across the life span. Most people in this group show steady but slow improvement in some of the core symptoms of autism, including (1) a greater "warming" to other people and some social interaction, (2) the development of some, albeit abnormal, language, and (3) less overactivity and eccentric behavior. This improvement usually starts after age 4 years.

The second developmental pattern, which accounts for almost all the remaining cases of autism, is marked by relatively normal functioning by adulthood. Those with Asperger's disorder, which is similar to autism but without the major cognitive and language deficits, often show this developmental pattern. However, even those in this group rarely work in occupations that demand a lot of personal interaction, and their social behaviors remain somewhat odd. Finally, the third developmental pattern, which is quite rare, is marked by a gradual deterioration in functioning, sometimes as a result of long-term institutionalization.

For each of these groups, the development of comorbid medical and mental disorder symptoms is common. The most prevalent comorbid medical condition is epilepsy, which is seen in up to one-third of cases (though not in Jennie) and seen throughout infancy, childhood, and adolescence (Wong, 1993). Comorbid mental symptoms include hypersensitivity, labile mood swings, inappropriate affect, and rarely, those related to schizophrenia (Wing, 1989).

The developmental course of children with mental retardation is linked closely to levels of cognitive functioning. These levels remain fairly stable over time, even during childhood and adolescence. Maisto and German (1986) reported, for example, that low scores on the Bayley Scales of Infant Development (the same ones given to Jennie) were predictive of low intelligence scores across childhood and adulthood. This seems to be true even if special education classes are a part of the child's life (Ross, Begab, Dondis, Giampiccolo, & Meyers, 1985).

Those with moderate, severe, or profound mental retardation tend to have very stable and poor cognitive development. Those with mild mental retardation, especially those with good verbal skills, tend to have a much better prognosis. In addition, those with Down syndrome or fragile X chromosome tend to develop their intelligence at a much slower rate than those with other types of mental retardation. Thus, greater impairment as one grows older may be the case here. With respect to adaptive behavior skills in those with mental retardation, a similar pattern of gradual growth is seen. However, a leveling off in skills is sometimes seen in middle childhood (Dykens, Hodapp, & Evans, 1994).

What about Jennie? To be sure, her limited language skills are a very poor prognostic sign (recall that this worried Ms. D'Angelo the most). Children without good language skills are more apt to withdraw, develop maladaptive behaviors to communicate, and fail to learn appropriate social skills. Indeed, in Jennie's case, Ms. D'Angelo strongly suspected that Jennie was sometimes aggressive as a way to communicate her desire to withdraw from a taxing situation. Unfortunately, Jennie did not have the means to show her frustration otherwise. The development of some type of language, perhaps involving sign language or extensive receptive language skills, was therefore made a top priority for Jennie.

On the other hand, Jennie had some good prognostic signs. Her parents, Mr. and Mrs. Hobson, expressed a strong desire to help their daughter in whatever way possible. They admitted that their current desire to help was partially in response to their guilt about having given Jennie a late start in her education. However, they also recognized that Jennie's difficulties were pervasive and that for any educational program to succeed, parents have to be active participants. Indeed, generalization of language and social skills is a key aspect of treatment for children with autism and mental retardation and tends to lead to better outcome. Mr. and Mrs. Hobson were already engaged in parent training classes at Jennie's school and were now extending the school's educational programs to their home environment.

Another good prognostic sign for Jennie was her enrollment in a specialized school that relied on behavioral strategies to address skills deficits. Indeed, her overall functioning was enhanced by the substantial attention now being paid to her behaviors. Such early and intensive intervention is crucial and had already been effective in reducing some of Jennie's overt behavior problems. For example, her on-task and self-injurious behaviors improved greatly after teachers began using tangible reinforcers. In addition, Jennie's aggression declined when she was kept on a regular schedule and became more familiar with her teachers. Her maladaptive behaviors also dropped suddenly after she was taught to use her picture book to make requests. Despite this progress, however, it was clear that Jennie still has a long way to go and that her long-term prognosis is not generally good.

Treatment

Treatment for children with autism and/or mental retardation tends to focus on (1) deficits of language, social skills, and adaptive behavior skills and (2) excess behaviors that are maladaptive in nature (e.g., aggression, self-injury, self-stimulation). Treatment may take one of two philoso-phies. First, autism may be treated as a global disorder, like depression, using medication. Second, autism may be divided into separate problems (e.g., language, social) that are addressed individually with behavior therapy.

Medication for children with autism has focused on fenfluramine, a drug that reduces levels of serotonin in the central nervous system (recall that many children with autism have high levels of serotonin, which is re-lated to motor behavior). Initially, fenfluramine was thought to help im-prove the cognitive and behavioral functioning of children with autism, but now the drug is considered useful only for controlling excess motor be-haviors (Campbell, 1988). Other drugs have been used in the treatment of autism as well, including neuroleptics like haloperidol, naltrexone, clo-mipramine, clonidine, and stimulant medication. Overall, these drugs im-prove motor behavior to some extent, but the hallmark symptoms of autism (e.g., language delays, poor social skills) are unaffected. In Jennie's case, medication was never used or considered.

Behavior therapy has instead been the mainstay of treatment for chil-dren with autism and is used to address specific problems. The remedia-tion of language problems in this population is usually considered a top priority for the reasons mentioned earlier. Sometimes, this involves shap-ing, or reinforcing successive approximations of a desired response (Lo-vaas, 1977). In shaping speech for a child with autism, any sound or vocalization is reinforced first. After the child vocalizes on a regular basis, these sounds are shaped into various phonemes that can later be formed into words. For example, a child could be rewarded with food every time he or she hums. This humming could then be shaped into the phoneme of "mmmm." Subsequently, this phoneme could be shaped into words like "mama" or "me." Other communication programs for children with autism emphasize more reciprocal language interactions, self-initiated questions, and self-management (Koegel & Koegel, 1996).

In Jennie's case, Ms. D'Angelo started a program whereby Jennie was reinforced every time she made her strange sounds. Over a period of time, however, Jennie's vocalizations increased only moderately. In fact, Jennie found the extra attention paid to her vocalizations aversive and often turned away when starting to make her sounds. Ms. D'Angelo further tried to shape Jennie's vocalizations into a short "o" sound, but many at-tempts over a 9-month period proved unfruitful. The teacher concluded that any language on Jennie's part would have to be developed from sign language and receptive skills, including the picture book.

As a result, Ms. D'Angelo implemented two language programs for Jennie that concentrated on these areas. Jennie had excellent motor skills, so she was initially taught some basic signs. Because many of Jennie's be-haviors were escape motivated, Ms. D'Angelo initially used functional communication training and taught Jennie the sign for "break" (Durand, 1990). This was a relatively simple sign (two fists placed side by side and then separated), and one reinforced by giving free time. Initially, Jennie was allowed to have a 10-minute break every time she formed the sign. At first, she had to be prompted and she became somewhat aggressive in re-action to the necessary physical contact (i.e., a teacher holding Jennie's fists together and "breaking" them). Following the prompted response, how-ever, Jennie was allowed to take a break.

Over a period of 2 months, Jennie successfully learned to sign "break" whenever she wanted to escape a particular task. After this 2-month pe-riod, Jennie was placed on a schedule in which she could ask for a maxi-mum of six breaks per day. Although this initially created some confusion and aggression on Jennie's part, she eventually caught on and used her break times selectively. Ms. D'Angelo noticed that, as a result, Jennie's escape-motivated aggression in the classroom dropped significantly. Un-fortunately, her use of the "break" sign did not generalize well to other ar-eas of the school or to home.

Ms. D'Angelo also tried to teach Jennie other signs, particularly those related to "bathroom" and "drink." Jennie had moderate success with these, but her performance was uneven. On some days, Jennie formed the signs and received reinforcement, but on other days she had no desire to use the signs. In addition, she never used the signs outside the classroom. Ms. D'Angelo also tried other concepts—"yes," "no," "eat," and "hello"—but Jennie never formed signs for these.

In conjunction with the sign language programs, Ms. D'Angelo wanted to expand Jennie's use of her picture book. This was met with much greater success, as Jennie was able to distinguish about a dozen pic-tures and point to them to request something. In addition to the pictures mentioned earlier (i.e., lunchbox, cookie, glass of water, one toy, toilet), the picture book now included articles of clothing, different foods, and certain playthings. A subsequent training program was added so that Jennie would carry her picture book with her and use it in other settings, espe-cially at home. Mr. and Mrs. Hobson, in their parent training classes, were taught to prompt Jennie to use the book at home and reward her for appro-priate requests. Later, they were asked to reward some of Jennie's basic signs as well.

Over several months, Jennie successfully used the book and a limited number of signs with prompting. However, she rarely used her skills with-out a prompt and seemed unable or unwilling to learn or express new words and concepts. In fact, Jennie often showed no motivation to use her current skills, and would occasionally become aggressive if someone was too avid in prompting her to do so.

To address Jennie's distaste for social interactions, Ms. D'Angelo sought to build some basic skills. Because Jennie essentially had no social behaviors, the establishment of eye contact was considered a top priority. Over a period of 3 months, Jennie was asked to look at the teacher. She initially failed to do so, and was therefore prompted by the teacher, who gently raised Jennie's chin and established brief eye contact. Jennie was subsequently rewarded. Although this process was somewhat aversive to Jennie, she did establish regular eye contact with a teacher on command after 5 months of training.

Ms. D'Angelo then extended Jennie's social skills training to include basic imitation and observation of others. This was done using both one-on-one instruction and participation in group activities. With respect to the former, for example, Jennie was asked to imitate two-step commands from the teacher like "stand up and go to the door." Over time, she was also asked to imitate more salient social behaviors like waving goodbye, smiling, and raising her hand to signal a desire to point to her picture book. Any social programs that required physical contact, however, were generally met with failure. In addition, Jennie was required to participate in simple group activities with other children at the school. Examples included rolling a ball toward others, playing basic games, and singing. Although Jennie interacted with her peers somewhat during these group activities, her behaviors were not extensively social in nature.

Ms. D'Angelo also concentrated on Jennie's adaptive self-help skills, and was largely successful in doing so. In a relatively short period of time, Jennie learned to do several things:

1. Dress herself fully (although her clothes still needed to be laid out)
2. Eat with a fork
3. Go to the toilet, re-dress, and wash without prompting afterward
4. Get in and out of a car without assistance
5. Organize her school materials

In addition, Jennie learned to bathe herself, although she did require a prompt to get out of the bathtub when finished.

Mr. and Mrs. Hobson expressed great satisfaction with Jennie's improved adaptive behavior skills and decreased maladaptive behavior. Indeed, Jennie's aggressive responses had dropped to almost zero by the end of the school year. However, she still screamed occasionally and tugged at her hair when upset. Ms. D'Angelo worked closely with Mr. and Mrs. Hobson during the course of the school year to help Jennie generalize her new skills to the home setting. In addition, Mr. and Mrs. Hobson were given a list of educational programs to practice during the summer so that Jennie could retain some of her skills. Fortunately, Mr. and Mrs. Hobson were able to maintain their daughter's overall level of functioning through the beginning of the next school year.

During the following school year, however, Jennie's level of progress remained flat. This applied especially to her language and social skills. Indeed, Ms. D'Angelo found that she had to spend considerable time working with Jennie just to retain what skills she had. Given Jennie's level of cognitive functioning, this scenario will likely be repeated in the coming years. This projection illustrates the difficulty in improving the long-term prognosis of children with autism, and the outlook for Jennie in the future remains cloudy.

Discussion Questions

1. In many cases, it is difficult to separate children with autism from children with moderate mental retardation, children with Asperger's syndrome, and children with severe learning disabilities. What symptoms and behaviors would you rely on most to make these distinctions?

2. Why do you think that autism and mental retardation are much more common in boys than girls? Be sure to explore the issue of gender stereotypes. Are any of your proposed reasons preventable, and how?

3. What recommendations would you make to Mr. and Mrs. Hobson for the care of Jennie at home? What do you think are the major ramifications of Jennie's condition for the family in general and her siblings in particular?

4. What do think is the best way to treat persons with severe disabilities within the public education system? Examine the pros and cons of segregated education and mainstreamed classrooms for all children involved.

5. A key issue in treating persons with disabilities is their (in)ability to give informed consent. Should a person with disabilities be subjected to educational, behavioral, or even aversive treatment without their expressed consent? What if the person is engaging in life-threatening behaviors?

6. How would you deal with an adolescent with a severe disability who commits a murder? Should that person be tried like anyone else or should he or she be given special considerations? What considerations, if any, would you recommend?

7. Too often, people rely only on intelligence tests to make a diagnosis of mental retardation. What could you do as a professional to help ensure that other methods are used to make this determination?

CHAPTER TWELVE

Pediatric Conditions

Symptoms

Andrew Barton was a 12-year-old multiracial (Caucasian and Brazilian) male referred to a psychology department training clinic at a local university. At the time of his initial assessment, Andrew was in seventh grade. He was referred to the clinic by his pediatrician, Dr. Morris, and his mother, Mrs. Barton, to address various somatic complaints that did not seem to have a largely organic basis. During the screening interview over the telephone, Mrs. Barton said that Andrew had recently missed several days of school, allegedly due to severe symptoms of asthma and abdominal pain. On each occasion, about 17 in the past 9 weeks, Andrew had been sent to the school nurse and later home, complaining of breathing difficulties or painful stomachaches.

During the initial assessment session, Andrew and his mother were interviewed separately by a doctoral student in clinical psychology. The student therapist interviewed Andrew first and found him to be somewhat meek and shy. Andrew was fairly quiet during the interview, and offered little more than yes-no answers to the therapist's questions. For more open-ended questions, Andrew provided information that was relatively vague or general. For example, when asked about the frequency of different symptoms at school, Andrew used phrases like "sometimes" or "I don't know." He was not hostile, however, and dutifully answered each of the questions put to him.

The therapist opened the interview by asking Andrew general questions about school, home, family, and friends. From the information first received, it appeared that Andrew was a fairly normal child who had a few close friends and who performed adequately at school. He did report some difficulties with his new middle school, however. For example, he was somewhat unfamiliar with the format of the school when he first started there and was surprised by the complexity and diversity of his schedule and classmates. Although several friends from elementary school were at the middle school with him, Andrew reported that he ate and spoke with them only occasionally; apparently, there was not much overlap in their schedules.

The therapist, aware of the reason why Andrew had been referred to the clinic, also asked more specific questions about his physical symptoms. Andrew reported that he often felt sick at school and needed to come home. In particular, he said he had asthma and would sometimes experience attacks that were severe enough to prevent him from doing his classwork. In addition, Andrew reported that he had frequent stomachaches while in school. When asked to identify the area that hurt, Andrew did not point to one area in particular, but instead rubbed his stomach and said that "it hurt all over." He also said that his asthmatic attacks and stomachaches did not occur at the same time, but that one or the other occurred almost every school day. He lied, however, when he said he'd missed only 5 days of school from September to December.

The therapist also spoke with Mrs. Barton individually. She was able to provide more detailed information but was careful not to place Andrew in a bad light. Mrs. Barton said first that she was quite concerned about Andrew's medical condition, as he had a history of asthma that was occasionally severe. His asthmatic condition had been problematic since preschool, when he was taught to use a portable bronchodilator to alleviate his breathing troubles. Although Andrew's condition had generally improved during his elementary school years, it had suddenly grown much worse this year.

Mrs. Barton speculated that Andrew's asthmatic attacks worsened because of several life stressors. These included Andrew's entry into middle school, Mrs. Barton's divorce from Andrew's father following a period of marital trouble, and her subsequent inability to spend much time with Andrew given her new work schedule (she worked odd hours that sometimes included early mornings and late nights). In general, Andrew was experiencing about one to three asthmatic attacks per week, some quite severe enough for him to be sent home from school. This was problematic for Mrs. Barton, however, as she felt obligated to leave work to attend to Andrew on these occasions.

During a typical asthmatic attack, Andrew would wheeze, cough, and clearly have trouble breathing. None of his attacks were life threatening, but Andrew was quite uncomfortable before he took his medication. Andrew's pediatrician, Dr. Morris, was at a loss to explain fully Andrew's sudden resurgence in asthmatic symptoms but attributed them somewhat to stress. In response to the recent attacks, Dr. Morris had adjusted Andrew's medication, but this seemed to have had little effect on his symptoms.

The therapist also asked about Andrew's stomach pains. Mrs. Barton seemed most concerned about this symptom, saying it was new and that the pediatrician could find no cause for the problem. Mrs. Barton reported that Andrew began complaining of stomachaches shortly after the start of the school year and that they had grown increasingly worse since then. On most occasions, the school had sent Andrew home when the symptom was especially acute. Interestingly, Andrew said that he didn't feel nauseous, just that a dull pain resonated in his abdominal region. He was scheduled for more medical tests the following week, but the pediatrician had suggested that the family try counseling as an adjunct treatment.

The therapist also explored recent family history, focusing especially on Mrs. Barton's previous marital relationship. Mrs. Barton reported that her husband had left the family 2 years before and that the final divorce was approved 8 months ago. She seemed somewhat baffled and depressed over the issue, attributing the situation to general feelings of disillusionment about marriage on her husband's part. She and Andrew did maintain contact with Mr. Barton, who now lived in Brazil, but this was only through infrequent calls and cards. No face-to-face contact had occurred in almost a year.

With permission, the therapist also contacted Dr. Morris, Andrew's pediatrician. Dr. Morris indicated that Andrew, Andrew's younger sister, and Mrs. Barton were an enmeshed family that seemed overly dependent on one another for emotional support. He knew that Andrew had real symptoms of asthma and suspected real symptoms of abdominal pain, but he speculated that Andrew was either stressed or exaggerating his symptoms for attention and release from school. At this time, he found no medical reason for Andrew's stomach pain or worsening asthma, and he hoped that counseling would change the family dynamics that seemed to maintain the problems. He offered to assist the therapist in whatever way possible.

The therapist also spoke, with Mrs. Barton's permission, to Andrew's school nurse and to several of his teachers. The school nurse, Ms. Ebersol, said that Andrew came to her office three to four times per week complaining of asthma symptoms or stomach pain. She was somewhat skittish about the symptoms and admitted that she often sent Andrew home after a brief examination. She also said it was difficult for her to pay close attention to Andrew given the sizable number of other children usually in her office. Andrew's teachers reported that he was a good student with excellent potential but one who was missing a lot of assignments due to his illnesses. All stressed that it was school policy to allow children to go to the nurse's office if they were ill, and all said that Andrew appeared ill whenever he asked to go to the office. Fortunately, each teacher wanted to know more about Andrew and his condition, and each was motivated to assist the therapist in his treatment program.

From the initial information gathered from several sources, the therapist made a preliminary conclusion that Andrew was likely experiencing an aggravated asthmatic condition and recurrent abdominal pain. He also felt, however, that significant psychological factors were affecting his medical conditions.

 Assessment

According to the *DSM-IV*, a problem that may be a focus of clinical attention involves psychological or behavioral factors that affect one's medical condition. These factors may, for example, aggravate a medical condition, interfere with treatment of the condition, serve as an added health risk, or trigger symptoms of the medical condition via stress (APA, 1994, p. 678). In Andrew's case, these factors were pertinent. For example, stress from school and other situations initially seemed to be aggravating his long-standing asthma and recent abdominal pains. These symptoms also interfered with Andrew's academic and daily life functioning. However, as discussed later, the major psychological factors that impinged on Andrew's symptoms were his attention-seeking and escape-motivated behaviors.

The assessment of youngsters with psychological factors that affect medical conditions (e.g., pediatric asthma, abdominal pain) is usually derived from a biopsychosocial perspective. This perspective assumes that the "interaction of developmental, personality, familial, social, and biological factors produce and are affected by the presenting psychosomatic problems" (Kager, Arndt, & Kenny, 1992, p. 309). With respect to the last factor, biological assessment is generally used to measure the severity of the medical condition and to guide biological treatment. In Andrew's case, he remained on a bronchodilator to control his severe asthmatic symptoms. However, no organic cause or treatment was identified for his recurrent abdominal pain.

The assessment of youngsters with psychological factors affecting medical conditions also involves the other factors mentioned above. With respect to developmental factors, for example, Kager et al. (1992) stated that one of the first avenues of assessment for this population should be an intellectual evaluation. This is done to see (1) whether a child has any major delays in cognitive functioning and (2) whether he or she would be able to understand a treatment program that involved techniques like cognitive restructuring or pain management. Although no formal intelligence test was used to assess Andrew, his teachers did report that he was fairly bright and quite talkative when in the mood.

Child personality factors should also be assessed, including those related to low self-image, external locus of control, dependency, and ability to handle stress. Instruments that may be useful in this regard include the Personality Inventory for Children (Wirt, Lachar, Klinedinst, & Seat, 1984), interviews, and self-report measures like the Piers-Harris Self-Concept Scale (Piers, 1984). In Andrew's case, the therapist conducted extensive interviews with his client over a period of several weeks and noted that the personality factors listed above seemed related to Andrew's physical conditions. For example, Andrew had a low self-image, often putting himself down about his appearance, academic status, and athletic prowess. In many ways, Andrew seemed depressed and socially withdrawn, conditions that are sometimes associated with somatic complaints.

The therapist also found Andrew to be dependent and unable to handle stress effectively. For example, he often preferred to be with his mother and sister and was clearly interested in gaining attention from both. In addition, Andrew was not self-sufficient in managing his asthma; he often called on his mother or the nurse whenever he had symptoms of wheezing or coughing. Andrew also had an external locus of control. He tended to blame his asthma and abdominal pain on school-related situations and on the quality of the air there. He would also induce guilt in his mother by saying that her marital problems were responsible for many of his current symptoms.

The assessment of children with psychological/medical conditions can also focus on specific reported pain. In Andrew's case, the therapist adopted Dolgin and Jay's (1989) suggestion to make an initial distinction between pain perception and pain behavior. Pain perception refers to thoughts and feelings regarding pain whereas pain behavior refers to how the child expresses pain. Common techniques for assessing these constructs include self-report measures (e.g., Comprehensive Pain Questionnaire and Pediatric Pain Questionnaire; McGrath, 1987; Varni, Thompson, & Hanson, 1987), global rating scales, and observational methods (e.g., Procedure Behavior Rating Scale and Observational Scale of Behavioral Distress; Elliot, Jay, & Woody, 1987; Katz, Kellerman, & Siegel, 1980).

Using interviews and observations in the office setting, the therapist noted that Andrew perceived his abdominal pain as a severe symptom that caused him great distress. He seemed to have a low tolerance for his pain and was often quite dramatic, even theatrical, when discussing the difficulty of his pain. He was also quite knowledgeable about medical information regarding his asthma. In addition, Andrew had a lot of pained facial expressions, verbal complaints, and requests to be taken to the medical doctor. Interestingly, he did not like his psychological therapist very much, indicating on occasion that the therapist did not fully appreciate his condition.

Family variables are also key in assessing children with pediatric conditions. The therapist in this case relied on interviews and the Family Environment Scale (Moos & Moos, 1986) to obtain information about the Bartons' family dynamics. In general, it was clear that Andrew was engaging in several attention-getting behaviors other than his physical symptoms. To get his way, for example, he sometimes threw tantrums, ran out of the house, and refused to do chores. Overall, Andrew was quite successful at forcing his mother to give in to his demands for attention. Mrs. Barton's tendency to rush home to attend to Andrew following his asthmatic attacks at school was a prime example of this coercion. Data from the Family Environment Scale also confirmed Dr. Morris's earlier statement that the Barton family was enmeshed and isolated from others. Indeed, few of the Barton family's recreational activities were conducted with outside members.

Mrs. Barton was also asked to complete the Child Behavior Checklist. The somatic complaints subscale of the CBCL may differentiate children whose pain has a psychological versus a physiological basis (Routh & Ernst, 1984). Andrew was rated very high on this scale, showing a clinical range of symptoms like headaches, nausea, vomiting, and fatigue in addition to his asthma and abdominal pain. The therapist also gauged Mrs. Barton's reactions to Andrew's physical symptoms. In general, she displayed a high degree of emotionality regarding her son's symptoms, sometimes crying and asking Andrew detailed questions about his physical state. In addition, it became clear that Andrew could successfully avoid different chores and responsibilities by complaining of asthma or pain. Overall then, Andrew displayed a wide range of symptoms to capture his mother's attention and/or to avoid obligations at school and home.

As part of an ongoing daily assessment, the therapist asked Andrew to rate his level of asthma and abdominal pain. Pain thermometers and checklists are available for doing so (Johnson, 1988), but the therapist simply had Andrew indicate what times of day his pain reached intolerable proportions. Andrew reported that most of his pain occurred during school hours. Few problems were apparent on weekends or holidays.

Causes and Maintaining Variables

The etiology of pediatric conditions like chronic asthma and abdominal pain can sometimes be difficult to pinpoint. This is so because each condition has its own set of different causal pathways. Asthma, for example, is a condition that often results from one or more of three physical pathways. First, the child may experience constricted bronchial tubes from spasms in the smooth muscle lining the airway. Second, the lining of the bronchial tubes may swell. Third, excess mucus may clog the airway. Each of these events can lead to a buildup of carbon dioxide and subsequent wheezing, coughing, gasping, and chest pain and tightness (Creer, Renne, & Chai, 1982). Severe cases may involve mucus secretion with spasms and/or swelling. In Andrew's case, however, his asthma was less severe and was characterized more by brief episodes of muscle spasms and swelling of the bronchial tube lining. His attacks rarely lasted more than a few minutes and, as mentioned earlier, were never life threatening.

Creer et al. (1982) described a variety of factors that can trigger asthmatic attacks in youngsters. These triggers can be generally divided into physiological and emotional factors. Physiological triggers include allergens and irritants such as dust, smoke, perfume, and paint. Other physiological factors to consider include exercise, infections, and aspirin and other medications.

Andrew's pediatrician, Dr. Morris, reported that Andrew had a mildly negative reaction to pollen and would sometimes have more trouble breathing during springtime. In addition, Andrew tended to have more difficulties with asthma whenever the wind blew particularly hard, stirring up more dust and other irritants than usual. No other physiological factors seemed pertinent, however, and Dr. Morris stressed that Andrew was not overly sensitive to pollen or dust. In addition, physiological factors could not explain why Andrew was suddenly experiencing more severe asthmatic attacks now than in the past. As a result, emotional or behavioral factors were thought to be the major causes and maintaining variables of Andrew's asthma.

Recurrent abdominal pain may also be the result of various physiological and psychological factors. Common physiological factors associated with this condition include autonomic nervous system hypersensitivity, excess muscle tension, irritable bowel syndrome, lactose intolerance, and lack of dietary fiber (Scharff, 1997). Andrew did seem to react to different events with more autonomic arousal than most children. In addition, he was tense and his diet was not monitored as well as it had been before his parents' divorce. Dr. Morris, after completing his remaining tests, believed that Andrew was occasionally constipated and therefore supplemented his diet with fiber pills. He suspected, however, as he did for Andrew's asthma, that psychosocial factors were largely responsible for the boy's recent symptoms.

Some of the most prominent psychosocial factors that affect youngsters with chronic pediatric conditions involve family variables. Potential family variables that most affect asthma include inconsistent parenting, conflict, and enmeshment. Children whose parents inconsistently give attention and discipline may learn to aggravate their physical symptoms for additional sympathy and tangible reinforcers. In Andrew's case, for example, his mother was clearly struggling to raise a family on her own and could not give her son as much attention as she had before Mr. Barton's departure. Andrew noticed, however, that his mother put aside her busy schedule and attended to his needs whenever he had an asthmatic attack.

Psychosocial factors may also help cause and maintain recurrent abdominal pain. Potential factors in this regard include anxiety, depression, perfectionism, shyness, stressful life events, and family enmeshment (Scharff, 1997). As mentioned earlier, Andrew did seem anxious in some situations, especially those involving new social interactions. In addition, his mother had reported that Andrew was sometimes depressed and withdrawn. It was unclear, however, whether Andrew's somatic symptoms resulted from anxiety and depression or whether these psychological symptoms resulted from his asthma and abdominal pain.

According to a popular structural family therapy model, conflict and enmeshment play key roles in causing and maintaining psychosomatic conditions in children. Minuchin described how poor boundaries between family members can lead to overprotectiveness, overinvolvement in one another's lives, and eventual conflict (Minuchin, Rosman, & Baker, 1978). Such conflict increases the amount of tension within the family and serves to cause or aggravate a child's illness. In Andrew's case, Mrs. Barton was clearly distressed by many factors, most notably her own parenting ability and Andrew's asthma and pain. As a result, she was somewhat overprotective, and sometimes argued with Andrew, but it was unclear whether the family conflict was actually leading to Andrew's symptoms. Instead, it seemed to be the other way around: Andrew's symptoms often led to Mrs. Barton's overprotectiveness, attention-giving, and frustration with her son.

Other family variables that affect children with chronic pediatric conditions include poor problem-solving skills, pessimism, lack of support, inflexibility, financial burden, isolation, modeling, and family member anxiety regarding the pediatric condition (Johnson, 1988). In Andrew's case, several of these seemed to apply. For example, he and his mother did not effectively solve problems, including the substantial amount of time he was missing from school. In addition, no consistent strategy had been formed about how to manage Andrew's asthma in school or how to prevent the condition in the first place. This was aggravated by Mrs. Barton's own symptoms of depression and pessimism about eventually resolving her son's symptoms. Mrs. Barton's divorce had also created a financial burden and isolation of the family members from others. She was overly dramatic when responding to Andrew's symptoms as well. As a result of these factors, considerable tension was building within the family, and few actions (outside of seeking therapy) had been taken to address any of the consequences that had arisen.

Although family variables are perhaps the major psychosocial factor that influences pediatric conditions, others include the child's adjustment to the illness, coping methods, and cognitive processes (Thompson, Gustafson, George, & Spock, 1994). In Andrew's case, his ability to cope with his medical conditions was generally and surprisingly poor. For example, he constantly asked for (1) assistance regarding his bronchodilator, (2) release to be sent home whenever he had even minor symptoms of distress, and (3) information about what to do if he experienced asthma or pain in a public setting. These questions may have been linked to his attention-seeking behavior, but Andrew had strange beliefs about his asthma and pain as well. For example, he was convinced that he would eventually die from the medical problems despite constant assurance otherwise. In addition, he continually overestimated the importance and severity of daily life stressors (e.g., talking to a teacher) and how these stressors would affect his asthma and pain.

Developmental Aspects

As children grow, their ideas about illness change as their cognitive development unfolds. Bibace and Walsh (1980) outlined seven major developmental stages that children generally progress through when grasping the concept of illness. These stages are closely linked to Piagetian stages of cognitive development. The first stage, incomprehension, refers to very young children (0–2 years) who clearly do not understand any concepts related to illness.

During the "prelogical explanation" phase, which typically occurs at ages 2 to 6 years, the child advances through two phases of thinking. The first, the "phenomenism" phase, is marked by poor explanations of illness. For example, a child might think that a cold comes from a plant or the sky. Usually, these explanations represent causes that are far removed from the child. In the second prelogical phase, "contagion," the child sees the cause of illness as something closer to him or her but nothing that actually produces direct contact. For example, the child may say that a cold comes from being outside, standing next to someone who is ill, or by magic.

During the "concrete-logical explanation" phase, which typically occurs at ages 7 to 10 years, an emphasis is placed on internal versus external causes of illness. The first, or "contamination," phase, is marked by a distinction between an external cause (e.g., cold temperature) and an internal effect (e.g., stuffed-up nose). The external cause may be another person or an event that harms the child by direct physical contact, or contamination. In the second concrete-logical explanation phase, "internalization," a similar process is seen. In this phase, however, the child (1) develops a clearer understanding of external causes and internal effects and (2) understands more readily that direct physical contact with an external source is not necessary to get sick. For example, the child may realize that one could "breathe in bacteria" to develop a cold.

Andrew, who was 12 years old, had clearly developed at least a concrete-logical explanation for his asthma. For example, he provided detailed scenarios of how the air quality at school, which contained dust and other irritants, would trigger different types of asthmatic attacks (he felt he had three different kinds of attacks). He also knew that if he avoided certain aggravating events like exercise or physical education class, an attack would be less likely to occur. Much of this information had been conveyed to him over the years by Dr. Morris, however. Therefore, it was unclear whether his conception of illness had developed normally or was enhanced by his extensive contacts with a pediatrician.

Andrew's detailed conception of asthma, however, did not generalize to a full understanding of his abdominal pain. When asked what he thought was causing his pain, Andrew would often shrug or say he didn't know. On other occasions, he would simply blame his mother or teachers, but he could not provide a direct link between their behaviors and his pain (as he could with his asthma). This might suggest that Andrew's conception of asthma, but not abdominal pain, had been inadvertently enhanced by the pediatrician. The therapist also found it interesting that Andrew asked his pediatrician many questions about his pain, possibly in an effort to add credibility to his claims of distress.

Bibace and Walsh (1980) claimed that in the final stages of understanding illness, adolescents progress through two "formal-logical" explanation phases. These phases are marked by even greater internal-external differentiation than before. The first, the "physiologic explanation" phase, is characterized by the child's realization that illness specifically affects internal organs or bodily processes. For example, the adolescent may describe a cold in terms of specific symptoms, lowered white blood cell count, or a suppressed immune system. The second formal-logical phase, "psychophysiologic," is characterized by the addition of a psychological component to illness. For example, the adolescent may come to realize that stress precipitates or aggravates a physical condition.

Andrew did not seem to grasp these latter, more detailed explanations for his asthma or recurrent abdominal pain. For example, he tended to stick to physical causes (e.g., air quality, pollen) to explain his asthma. On some occasions, he did blame others for his physical conditions but could offer only vague explanations for how they were causing his illnesses. For example, he once claimed that his teacher put him in an area of the classroom that was particularly dusty. On other occasions, he complained that the teachers made him walk too fast or did not give him enough time to use the bathroom, thus causing him to experience asthma or abdominal pain.

Developmental factors also influence children's conceptions of treating illness. For example, younger children are often quite afraid of medical doctors and procedures because they have not made a link between illness and treatment. In addition, young children tend to have cognitive distortions regarding treatment. For example, they may believe that one can bleed to death following an injection (Kager et al., 1992). Older children and adolescents obviously make a better connection between illness and the benefits of medical treatment. Some, in fact, start to take advantage of this; children learn at a young age that a need for treatment is a legitimate way of excusing oneself from something. For example, Andrew knew early on that one way to relieve symptoms, get attention, and be released from class was to ask to see the nurse.

Kager et al. (1992) also stated that other variables related to illness change from childhood to adolescence. As they grow, for example, children become more tolerant of pain, more knowledgeable about preventing illness, more attuned to rules of health, and more aware of their bodily sensations and changes in their bodies (especially during puberty). Developmental changes are also pertinent to one's adherence to treatment, although these likely interact with peer and other influences (La Greca, 1988). In addition, children change rapidly in their physical development, which necessitates frequent reassessments of their medication and other treatments. This applied somewhat to Andrew, who seemed to require a stronger bronchodilator than he had needed the year before.

Another variable important to child illness that changes significantly over time is the child's ability to cope with health problems. In general, children learn to cope with pain and other conditions better as they grow older. This is most likely a function of greater experience and a better cognitive understanding of what to do. Different coping methods include distraction, exercise, cognitive activities like reading, talking about nonpain topics, and imagining events incompatible with pain, among others. As indicated earlier, Andrew's coping skills were not very good. His first response to asthma or abdominal pain was to alert an adult and complain about his symptoms in dramatic fashion. As such, Andrew focused more on the reinforcers for his symptoms (e.g., attention) than alleviating the symptoms himself. Unfortunately, this is a poor prognostic sign for Andrew. Some have found, for example, that recurrent abdominal pain in childhood is linked with somatization disorder in adulthood (Coryell & Norton, 1981).

Treatment

The treatment of children with asthma often involves a combination of medical and psychological approaches. In addition, such treatment often includes as many relevant people as possible to address the problem. In Andrew's case, the therapist initially set up a meeting that included Andrew's mother, pediatrician, teachers, and school nurse. During the meeting, Andrew was asked to wait outside. However, he was apprised of all procedures afterward.

The general purpose of the meeting was to design a strategy for recognizing Andrew's asthma symptoms and for responding effectively to them. Dr. Morris, Andrew's pediatrician, taught the group what to look for during the initial stages of an asthmatic attack. This included tightness of chest and shortness of breath followed by coughing and wheezing. However, these symptoms may or may not lead to a full-blown asthmatic attack. According to Creer et al. (1982), coughing and wheezing may stop if a child is allowed to calm down, stop exercising, or remove a foreign substance from the throat. In this case, no further treatment is necessary.

Everyone at the meeting was therefore encouraged not to jump to any conclusions regarding Andrew's symptoms. Instead of sending Andrew to the nurse's office after some minor wheezing, for example, they were encouraged to wait about 2 minutes to see whether Andrew's symptoms worsened. If it was clear that Andrew had severe symptoms to begin with or if he was continuing to have minor symptoms after 2 minutes, then he would be sent to the nurse. In turn, the nurse was instructed to give Andrew (1) his bronchodilator and let him rest for at least 10 minutes or (2) some warm liquids to enhance bronchodilation.

The therapist also described Andrew's attention-seeking and escape-motivated behavior and asked whether Andrew could be kept in school as much as possible. This question was primarily directed toward the nurse, who agreed to send Andrew home only if his symptoms seemed particularly dire. Otherwise, he would be asked to return to class or at least complete his work under the nurse's supervision in her office. Mrs. Barton expressed concern that Andrew might be in physical danger using this procedure, but Dr. Morris graciously offered to receive the nurse's call at any time if Andrew seemed to be having a particularly bad asthmatic attack. This never became necessary, however.

Separate therapy sessions were also held with Mrs. Barton regarding her treatment of Andrew at home. For example, if Andrew did have to come home after a severe asthmatic attack, Mrs. Barton was asked not to give her son any extra verbal or physical attention. In addition, Andrew would not be allowed any tangible reinforcers like television, videogames, or reading. Instead, he would be required to stay in bed and/or complete his homework for that day. In addition, Mrs. Barton was to treat Andrew in a matter-of-fact way and make it clear that he would be expected to attend school the following day.

The therapist also worked with Dr. Morris and Andrew to fine-tune the boy's ability to use his bronchodilator when necessary. This way, he could become more independent in treating his symptoms. The therapist also engaged in relaxation training with Andrew, teaching him to tense and release different muscle groups whenever he felt stressed. In addition, Andrew was taught to control his breathing better during exercise and to calm himself afterward. However, the therapist also made it clear that Andrew would no longer be released from school or receive extra tangible rewards for his general asthmatic attacks. Instead, a series of reinforcers were established for asthma-free days, completion of homework, and classroom attendance.

According to Creer et al. (1982), the psychological treatment of children with asthma could also include self-observation, self-instruction, decision making, and self-induced stimulus or response change. These are used primarily to prevent attacks or to promote a child's health. Self-observation involves having the child track his or her asthmatic attacks and required medication. In this way, the child becomes a better monitor of his or her behavior. However, this was not done in Andrew's case because he was already monitoring and dramatizing his asthma symptoms too much.

Self-instruction involves self-statements that a child can use to control his or her behavior. For example, a child can repeat statements like "I am okay," "I can take care of myself," and "I've been through this before, and I can get through it again." These were tried with Andrew but had little effect on his behavior. In addition, Andrew was taught different strategies for controlling minor symptoms of coughing and wheezing on his own. Andrew and the therapist also worked on (1) improving his decision-making skills so that Andrew could accurately judge when to stop exercising and (2) changing stimulus conditions that triggered asthma by having Andrew avoid areas with excessive cigarette smoke or dust.

Initially, Andrew responded poorly to the contingency management program implemented by his teachers, nurse, and mother. For example, he threw four major temper tantrums during the next week of school, demanding that he be sent home because of his symptoms. Fortunately, the therapist had warned the nurse that this behavior "burst" was likely to happen, and she was able to downplay Andrew's petulance. Andrew compensated by staying in the nurse's office most of the day almost every day, but he was still required to do his homework. In addition, his antics at school were met with a strict revocation of privileges at home. As a result, Andrew's misbehavior eventually declined over a 3-month period and he had only one asthmatic attack during the last 3 weeks of this period.

Treatment during this time also focused on Andrew's recurrent abdominal pain. In addition to the fiber pill supplement mentioned earlier, contingency management was again used. For example, Andrew was not allowed to leave school even if he reported his pain to be severe (Dr. Morris had already concluded that Andrew's constipation was not serious). He was also required to complete his chores and schoolwork at home despite complaints of pain.

Other psychological treatments for children with recurrent abdominal pain include time-out, electrical shock, and reducing parent complaints of pain (Scharff, 1997). However, these were not pertinent to Andrew's case. Instead, the therapist encouraged Mrs. Barton to ignore "sick role" behaviors like pained facial expressions, verbalizations of pain, and whining. Conversely, whenever Andrew showed positive behaviors like working through his pain, Mrs. Barton was to give him considerable praise.

Therapy over a 3-month period also focused on Mrs. Barton's enmeshed relationship with her son as well as strategies for responding to his general noncompliance at home. In addition, Mrs. Barton was able to change her work schedule to better monitor Andrew's behavior and to develop more social contacts outside the family. The school's guidance counselor also changed Andrew's class schedule so that he could spend more time with his old friends. By the end of therapy, Andrew's problems regarding his asthma and recurrent abdominal pain were largely under control. He still complained occasionally of symptoms but came to realize that this behavior would bring him little reward. General conflict between Mrs. Barton and her son remained problematic, but Andrew's overall functioning 6 months after therapy was determined to be good.

Discussion Questions

1. How might you distinguish between children with asthma triggered by physiological factors and children with asthma triggered by emotional factors? How would you assess and treat these types of children differently, if at all?

2. Explore how psychological factors can impinge on disorders traditionally thought to be mostly biological in nature. What psychological factors other than stress could trigger pain and other physical responses? How does your own personality and behavior affect your body's functioning?

3. Certainly one issue of great concern in treating children with pediatric conditions is adherence to treatment. How would you go about helping a child keep up with medical doctor appointments, physical therapy assignments, and prescriptive drug regimens?

4. How might treatment differ for Andrew if he had other pediatric conditions? Explore in particular the specific issues related to childhood diabetes, visual and auditory handicaps, cancer, and headaches.

5. Obviously one of the most serious pediatric conditions involves children with AIDS. As a therapist, what would you need to focus on most when addressing a family with such a child?

6. Many children are terrified of surgical, dental, and other medical procedures that are necessary for their care. How might you go about reducing a child's fear in these situations? What could hospitals do to ease the treatment of children with pediatric conditions?

7. Explore the issue of social support and its influence on medical problems in a child as well as family members who care for the child.

CHAPTER THIRTEEN

Effects from Sexual Abuse

Symptoms

Joline Kennington was a 12-year-old Caucasian female referred to treatment by her mother, Mrs. Kennington, and a social worker from a state family services department. Joline was referred to a private practitioner, a female clinical psychologist who specialized in youngsters who have faced traumatic circumstances. Joline's circumstances involved alleged sexual abuse by her father, who was incarcerated at the time. Both Mrs. Kennington and the social worker felt it was important for Joline to receive therapy to deal with her current trauma and the loss of her father.

During the initial interview, the psychologist tried to speak with Joline individually. She found, however, that the girl was reticent and made little eye contact. At first, Joline responded only briefly to questions that had nothing to do with the recent abusive situation. For example, she talked about her dog and her favorite television shows and foods. After the psychologist felt she had good rapport with Joline, she asked about recent events. At this point, Joline cried softly and would not speak. The psychologist comforted Joline and thanked her for coming in. She also secured a promise from the girl to meet again the following week.

The psychologist interviewed Mrs. Kennington next and found that she had a lot to say about the current situation. She reported that Joline's father had been accused of sexually abusing his daughter about 10 months earlier. Mrs. Kennington had apparently been suspicious of her husband when he would go into Joline's bedroom, shut the door, and stay there for long periods of time. Mrs. Kennington insisted that she only noticed her husband's odd behavior just before calling the police. She said she asked Joline about the situation, and that her daughter had started crying and said that "Daddy keeps touching me in bad places." Mrs. Kennington reiterated that she immediately called the police, who in turn contacted the family services department. Following interviews with Mr. and Mrs. Kennington and Joline, the father was arrested on charges of child molestation and was in jail awaiting trial.

Mrs. Kennington brought Joline in for counseling because the girl was upset that her father was to go on trial the next week and that she, Joline, might have to testify. Mr. Kennington was vigorously denying the charges, but Mrs. Kennington said he was a "pathological liar" who would "say anything to save his skin." Interestingly, the psychologist noticed that Mrs. Kennington was more concerned about Joline's performance on the witness stand than she was about her daughter's emotional state following the performance. In particular, Mrs. Kennington was concerned about how Joline would look to the jury, whether she would appear credible, and whether she would be intimidated by her father.

The psychologist also noted that Mrs. Kennington had a detached relationship with her family. For example, she and her husband had experienced deep marital problems for a number of years and often argued about finances, childrearing, and sex. Mrs. Kennington described her husband as abusive, brutish, and coarse. In addition, Mrs. Kennington was unaware of many of Joline's day-to-day activities like her schoolwork. However, she was effusive in her praise for Joline and insisted that she and her daughter had a close, loving relationship. Finally, Mrs. Kennington was not close to her two sons either, both of whom reportedly reminded her of her husband. Her sons, 17 and 19 years old, were not living at home at the time of their father's arrest. Although they had no knowledge about recent family events, "the boys," Mrs. Kennington said, "will be on their father's side."

The psychologist also spoke with the family services social worker who was in charge of Joline's case. The social worker, Mrs. Tracy, seemed to provide a more balanced view of the situation than Mrs. Kennington. Mrs. Tracy admitted that the entire situation was cloudy and that the police and family services department had acted largely on Joline's self-report after her mother called police. At that time, Joline said that her father had been coming into her bedroom and fondling her. Specifically, he was allegedly caressing his daughter's body and then asking her to do the same to him. Mrs. Tracy reported that Joline went as far to say that her father touched her genital area and asked her to fondle his. No kissing, vaginal penetration, or oral sexual contact were initially reported, however.

At the time, Joline was asked how often and how long the fondling had taken place and was unable to give a clear answer. She initially said the abuse had been going on since her 10th birthday about 15 months earlier. However, when reinterviewed in front of her mother, Joline said the abuse had lasted only one month. Also during this second interview, Joline reported more thorough abuse, including extensive kissing and oral sexual contact. Therefore, it was unclear exactly what had happened. During subsequent interviews, Joline's accounts of events wavered even more, but she always insisted that her father had caressed her and asked her to do the same. In recent interviews, she said she could not remember whether the kissing and oral contact had actually taken place.

Mrs. Tracy conveyed her suspicions that Mrs. Kennington influenced her daughter's answers. In particular, it seemed that Mrs. Kennington was trying to punish her husband for past offenses by encouraging Joline to magnify the seriousness of the alleged abuse. Conversely, it seemed that Mrs. Kennington was trying to minimize the length of the alleged abuse to avoid blame for any reporting delays. At the present time, it remained unclear as to what had actually happened, if anything, to Joline. Mrs. Tracy said her "gut reaction" was that some abuse had occurred but that the nature of the abuse was unknown. Mrs. Tracy expressed concern that different accounts of what happened might jeopardize the district attorney's chances for a conviction in the case.

Mrs. Tracy also reported that Joline was suffering from various problems in past months. In particular, her schoolwork had suffered dramatically, as her "B" average had slipped to "D" and "F" grades. In addition, Joline apparently had enormous guilt and sadness over the loss of her father, as well as anger toward him and her mother. With respect to her mother, for example, Joline had told the social worker at one point that her mother "waited too long" and ignored her complaints about her father. After further conversations with Joline, Mrs. Tracy suspected that Mrs. Kennington had indeed called police only after a major argument with her husband about another issue. Finally, Joline was experiencing a lot of nervousness about the possibility of testifying in court.

With Mrs. Kennington's permission, the psychologist completed her initial assessment by interviewing Joline's schoolteacher. The teacher, Mrs. Ecahn, said that Joline was a bright child who was clearly having trouble concentrating on her work. She also appeared agitated and occasionally cried during class. Mrs. Ecahn and other school officials were aware of Joline's situation, so accommodations were made to assist her. In particular, the teachers gave her a lot of emotional support and after-school tutoring.

Based on information from all these sources, the psychologist suspected that some form of abuse had indeed occurred and that Joline was suffering from its aftereffects. In particular, the psychologist suspected that Joline was displaying symptoms of posttraumatic stress disorder.

Assessment

According to the *DSM-IV*, the essential feature of posttraumatic stress disorder (PTSD) is "the development of characteristic symptoms following exposure to an extreme traumatic stressor involving direct personal experience of an event that involves actual or threatened death or serious injury, or other threat to one's physical integrity; or witnessing an event that involves death, injury, or threat to the physical integrity of another person; or learning about unexpected or violent death, serious harm, or threat of death or injury experienced by a family member or other close associate" (APA, 1994, p. 424). In addition, a person's response to the trauma must involve some intense fear, helplessness, horror, or in youngsters, disorganized or agitated behavior (p. 428). Other PTSD-related symptoms that may occur in those who have been sexually abused include self-destructive and impulsive behavior, somatic complaints, shame, depressive behaviors, social problems, feeling "damaged" or threatened, and personality changes (p. 425).

A key aspect of PTSD is that the traumatic event is constantly reexperienced in the form of memories, dreams, a sense of reenactment, or physiological or psychological distress when a person is faced with cues that remind him or her of the trauma. Young children may also relive the trauma through repetitive play and manifest beliefs that their lives will be shortened or that they can foresee negative events. In addition, someone with PTSD generally experiences increased arousal and avoids stimuli that are linked to the traumatic event. To qualify as PTSD, these symptoms must last longer than one month and must cause significant impairment in functioning. PTSD is considered chronic if the symptoms last longer than 3 months (APA, 1994).

In Joline's case, she appeared to meet some diagnostic criteria for PTSD. For example, the reported abuse seemed to involve a threat to physical integrity, as Joline had told the social worker that she felt endangered and "dirty" as a result. Specifically, she reportedly felt helpless during the abusive episodes, daring not to resist her rather large father. Since the alleged abuse, Joline had also experienced nightmares about the abusive episodes and anxiety when confronted with the fact that she might have to face her father in court. In addition, she (1) often avoided talking further about the abuse, (2) was disinterested in activities that used to make her happy, and (3) was detached from others. Symptoms of PTSD were also evident in Joline's anger and concentration problems. As a whole, these symptoms were affecting Joline's social and academic functioning, so a consideration of PTSD seemed warranted. About one-third of youngsters who experience sexual abuse later develop PTSD (Kendall-Tackett, Williams, & Finkelhor, 1993).

The assessment of youngsters who have endured sexual abuse and who experience symptoms of PTSD usually involves some type of interview. For obvious reasons, interviewers usually focus on the child and must do so carefully and without forcefulness. The interviewer must develop rapport with the child and provide a safe, confidential environment where the child feels comfortable expressing very personal issues. In Joline's case, the psychologist met with Joline and the social worker, who already had a special rapport with the girl. After a few sessions, Joline said she felt comfortable talking with the psychologist individually about her abuse. In the meantime, the legal case against Mr. Kennington had been delayed because of Joline's unwillingness to testify.

The psychologist's first task was to clarify whether any abuse had occurred and, if so, what type. After much discussion and reassurance about confidentiality, Joline repeated her original version of events. She said that for several months, her father entered her bedroom at night, talked to her about her day, and began some type of physical contact. Initially, this was in the form of body massages but later progressed to full-body caressing. In later stages of the abuse, Mr. Kennington told Joline to reciprocate and had directed her hand to his genital area. In addition, as these events progressed, Mr. Kennington told his daughter that she should not tell anyone about their "special time together." However, no overt threats were made.

When asked if anything else had occurred, Joline said that no kissing or other activity had taken place. She admitted lying to police after her mother had told her to "make the story as painful as possible." She complied, but had later mixed up her accounts of these nonexistent events. Joline also claimed that she told her mother several times what was going on before the police were contacted but that her mother had taken no action until the night of her big argument with Mr. Kennington.

According to Wolfe (Wolfe & Birt, 1997; Wolfe & Wolfe, 1988), the assessment of children following disclosure of abuse should focus on several elements:

1. Behavior patterns that may lead to future revictimization (e.g., delinquency, truancy)
2. Symptoms of PTSD and general anxiety
3. Sexual and peer relationships
4. Causes and feelings about the past abuse
5. Level of general disorganization
6. Current family atmosphere

In Joline's case, no disruptive behaviors, substance use, stealing, or aggression were reported. Instead, depressive symptoms of social withdrawal, guilt, and suicidal ideation were present. Joline said she felt her classmates were looking at her "funny," that she was the one who had gotten her father into trouble, and that the family "might be better off if I was dead." The psychologist developed a verbal contract with Joline to ensure that Joline would speak to the psychologist if she had any suicidal thoughts or prior to any suicide attempt.

Joline was also reportedly anxious about going to school and about testifying in court. In fact, this latter symptom persisted for so long that Joline eventually refused to testify and the charges against Mr. Kennington were dropped (he moved out of state thereafter and had no further contact with Joline or Mrs. Kennington). The psychologist suspected that Joline had refused to testify as well because of her guilt about the situation. Joline actually blamed herself for some aspects of the abuse, even saying that if she hadn't lived in the apartment, her father wouldn't have gotten into trouble.

The psychologist also discussed Joline's current relationship with her peers and family members. Joline said that her friends and people at school were generally supportive, but that she felt uncomfortable with them given recent media attention about the case. Her relationship with her mother was strained because Mrs. Kennington was upset that Joline would not testify in court. In addition, Joline remained angry at her mother for waiting so long to do anything about the abuse. In general, the psychologist felt that Joline was learning to adjust to the major changes in her life but that she would have to work through many of her negative feelings.

The assessment of youngsters who have been sexually abused may be assisted by the use of anatomical dolls. They are usually used in cases where the youngster is unwilling or not verbal enough to describe abusive events fully. Typically, the child is taught to draw the human body and identify different body parts. The doll is then introduced to the child and different questions are asked about what the offender may or may not have done. Research indicates that using dolls facilitates memory for details of abusive events but is not helpful if the child has completely forgotten what happened. In addition, the use of dolls tends to reveal aggressive and sexual play among those who have been sexually abused. Finally, the use of dolls does not appear to entice children to make up stories of abuse, a source of great controversy in this area (White & Santilli, 1988). In Joline's case, however, dolls were not used.

Causes and Maintaining Variables

Although no child is immune from abuse, Finkelhor (1984) and Wolfe and Wolfe (1988) summarized some of the major risk factors that precipitate the sexual abuse of youngsters. These factors include low family income, isolated families, presence of a stepfather, patriarchal attitudes on the part of the father, lack of social contact on the part of the child, sexually restrictive family attitudes, and a poor mother-child relationship. This relationship may have several features:

1. A past situation in which the child has lived away from his or her mother
2. Emotional detachment on the part of the mother
3. Poor supervision of the child

4. The mother's punitiveness regarding her child's sexual development

Some of these characteristics certainly did *not* apply to Joline and her family. For example, the family's socioeconomic status was middle class, Mr. Kennington was Joline's natural father, Joline did have several close friends, Joline and her mother had never been separated for a long time, and the family was not isolated from others. In fact, they lived in an urban environment and interacted regularly with other families. In addition, it was not clear whether the family as a whole had sexually restrictive attitudes, although this did seem to be the case for Mrs. Kennington.

Conversely, some of the other characteristics mentioned above *did* apply to Joline and her family. For example, Mr. Kennington was reportedly very traditional and conservative regarding family structure. He disapproved of his wife's career and time spent away from home, and apparently fought a lot with his wife about their lack of sexual activity and affection. In addition, it was clear that Joline and her mother had a problematic relationship. The social worker speculated that Mrs. Kennington had always resented her husband's affection for his daughter and may have even postponed calling the police about the abuse to deliberately poison the husband-daughter relationship. Mrs. Kennington also seemed nervous about her daughter's potential sexual development, telling the social worker at one point that she felt uncomfortable talking to Joline about dating and sex.

Finkelhor (1984) and Wolfe and Wolfe (1988) also discussed four preconditions that must be met before sexual abuse occurs. First, the perpetrator must have motivation to abuse a child sexually. Although many people believe that sexual abuse is about sexual gratification, it is more often the result of a desire for power and the need to humiliate others. The psychologist in Joline's case speculated that Mr. Kennington's recent occupational difficulties, loss of the boys from the house, and arguments with his wife may have created a sense of lack of power that was assuaged by controlling his daughter. However, because Mr. Kennington was never interviewed, no direct evidence existed of this need for power or any desire to humiliate Joline.

A second precondition for sexual abuse is that the perpetrator must overcome his or her inhibitions regarding sexual activity with a child. To do so, the person may engage in alcohol use, deny negative consequences of the abuse, accept child pornography as a legitimate medium, attribute the behavior to poor self-control, or believe that a parent may do as he or she wishes with a child. In Joline's case, the latter certainly applied, but no evidence was available regarding the other factors. For example, it was not known whether Mr. Kennington actually believed that sexual interactions with his daughter were based on affection and were not abusive.

A third precondition for sexual abuse is that the perpetrator must overcome external obstacles to the sexual behavior. Major obstacles, of course, include discovery and arrest. This was not initially difficult for Mr. Kennington because his wife allowed him to spend considerable time alone with Joline and did not care to listen to Joline's complaints about the sexual activity. In addition, Mr. Kennington apparently thought, wrongly so, that his appeals to Joline to remain silent about their "special time together" would be sufficent to prevent his eventual arrest.

Finally, to commit abuse, the perpetrator must overcome the child's resistance to sexual contact. In Joline's case, Mr. Kennington took advantage of Joline's initial confusion about the difference between normal parent-child affection and exploitation. In addition, the extra attention that he gave Joline may have placated the girl for some time before she reported the abuse to her mother.

Researchers have also developed etiological models of posttraumatic stress disorder (PTSD) in youngsters. For example, some claim that PTSD symptoms are maintained by continual avoidance of thoughts associated with the trauma (Gilbert & Dollinger, 1992). Instead, the person must fully assimilate these thoughts into his or her psyche if PTSD symptoms are to be reduced. This model may have been applicable to Joline, who was initially hesitant about sharing her account of the sexual events. In addition, Janoff-Bullman (1985) claimed that traumatic events trigger feelings of vulnerability, helplessness, fear, anxiety, and guilt from self-blame. These feelings then trigger symptoms of PTSD like physiological arousal and negative views about the future. Certainly Joline had many of these feelings, which the psychologist felt were maintaining her PTSD symptoms.

Other etiological theories of PTSD involve a more integrated approach. For example, Fletcher (1996) outlined a working model for the etiology of childhood PTSD that includes traumatic events, emotional and biological responses, attributions, individual characteristics, and characteristics of the social environment. Fletcher (1996) stated that, for an event to be traumatic, it would typically involve death, injury, loss of physical integrity, suddenness, unpredictability, uncontrollability, chronic or severe exposure, close proximity, and/or social stigma. Several of these certainly applied to Joline's situation.

Emotional responses of PTSD include fear, horror, and helplessness, whereas biological responses include changes in neurotransmitters like norepinephrine, dopamine, serotonin, and acetylcholine. Attributions linked to PTSD include (1) an appraisal of the traumatic situation as inescapable, (2) a belief that one's safety will always be threatened, or (3) an attitude that one's future will forever be tainted by the traumatic experience (Fletcher, 1996). To some extent, these beliefs were evident in Joline.

Individual characteristics that may help cause PTSD include a biological predisposition toward negative reactivity to stressful events, psychological vulnerabilities based on past experiences, and an inability to cope with stressors. Finally, characteristics of the social environment may lead to PTSD as well. These characteristics include negative family reactions to the trauma and to the person, poor community support, and financial difficulties.

In Joline's case, her coping skills were actually quite good given her circumstances, although she continued to display many negative emotions and poor school performance. In addition, she often became upset about new changes in her life and remained upset for long periods of time. Joline's condition was also not helped by her strained relationship with her mother and the family's problematic financial situation. However, positive community support from school officials, the family services department, Joline's friends, and the psychologist likely prevented the develop- ment of some long-term PTSD symptoms.

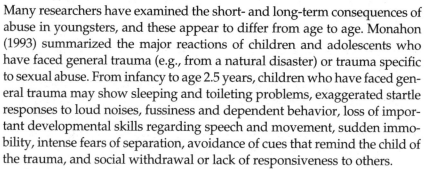

Developmental Aspects

Many researchers have examined the short- and long-term consequences of abuse in youngsters, and these appear to differ from age to age. Monahon (1993) summarized the major reactions of children and adolescents who have faced general trauma (e.g., from a natural disaster) or trauma specific to sexual abuse. From infancy to age 2.5 years, children who have faced general trauma may show sleeping and toileting problems, exaggerated startle responses to loud noises, fussiness and dependent behavior, loss of important developmental skills regarding speech and movement, sudden immobility, intense fears of separation, avoidance of cues that remind the child of the trauma, and social withdrawal or lack of responsiveness to others.

With respect to very young children who have been sexually abused, reactions may include inappropriate touching of other children, unusual attention to one's own genital area (e.g., massaging), demonstration of sexual knowledge highly advanced for the child's age, or genital pain or sexually transmitted disease. The latter, of course, may be present at any age. Monahon (1993) also indicated that a child's play may be a reenactment of abusive trauma and that the child, if verbal enough, may suddenly discuss issues surrounding the abuse.

From 2.5 to 6 years of age, children who have faced general trauma may show separation anxiety, social withdrawal, nightmares, magical thinking to explain "bad" events, somatic complaints, unpleasant visual images, regressions in language and self-care skills, retelling of the traumatic event, involvement of the traumatic events in play and with playmates, changes in mood and personality, and fear that the trauma will recur. In addition, the child may become more sensitive to anniversaries that remind him or her of the trauma. Children in this age group who have been sexually abused tend to show sexualized play, sudden and specific fears of a particular gender or place, aggressive touching of others, and overconcern with masturbation and their own genital area. In addition, children from 2.5 to 6 years of age have better memories of traumatic events than younger children (Monahon, 1993).

From 6 to 11 years of age, children who have faced general trauma tend to reenact the trauma in detailed stories and play. In addition, these children have specific fears and unwanted visual images, distractibility, poor concentration, guilt about their own role in the traumatic event, and sensitivity to parental reactions. Of course, any of the reactions mentioned for younger children (e.g., regressive behavior) may also apply to 6- to 11-year-olds. Children in this age group who have been sexually abused may show overt sexual behaviors, hint about their own sexual experience, verbally describe the abuse, or act like younger sexually abused children. In addition, they have better recall than preschoolers, so their memories of abuse are more detailed and long-standing (Beitchman, Zucker, Hood, da-Costa, & Akman, 1991; Monahon, 1993).

Adolescents who have faced general trauma can have several common reactions, including these:

- Delinquent, reckless, or risk-taking behavior
- Accident proneness
- Vengefulness
- Shame and guilt
- A sense of humiliation
- Intense memories
- Depression and pessimism
- Problems in interpersonal relationships
- Extreme social involvement or withdrawal

For adolescents like Joline who have been sexually abused, common reactions also include sexual promiscuity or abstinence, running away from home, and/or sexual aggression toward younger children (Kendall-Tackett et al., 1993; Monahon, 1993).

In Joline's case, her most prominent reactions were guilt, social withdrawal, embarrassment, depressive symptoms, and sexual repressiveness. With respect to the last one, Joline was clearly uncomfortable talking about sexual issues, although this is often normal for a 12-year-old. She also had a tense relationship with her mother, wanted to skip school, and sometimes avoided social outings with her friends. In addition, as the psychologist had noted before, Joline continued to blame herself for her father's absence and occasionally thought about suicide.

As adults, those who have been traumatized, especially those who have been sexually abused, tend to marry and have children at a younger age than the general population, leave school, fear independence, and seek a different social group. Common long-term problems include anxiety and depression, feelings of isolation, substance abuse, sexual problems, poor self-esteem, and eating and sleeping disorders. In addition, women who have been sexually abused are at greater risk of being revictimized through rape or spousal abuse (Bonner, Kaufman, Harbeck, & Brassard, 1992). This may be due to their compromised ability to judge the trustworthiness of others following abuse.

In related fashion, there are key developmental aspects of PTSD that may indicate how severe the disorder will be. As noted earlier by Fletcher (1996), a child's level of cognitive and social development is certainly critical. Children with more advanced cognitive development, for example, may appraise an event as more traumatic, have more self-defeating thoughts, be more susceptible to depression, fear more abstract consequences of the trauma, and have better memories of the trauma than would younger children. However, older children and adolescents with better cognitive development also tend to have better coping skills. With respect to social development, younger children with poor social skills may not develop a wide support network or effectively communicate their fears and worries about the future. Conversely, adolescents with good social skills can soften PTSD symptoms by talking with their friends and escaping aversive family situations.

Developmental differences can also influence how a youngster reacts to traumatic events. Children tend to react worse to traumatic events because they have less control (and perceived control), more disorganized behavior, and greater sensitivity to reminders of the event than adolescents (Fletcher, 1996). However, younger children are better at dissociating themselves from a traumatic event, and this may protect them somewhat from developing PTSD symptoms. This characteristic may also explain why children who have been severely abused sometimes develop dissociative identity (multiple personality) disorder.

In general, Joline's cognitive and social development were good. This proved to be a double-edged sword, however. For example, her cognitive skills allowed her eventually to understand that the sexual abuse was not her fault and that her mother, though not blameless, was also a victim of these circumstances. However, Joline also came to fear men in general, regarded sexual behavior and activity as somewhat repulsive, and continued to have unpleasant memories of the abusive episodes. In similar fashion, Joline's positive social development allowed her to build coping skills, rely on a support network, and become more self-reliant than before. However, Joline's ongoing attachment with her friends came at the expense of a continually strained relationship with her mother and less concern for her academic performance.

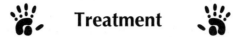

Treatment

The treatment of abused children often focuses on the parents and the child. In many cases, treatment is aimed toward the remaining parent because, as in Joline's situation, one has been removed from the family. Parent-oriented treatment often involves building better methods of discipline through modeling, role-play, and instructions regarding time-out and appropriate positive reinforcement. Other parent treatment components include cognitive therapy to modify irrational thoughts about a child's behavior, anger/self-control training, and general coping skills training (Azar & Wolfe, 1989; Deblinger & Heflin, 1996). In Joline's case, parent training was not emphasized because Mrs. Kennington had not engaged in any overt abuse toward Joline, and she did not wish to be an active participant in Joline's treatment. However, some might argue that Mrs. Kennington's neglect of Joline's trauma was abusive itself and worthy of some intervention.

Child-oriented treatment for youngsters who have been abused, especially those who have been sexually abused, depends largely on the age of the child. For preschool children without fully developed cognitive or social skills, play therapy may be most useful. Play therapy involves having the child interact with different recreational items (e.g., doll houses, puppets, paints, clay, building materials) that allow for expression in a comfortable setting. According to Schaefer (1993), play therapy is effective for overcoming resistance to therapy, enhancing communication about certain events, promoting creative thinking and fantasy, and releasing emotions. As a child engages in pretend play, for example, questions can be raised about hypothetical scenarios (e.g., inappropriate requests from others) and how the child might protect himself or herself (e.g., tell others about "bad" touches).

Bonner et al. (1992) indicated that treatment for sexually abused preschoolers can also focus on having a child talk about traumatic events. This is done to lower the child's apprehension and identify different people whom a child can trust. Emotive imagery techniques can be used to address nightmares. Here, a child is asked to imagine teaming up with a favorite superhero to battle a nightmare villain. In addition, it is helpful to educate a child about what touching behaviors are inappropriate and how to say "no" to unwanted touches. In Joline's case, however, these latter techniques were not necessary.

For school-age children who have been sexually abused, child-based treatment often focuses on impulse and anger control, emotional expres-

sion, problem-solving training, gradual exposure to feared stimuli with relaxation training, improving self-esteem, increasing social activity to
reduce isolation or depression, and cognitive therapy. Education about
sexuality, sexual abuse, and personal safety is also important (Deblinger &
Heflin, 1996). Group therapy may be helpful for education, emotional expression, and building social support. Another common treatment technique is to have a child write letters to hypothetical victims or family
members to describe his or her current feelings and achieve mastery of the
feelings (Karp & Butler, 1996).

In Joline's case, the psychologist asked her to write a letter to a hypothetical 12-year-old girl who had been abused by her father. The psychologist asked Joline to write about her own feelings and give advice to the
"other" child. Joline wrote several short letters about her feelings of guilt
and sadness, and fortunately told the "other" child that she shouldn't
blame herself for any of the abuse that happened to her. She also gave advice about how to talk with friends, see a therapist, and live life "one day at
a time." As Joline wrote the letters, the psychologist talked to her about her
feelings and helped ease her guilt and anger.

A more controversial topic that arose during therapy was Joline's desire to write a letter to her father. This was adamantly opposed by her
mother, who insisted that Joline have no contact whatsoever with Mr. Kennington. The psychologist offered a compromise, suggesting that Joline
write the letter but send it to the psychologist instead. Joline agreed, and
wrote a long, rambling letter about her anger toward her father, her hopes
that he was okay, and her wish to see him again at some time in the future.
Mrs. Kennington reported that it took Joline several days to complete the
letter, during which time she often cried. Although Mrs. Kennington saw
this as a destructive process, the psychologist recognized that Joline
needed to express these feelings if she were to put the abusive events behind her. Indeed, Joline's overall mood did improve somewhat following
the letter-writing exercise.

Treatment with Joline also focused on her feelings of isolation, general
fears of men, and questions about dating and sex. First, the psychologist
engaged in cognitive therapy to reduce Joline's interpretation of others' actions as threatening or mean. This applied especially to others who were
close to her, including her peers and mother, and was a natural result of
her father's betrayal. For example, Joline often felt that her friends looked
at her strangely and did not want to interact with her. However, Joline
came to recognize that others were perhaps uncomfortable around her because they didn't know what to say. Following the psychologist's suggestion that three of Joline's close friends attend therapy, this issue regarding
her peers was largely resolved. Therapy, however, did not improve Joline's
relationship with her mother.

The psychologist also helped Joline identify "good" men in her life to help her see that abusive behavior was not a part of every man's nature. In particular, her brothers, pastor, and guidance counselor at school were identified as positive role models. Finally, the psychologist answered Joline's questions about dating and sex, and appropriate and inappropriate sexual contacts were discussed at length.

The initial treatment of youngsters with symptoms of PTSD involves ending the trauma and helping them recover in a safe environment. Subsequent treatment may then resemble components for treating sexually abused children, including emotional expression, family therapy, and exposure to thoughts and cues that surround the trauma. In Joline's case, she had persistently avoided the old apartment where her father had molested her. When the psychologist felt that Joline was ready, they took a tour of the old apartment together. Joline pointed out different aspects of the place and entered her old bedroom last. She cried for an extended period of time, but eventually became calm. Following this experience, Joline wrote another unsent letter to her father, but kept this one confidential.

The long-term prognosis for those who have been abused or who have PTSD depends largely on their degree of emotional expression (catharsis), level of family and social support, exposure to cues that remind the person of the trauma, and development of coping skills. Joline remained in therapy for 7 months, after which treatment was ended when she and her mother moved to a different city. By the end of treatment, however, Joline's grades at school had generally improved, and she had adjusted well to past events and to her new life. The psychologist felt that Joline's long-term prognosis was probably good.

Discussion Questions

1. About one in four girls and one in six boys are sexually abused by the time they reach age 18 years. Why do you think sexual abuse is so prevalent? Also, why do you think that most victims of childhood sexual abuse are girls aged 4 to 12 years?

2. If you were to interview a child who had been severely abused, what themes would be most important to cover first? What characteristics about yourself should you think about when talking to an abused child?

3. What types of trauma do you think are most likely to lead to posttraumatic stress disorder (PTSD)? Why do some people experience PTSD following a terrible event whereas others do not? Explore personal, family, and social issues to address this question.

4. What events in your own life might you describe as traumatic? What about the event made you feel that way?

5. Given Mrs. Kennington's role in the case just described, do you feel it was appropriate for Joline to stay with her mother after her father left? Explore the advantages and disadvantages of this situation.

6. If you could speak to Joline about her situation, what would you most like to say? If you were a therapist and had been abused in the past, would you self-disclose this as part of therapy to help your client? Defend your answer.

7. Can memories of past abuse be repressed and later remembered? Support your answer. What are the ramifications of this (e.g., judicial)?

8. Explore the usefulness or desirability of self-help groups in treating people who have been sexually abused. In particular, discuss the pros and cons of using support groups rather than a trained professional who has never experienced abuse personally.

CHAPTER FOURTEEN

Mixed Case Two

Symptoms

Cindy Wellers was a 14-year-old Caucasian female referred to an outpatient clinic for youngsters with school refusal behavior. At the time of her initial assessment, Cindy was in ninth grade. She was referred by her mother, Mrs. Wellers, after a school official notified the family that Cindy had missed 28 days of school since the beginning of the academic year (it was now November). Most of these days were partial absences involving a skipped afternoon. In accordance with school policy, however, the principal had referred Cindy's case to juvenile court. There, Cindy would face charges of truancy and her parents might face charges of educational neglect. The principal informed Mrs. Weller that, historically, the court looked more favorably on families with such problems if they agreed to seek therapy. Mrs. Weller then made an initial appointment at the clinic for Cindy, herself, and her ex-husband.

During the first assessment session, Cindy and her parents were interviewed separately by a clinical psychologist. Cindy was interviewed first but was initially vague when providing information. For example, when asked about how many days she'd missed, Cindy testily reported that "it wasn't that many." However, she was aware of the school's policy to refer a student to court after 20 absences in a semester. After being reassured of confidentiality, especially with respect to her parents, Cindy was more forthcoming. She said that she didn't like school and generally found it boring. More specifically, she said she didn't like her classmates, teachers, subjects, or the new high school in which she had been placed. When asked if there was anything about school she *did* like, Cindy reported that she enjoyed only the free times with her friends.

The psychologist also questioned Cindy about her activities outside of school. Cindy replied that she and her friends would often skip school to "hang out and smoke weed" or stay at someone's house to watch television or play videogames. This occurred about two or three times per week. In addition, she would sometimes cruise a local shopping mall or go back home to sleep. On weekends, this routine was usually the same. The psychologist explored Cindy's drug use further and found that she sometimes used crack and powder cocaine in addition to marijuana. However, outside of missing school, none of Cindy's reported drug use appeared to interfere significantly with her daily life functioning. For example, she never missed family or doctor appointments because she was intoxicated. In addition, nothing suggested that Cindy placed herself in dangerous situations because of her drug use. For example, she didn't ride in a car with intoxicated friends or drink alcohol when using other drugs.

The psychologist also delved into past areas of Cindy's life. Cindy reported that her parents had divorced about one year earlier following a period of intense fighting. In particular, she described how Mr. and Mrs. Weller would argue and become physically violent with one another. In fact, Cindy had called the police twice to intervene. Ironically, following the divorce, Mr. and Mrs. Weller remained in close contact and often consulted one another about Cindy (note that both had come to the clinic). Cindy described the divorce as a "good thing" and was reportedly glad that her father was out of the house. However, it was clear also that she and her mother did not get along. Cindy said that she often argued with her mother and that Mrs. Weller "was counting the days until she could kick me out." As a result, Cindy avoided her home and interactions with her mother as much as possible.

Returning to more recent events, Cindy was insistent about her need to spend time with her friends and hinted that she might never go back to school. Cindy was reportedly anxious about her performance in several classes, claiming that she did not understand the work and could not see its relevance to her life. She said she felt "out of place" during many of her classes and therefore skipped school to be with more supportive friends. She denied any emotional distress outside of school, but the psychologist saw that Cindy was concerned about what would happen in court and that her mood was somewhat depressed. For example, she shrugged her shoulders in response to several questions and was tearful when asked about her future plans. In addition, Cindy provided no ideas regarding treatment goals.

During the parents' interview, Mrs. Weller was eager to give information and criticism regarding Cindy. She began by placing the blame for recent problems squarely on her daughter, whom she called "troubled." She outlined Cindy's long history of school refusal behavior, reporting that her daughter had missed 17 days during seventh grade and 50 days the previous year during eighth grade. However, no legal action had been taken by the school district until now. Mrs. Weller said she was surprised by the school's policy regarding absenteeism and complained about her own upcoming loss of work time from required court and therapy appearances.

When asked why Cindy was refusing school, Mrs. Weller shrugged and said that her daughter was "becoming a drug addict." Mrs. Weller had reportedly found marijuana and cocaine in her daughter's room the previous summer and had briefly kicked Cindy out of the house before relenting and allowing her to come home. Moreover, she felt that Cindy skipped school to be with her friends and "party it up." Mrs. Weller was also concerned that Cindy was about to join a gang and start shoplifting. In addition, she claimed that Cindy no longer listened to her and was "out of control" and "headed for big trouble." She also expressed doubt that the psychologist would be able to help in any substantial way.

Mr. Weller, who was quiet until this point, adopted a softer tone. He said his divorce from Mrs. Weller had been particularly difficult on Cindy and that she was probably "rebelling" against him and his ex-wife. He admitted past accounts of marital conflict and physical violence, and he speculated that Cindy was "scarred" by this in some way. With respect to recent events, Mr. Weller said that Cindy still argued frequently with him and his ex-wife, at times using highly obscene language. In addition, she sometimes threatened to run away from home and had actually done so twice. On both occasions, she had stayed at a friend's house for 4 days before returning. Mr. Weller agreed with his ex-wife that Cindy was "headed for big trouble."

With Mr. and Mrs. Weller's permission, the psychologist also spoke with various school officials. From them, a different clinical picture emerged. Several teachers, for example, described Cindy as anxious, depressed, and withdrawn. No one said she was disruptive in class, although one teacher complained that Cindy seemed "out of it" and would shrink when asked a question. All reported that Cindy was currently failing their classes. Her guidance counselor, Mrs. Arias, also reported that Cindy had threatened to hurt herself at the beginning of the year if she did not get the class schedule she wanted. Although the threat was not deemed serious, Mrs. Arias voiced her concern about Cindy's family and social life and described her as an "at-risk" student.

Following this initial assessment process, the psychologist concluded that Cindy had internalizing, externalizing, and academic difficulties. However, school refusal behavior was thought to be the most serious and immediate problem. Other problems that would have to be addressed in therapy included depression, substance use, noncompliance, and family conflict, among others.

Assessment

School refusal behavior refers to a child-motivated refusal to attend school or difficulties remaining in classes for an entire day. Specifically, the behavior refers to children and adolescents 5 to 17 years old whose behavior fits one or more of these categories:

1. They are completely absent from school.
2. They go to school but then leave during the course of the day.
3. They go to school only after severe behavior problems (e.g., tantrums) in the morning.
4. They go to school with great dread and ask repeatedly to be excused. (Kearney & Silverman, 1996)

Although terms like *school phobia* or *truancy* have been used earlier to describe this population, the term *school refusal behavior* is preferred because it covers all youngsters who have trouble going to school. School refusal behavior is different from school withdrawal, in which a parent deliberately withholds a child from school for economic purposes or to prevent harm to the child (e.g., kidnapping by an ex-spouse).

In Cindy's case, she was secretly refusing school of her own volition. In fact, her parents knew very little about her absenteeism until school officials produced her records. In addition, Cindy's school refusal behavior was largely of the second type: she often went to school but skipped out during the day to be with her friends. Her problem going to school could probably be classified as chronic as well because the behavior had lasted on and off for 3 years. This year, however, was worse than previous ones, and significant interference in family and academic functioning was evident.

Most cases of school refusal behavior involve a complex pattern of internalizing and externalizing behaviors (Kearney & Silverman, 1996). Common internalizing behaviors include fear, anxiety, depression, social withdrawal, suicidal ideation, fatigue, and somatic complaints. The latter often involve stomachaches, headaches, trembling, and nausea. However, it's not often clear whether a youngster has real somatic complaints because of school, or exaggerates these complaints to avoid school. In Cindy's case, no somatic complaints were reported. However, she did report a sense of general anxiety and depression when in school. This applied especially to situations where she had to interact with classmates she didn't know or had to perform in front of others. Cindy was definitely a "follower" and avoided situations in which she would have to initiate social contact or be the center of attention.

Common externalizing behaviors in youngsters who refuse school include verbal and physical aggression, noncompliance, running away from home or school, and temper tantrums. These were generally evident in Cindy's case, as she was clearly noncompliant with many parent and teacher requests and had a history of leaving home and school. In addition, Mr. and Mrs. Weller said that Cindy would become verbally and physically abusive when she didn't get her way. They recalled one incident, for example, when Cindy tried to push her mother down the stairs so she could leave the house and be with her friends.

The assessment of youngsters with school refusal behavior must therefore concentrate on many areas of functioning. For internalizing problems, several self-report and parent/teacher questionnaires were used in this case. On the Children's Depression Inventory (Kovacs, 1992), for example, Cindy's score was in the normal range but she did give a high rating to several items. These items involved poor schoolwork, feeling unloved, depressed mood, fatigue, and thoughts about suicide. To address the last one, the psychologist made a contract with Cindy in which Cindy promised to contact him if she had any serious thoughts or impulses regarding suicide.

Cindy also reported moderate to high levels of general and social anxiety on the Revised Children's Manifest Anxiety Scale (Reynolds & Paget, 1981) and Social Anxiety Scale for Children-Revised (La Greca & Stone, 1993). Cindy was most anxious around people she did not know well, and she was concerned about how others assessed her appearance and behavior (this is often normal for a 14-year-old, however). This concern partially explained why she stayed close to her small group of friends who missed school. In addition, Cindy's scores on the Piers-Harris Self-Concept Scale for Children (Piers, 1984) revealed personal reservations about her popularity, performance in front of others, inner strength, and intelligence.

Cindy was also asked to complete the School Refusal Assessment Scale (SRAS; Kearney & Silverman, 1993), a measure of the strength of four functional conditions that surround school refusal behavior. This measure revealed that Cindy was missing school primarily for positive tangible rewards like visiting her friends, engaging in drug use, and watching television at home. However, a secondary concern was Cindy's desire to escape aversive social and evaluative situations at school, including meeting new people and performing athletically and academically in front of others. Therefore, Cindy had more than one reason for missing school. In general, it is more difficult to treat a youngster who is chronically refusing school for multiple reasons, as Cindy was, than a youngster who has just started refusing school for only one reason.

Parent/teacher questionnaires for general externalizing behaviors were also used in this case. On the Child Behavior Checklist, for example, Mr. and Mrs. Weller endorsed several items on the "delinquent behavior," "aggressive behavior," "anxious/depressed," and "social problems" factors. In particular, they noted Cindy's frequent noncompliance, arguing, swearing, crying, worrying, nervousness, and failure to get along with others. It is interesting that their assessment confirmed Cindy's report of mixed internalizing and externalizing symptoms. In addition, Mr. and Mrs. Weller completed the parent version of the School Refusal Assessment Scale. They rated Cindy very high on the "positive tangible reinforcement" dimension, convinced that she was refusing school to have more fun outside of school.

Cindy's guidance counselor, Mrs. Arias, was asked to complete the Teacher's Report Form. Her ratings closely mirrored those of Mr. and Mrs. Weller. In addition, she released Cindy's academic records, which revealed good attendance for morning classes (computer science, English, social studies) but poor attendance for afternoon classes (choir, math, earth science, and physical education). Although Cindy was failing each class, her computer science, English, and social studies teachers said that only some make-up work was needed to boost her grade to a passing level.

The assessment of youngsters with school refusal behavior may also involve direct observation of behavior. As part of the clinic's procedure, Cindy was observed twice from 6:00 A.M., when she was supposed to rise from bed, until 8:15 A.M., when she was supposed to enter her first class. These observations revealed a lot of conflict between Mrs. Weller and Cindy, who had a tough time getting out of bed and getting ready for school. Once she arrived at school, however, she went to class without incident. In addition, Mrs. Arias secretly observed Cindy on 2 days after she left her social studies class. Both times, Cindy ate lunch with three friends before slipping out of school. Mrs. Arias extended her observation to a third day, hoping to catch Cindy in the act of leaving school without permission. She did so, and gave Cindy 4 days of detention as a result.

Causes and Maintaining Variables

The precursors to school refusal behavior are not always clear, but major triggers include entering a new school building, onset of a stressful school year, disagreements with a teacher, trouble with peers, separation anxiety, and serious illness. Family variables can also provoke school refusal behavior and are discussed at length in the next section. In Cindy's case, her entry into high school had been a troubling one, as she was initially confused about finding her classes and knowing how to do her homework. In addition, she felt that some of her teachers were distant and mostly concerned with the best students. She also complained of the school's racial composition.

According to Kearney and Silverman (1996), youngsters continue to refuse school for one or more of four reasons or functions. First, youngsters may refuse school to get away from strange or negative emotions they feel when in school (avoidance of stimuli that provoke a general sense of negative affectivity). This usually refers to younger children who are absent because they generally feel anxious or upset about the school setting. These children often cannot point to one thing that makes them upset but sometimes report an overall feeling of malaise about the size and scope of the school building. In many cases, these children also report aversive physical symptoms like stomachaches. In addition, they tend to be more sensitive, reactive to stressors, and dependent than children who do not refuse school. A child in this group may also have a specific phobia of a school-related object or situation, but these cases are rare and not representative of those who miss school.

A second reason or function for school refusal behavior, and one that applied more to Cindy, is escape from aversive social and/or evaluative situations. This usually refers to adolescents who skip school to avoid situations that require social interaction or performance in front of others. These youngsters may avoid people like peers, teachers, and other school officials. In addition, they may avoid situations like tests, oral presentations, writing in front of others, recitals, athletic settings, walking into class or hallways, eating in the cafeteria, group events, large crowds, or any other setting involving social interaction or evaluation. In many cases, these youngsters show high social anxiety and personalization. With respect to the latter, for example, they may assume that two people whispering in a hallway are necessarily talking about them. Social anxiety in adolescents is common, of course, but problematic if it interferes with school attendance.

In Cindy's case, she did skip school partly to escape aversive social and evaluative situations. She was reportedly nervous in front of others, especially when meeting new people. She also worried about the consequences of returning to class full-time and getting strange looks from her classmates and teachers. Cindy found it easiest to skip school during the afternoon, when several of her classes involved more social interaction and evaluation. For example, Cindy liked to skip physical education class so she wouldn't have to perform athletically in front of others. She also skipped choir so she wouldn't have to sing in front of others. In addition, she liked to skip math so she wouldn't have to write and solve problems on the board. Cindy's school refusal behavior was not always limited to her afternoon classes, however. For example, she skipped all her morning English classes that involved student oral reports. Overall, Cindy preferred to be with her small group of friends and often shied away from others.

A third reason why many children refuse school is to receive attention from parents or other caregivers. This usually refers to younger children who show behavior problems in the morning to stay with parents at home. Common behaviors to do so include refusal to get out of bed (e.g., being "dead weight"), locking oneself in a room or car, clinging, tantrums, and running away from the school setting. These children may show high levels of separation anxiety as well (school refusal is one symptom of separation anxiety disorder), but attention-getting is the larger issue. In general, these youngsters are fearful, noncompliant, manipulative, and dependent. In Cindy's case, however, this functional condition clearly did not apply either now or in the past. Indeed, she wanted to be as far away from her parents as possible.

Finally, Kearney and Silverman (1996) indicated that some youngsters may also refuse school for positive tangible reinforcement. This usually refers to adolescents who skip school to pursue the many attractions of being out of school. As mentioned earlier, these attractions include time with friends, sleeping, and watching television, among others. In most cases, these youngsters have no anxiety about school but are more prone to show symptoms of oppositional defiant or conduct disorder. For example, common behaviors associated with this function include aggression, substance use, lying, and running away from home.

In Cindy's case, she was certainly refusing school for positive tangible reinforcement. This pattern began the previous year when Cindy skipped school to go shopping with her friends. The pattern was then reinforced when Cindy found that she could leave school without much consequence. For example, her parents were rarely notified of her absences by school officials. In many large school settings like Cindy's, absenteeism is difficult to track consistently. Regrettably, therefore, problems like Cindy's may develop for some time before action is taken.

The first two functional conditions, (1) avoiding negative emotions or physical symptoms associated with school and (2) escaping aversive social/evaluative situations, represent youngsters who refuse school for negative reinforcement (i.e., to get away from something unpleasant at school). The last two functional conditions, (1) attention-getting and (2) positive tangible reinforcement, represent youngsters who refuse school for positive reinforcement (i.e., to pursue something pleasant outside of school). Many youngsters refuse school for multiple reasons as well. For example, a child may initially miss school to avoid social interactions there, but then discover the positive aspects of staying home alone (e.g., watching television, talking on the telephone without interruption). Conversely, an adolescent may skip long periods of school to be with friends but then become anxious about having to return to new classes, peers, and teachers. As mentioned earlier, therapy for those who refuse school for multiple reasons requires a complex treatment strategy.

In Cindy's case, the complex scenario seemed to apply. Although clearly refusing school for tangible rewards outside of school, Cindy was nervous about returning to classes she hadn't attended in some time. The psychologist thought that Cindy was perhaps more willing to return to school than she admitted, but also that she was greatly worried about what would happen if she did return (e.g., being asked intrusive questions by others). The psychologist also recognized that other behaviors might interfere with Cindy's return to full-time attendance. These behaviors included frequent drug use, deteriorating family relationships, and depressive symptoms. Comorbid problems like these generally complicate the treatment for youngsters with chronic school refusal behavior.

🖐 Developmental Aspects 🖐

School refusal behavior, as indicated above, is maintained by different child factors or functions. However, certain dysfunctional family dynamics may set the stage for the development of school refusal behavior in the first place. Kearney and Silverman (1995) summarized the major family patterns that characterize children who refuse to go to school. A well-known pattern is enmeshment, which is marked by overinvolvement of family members in one another's lives. Typically, these families are characterized by parental overindulgence and overprotectiveness, dependence, hostility, and withdrawal on the father's part. This pattern often leads to a child's separation anxiety and attention-getting behavior and is triggered most when the child first enters school. In Cindy's case, however, she was never particularly close to her parents. She had gotten into trouble in the past to get her parents to stop fighting, but she currently avoided them whenever possible. Thus, her family could not be described as enmeshed.

Another family pattern characteristic of youngsters who refuse school is isolation, which is marked by little outside contact on the part of its members. For example, children in an isolated family spend most of their recreational time with their parents and therefore develop fewer friendships than most children their age. These families are also less likely to seek treatment for a child's behavior problem. This pattern was somewhat evident in Cindy's case and is often associated with those who refuse school to escape aversive social/evaluative situations. In Cindy's case, for example, her parents often isolated themselves from others, and Cindy spent much of her time at home during her early school years. Even now, Mr. and Mrs. Weller remained in close contact with one another and did not socialize much with others. This early family isolation may have led Cindy to develop social anxiety and become a "follower." As a result, she spent time with only a small group of friends and ended up following those who skipped school.

A third family pattern common to those who refuse school is detachment. Detached family members are poorly involved in one another's lives and pay little attention to each member's wants and needs. In general, detached parents usually wait a long time before responding to a child's behavior problems. Poor communication patterns and little emotional expression are also present. In Cindy's case, this pattern seemed especially pertinent. Mr. and Mrs. Weller had little positive communication with their daughter. In addition, Mrs. Weller often let Cindy's misbehavior continue undisciplined until her own life was affected. For example, Mrs. Weller was initially unconcerned about Cindy's school attendance even though Cindy had a long history of school refusal behavior. She intervened only after receiving a notice from the school about upcoming legal action.

Conflict is another family pattern seen in youngsters with school refusal behavior. This family type is marked by verbal and physical fighting, poor problem-solving skills, and coercive processes. This antagonism is often the result of marital problems, which may lead to inconsistent child discipline and later problems like school refusal behavior. Conversely, however, a child's school refusal behavior may trigger marital fighting as parents disagree about how to address the situation. Kearney and Silverman (1995) reported that conflict is most characteristic of youngsters who refuse school for positive tangible reinforcement. For Cindy, who did refuse school for positive tangible reinforcement, conflict among family members was certainly a long-standing pattern.

How might all these family patterns interact to produce Cindy's school refusal behavior? One possible scenario is that Mr. and Mrs. Weller were relatively withdrawn people who stayed mostly to themselves and required Cindy to do the same. This might explain why Cindy initially developed few friends and would later become anxious in new social situations. Over time, family stressors and little outside social support may have created an atmosphere of conflict that deprived Cindy of parental attention. Much of her reinforcement then came from external sources. For example, as her parents split up, Cindy became more interested in enjoying the material things that were available to her friends (e.g., videogames, drugs). As her friends began to skip school to enjoy these activities more, Cindy increasingly went along. Following the divorce, Mrs. Weller then became more detached from her daughter and even blamed her for some of the marital problems. As this detachment grew, Cindy was able to skip school and pursue tangible reinforcers with even greater vigor than before. This also allowed her to skip classes involving extensive contact with others.

What about the long-term developmental prognosis for youngsters who refuse school? Follow-up studies indicate that adults who refused school as adolescents are at risk for occupational and marital problems, anxiety and depression, alcohol abuse, and criminal behavior (e.g., Berg & Jackson, 1985; Flakierska, Lindstrom, & Gillberg, 1988). In addition, of course, those who drop out of school are less likely to attend college and achieve economic success.

What is the likely long-term prognosis for Cindy? Although her treatment program was moderately effective, as discussed next, her chronic school refusal behavior certainly places her at risk for further delinquent behavior and eventual dropout from school. These effects, in turn, could impair her long-term academic and financial success. Cindy's social avoidance, depression, substance use, and poor parental support might also predispose her toward problems in adulthood.

Treatment

Cindy's treatment program was designed by the psychologist to address her multiple behavior problems, but focused primarily on reducing her school refusal behavior. This was done in the hope that some of her secondary behaviors (e.g., social anxiety, depression, substance use) would then decline on their own. Kearney and Silverman (1996) outlined different treatments for youngsters with school refusal behavior based on the functions described earlier. As mentioned, for example, some children refuse school to get away from negative emotions or physical symptoms experienced there. These children might receive relaxation training, breathing retraining, and gradual reexposure to the school setting. Relaxation training and breathing retraining are used to help children control physical, school-based anxiety symptoms like muscle tension or hyperventilation. In addition, these children may be gradually reintroduced to their classroom and other settings to associate relaxation and normal breathing with school-related stimuli. This treatment was not applied to Cindy, however.

For youngsters who refuse school to escape aversive social/evaluative situations, as Cindy partially did, Kearney and Silverman (1996) recommended a treatment regimen of modeling, role-play, and cognitive therapy. Modeling and role-play are often used to build social skills. In Cindy's case, her social skills were relatively good, but she often withdrew and did not show the skills frequently enough. The psychologist believed this withdrawal was due to Cindy's depressive behaviors and social anxiety. At the heart of these symptoms were cognitive distortions that Cindy had about herself and her interactions with others.

As a result, the psychologist worked with Cindy first to identify distorted thought processes that maintained her depression and social anxiety. As mentioned earlier, Cindy was quite self-conscious about her appearance and behavior before others. She sometimes assumed that others were negatively judging her even when she had no evidence to support this assumption. For example, she speculated that the psychologist, on meeting her for the first time, thought about her messy hair, problematic complexion, and large nose. In addition, Cindy thought that others would judge her harshly, as her mother had done in the past, whenever she tried new things on her own. As a result, she often avoided new situations and rarely attempted to do things differently from before.

The psychologist then helped Cindy try new ways of interacting with her environment. In doing so, he gave Cindy substantial encouragement and invited her parents to do the same. Over time, Cindy was asked to engage in new situations involving her school (i.e., talking to others outside her group), church (i.e., joining the youth group), and family (i.e., initiating more conversations with her mother). During each situation, Cindy examined her own thoughts and changed irrational ones. In addition, when meeting people for the first time, Cindy was taught to attend to both the positive *and* negative feedback that she received from them. These efforts were designed to help her think more realistically, increase her activity level, and reduce her social anxiety and withdrawal. Over a period of several weeks, Cindy gradually took more social risks and engaged others more actively.

For youngsters who refuse school for attention, Kearney and Silverman (1996) recommended parent training in contingency management. In this approach, parents are encouraged to set regular morning and evening routines for the child, issue commands more clearly, actively reward prosocial or school attendance behaviors, and punish or ignore inappropriate school refusal behaviors. This treatment program is used primarily for younger children but certain aspects may be applied to adolescents as well.

In Cindy's case, the psychologist helped Mrs. Weller improve the clarity of her statements to her daughter. For example, she was encouraged to say, in unequivocal terms, what she wanted Cindy to do regarding chores, curfew, and school attendance. In addition, Cindy and her mother agreed on times when Cindy should rise from bed, go to school, arrive home from school, and associate with friends. Mr. and Mrs. Weller were also encouraged to praise Cindy for her positive behaviors and avoid sarcastic or hurtful comments. Over time, the psychologist saw that Mr. Weller was generally able to improve his relationship with Cindy. However, Mrs. Weller's attitude toward her daughter remained negative. As a result, her relationship with Cindy continued to be strained.

For youngsters who refuse school for positive tangible reinforcement, Kearney and Silverman (1996) recommended a family therapy approach. This approach emphasizes contracting and the development of problem-solving, communication, and peer refusal skills. Because the psychologist's first goal was to reestablish Cindy's full-time school attendance, the family's initial treatment sessions involved contracting. The written contracts had conditions under which Cindy would attend school in exchange for the opportunity to do chores at home for money. Specifically, Cindy could earn the chance to vacuum the house and clean the bathrooms for a certain amount of money *if* she attended school full time for one week. If she missed any amount of school, she would have to complete the chores without getting paid. If she then refused to do the chores, she would be grounded for the weekend. To monitor Cindy's school attendance, a clinic staff member contacted the school on a daily basis and let Mr. and Mrs. Weller know of any absence on Cindy's part.

Unfortunately, Cindy had great trouble complying with these initial contracts. In the first 2 weeks, for example, she left school on four different occasions. The psychologist then warned Cindy that one of her parents or a school official would escort her from class to class if she did not attend. Despite this warning, Cindy missed 15 afternoon classes over the next 2 weeks. Subsequently, Mr. Weller and Mrs. Arias, the guidance counselor, took turns walking Cindy to each of her afternoon classes. Cindy did attend school under this condition and was given the rewards from her contract as a result. Toward the end of therapy, this procedure was gradually faded, although Mrs. Arias asked Cindy's teachers to keep an eye on her as she went from class to class.

In conjunction with the contract and escort procedure, the psychologist focused on Cindy's peer refusal skills. This involved behaviors and statements that Cindy could use to decline offers to skip school without feeling rejected. For example, Cindy was encouraged to avoid lingering in hallways where she was likely to face such offers. In addition, her lunchtime was changed so she would not be tempted by certain peers to leave school. The psychologist also helped Cindy form statements to respond to those who wanted her to skip class. For example, Cindy was encouraged to say no because she wanted to earn money for chores by attending school (i.e., adhere to the contract). Another goal of this approach was obviously to reduce Cindy's time with people who skipped school. Cindy compensated for this, however, by spending extra time with her friends on the weekends.

The psychologist also worked with Cindy and her parents to improve their level of problem-solving and communication skills. The Wellers were essentially taught to define current problems, develop solutions, communicate with one another respectfully, and implement and evaluate solutions. Much of this process was done as the family formed the school attendance contracts. These procedures generally eased family tensions, but no major improvements in overall communication were noted. For example, family members continued to interrupt one another over time.

During the course of therapy, the psychologist also focused on Cindy's drug use. Cindy was educated about the potentially harmful effects of marijuana and cocaine, and the psychologist designed a schedule so that Cindy could reduce her drug use comfortably over time. However, this was met with no success. Instead, Cindy slightly *increased* her drug use, albeit mostly on the weekends. The only saving grace was that Cindy continued to abstain from alcohol.

Treatment in Cindy's case lasted almost 4 months, during which time her school attendance gradually improved. By the end of therapy, she was attending school about 90% of the time and all her grades except two were passing. This included English, as Cindy did make up her oral presentation assignments. In addition, her levels of social anxiety and depression had generally declined. However, the family's interactions and problem-solving abilities remained mediocre. Cindy was taken out of therapy when Mrs. Weller decided it was no longer necessary—in other words, she was no longer faced with legal actions regarding Cindy's behavior. Informal telephone contact with Cindy 6 months later revealed her overall functioning to be fair. In particular, her school attendance remained stable, although her relationship with her parents remained distant. In addition, no changes were reported in Cindy's level of drug use.

Discussion Questions

1. Do you think Cindy meets diagnostic criteria for any *DSM-IV* disorder? If so, which one(s)? Defend your answer. Also, what are the advantages and disadvantages of assigning a mental disorder to a case, like this one, that involves multiple behavior problems?

2. Explore the issue of comorbidity or the occurrence of multiple problems in an individual. What childhood problems are most closely related?

3. Compare Cindy's behavior problems to the others described in this casebook. For example, compare her social anxiety to Bradley's in case two, her depression to Anna's in case three, her substance use to Jennifer's in case nine, and her family conflict to the Simington family in case ten. Discuss which case was more serious and why. How might a specific treatment be used differently for Cindy's case compared to the others listed here? Also, how might Cindy's prognosis differ from these other cases?

4. How might you change your assessment protocol for a youngster with multiple behavior problems? What questions become more pertinent?

5. How might you change your treatment program for a youngster with multiple behavior problems? How should dual therapy procedures be conducted? Why and how might family therapy become more crucial?

6. Cindy's case appeared to be chronic in nature. How might you alter your assessment or treatment of a youngster if you know his or her problems have been going on for a year or longer?

7. What procedures would you recommend for *preventing* chronic or multiple problems like Cindy's? What procedures would you recommend *following* therapy for a youngster with chronic or multiple behavior problems?

8. Which treatments for children do you feel are most effective, and why?

9. Which child in this casebook would you most want to work with, and why?

REFERENCES

Abramson, L. Y., Seligman, M. E. P., & Teasdale, J. D. (1978). Learned helplessness in humans: Critique and reformulation. *Journal of Abnormal Psychology, 87,* 49–74.

Achenbach, T. M. (1991a). *Manual for the Child Behavior Checklist/4-18 and 1991 profile.* Burlington: University of Vermont Department of Psychiatry.

Achenbach, T. M. (1991b). *Manual for the Teacher's Report Form and 1991 profile.* Burlington: University of Vermont Department of Psychiatry.

Achenbach, T. M. (1991c). *Manual for the Youth Self-Report and 1991 profile.* Burlington: University of Vermont Department of Psychiatry.

Aiken, L. R. (1996). *Assessment of intellectual functioning* (2nd ed.). New York: Plenum.

Albano, A. M., Chorpita, B. F., & Barlow, D. H. (1996). Childhood anxiety disorders. In E. J. Mash & R. A. Barkley (Eds.), *Child psychopathology* (pp. 196–241). New York: Guilford.

Algozzine, B. (1977). The emotionally disturbed child: Disturbed or disturbing? *Journal of Abnormal Child Psychology, 5,* 205–211.

American Psychiatric Association. (1994). *Diagnostic and statistical manual of mental disorders* (4th ed.). Washington, DC: Author.

Azar, S. T., & Wolfe, D. A. (1989). Child abuse and neglect. In E. J. Mash & R. A. Barkley (Eds.), *Treatment of childhood disorders* (pp. 451–489). New York: Guilford.

Azrin, N. H., & Besalel, V. A. (1979). *A parent's guide to bedwetting control: A step-by-step method.* New York: Simon & Schuster.

Azrin, N. H., & Foxx, R. M. (1974). *Toilet training in less than a day.* New York: Simon & Schuster.

Babor, T. F., Ritson, E. B., & Hodgson, R. J. (1986). Alcohol related problems in the primary health care setting: A review of early intervention strategies. *British Journal of Addiction, 81,* 23–46.

Bakwin, H. (1973). The genetics of enuresis. In I. Kolvin, R. C. MacKeith, & S. R. Meadow (Eds.), *Bladder control and enuresis* (pp. 73–77). Philadelphia: Lippincott.

Barkley, R. A. (1990). *Attention-deficit hyperactivity disorder: A handbook for diagnosis and treatment.* New York: Guilford.

Barkley, R. A. (1996). Attention-deficit/hyperactivity disorder. In E. J. Mash & R. A. Barkley (Eds.), *Child psychopathology* (pp. 63–112). New York: Guilford.

Barkley, R. A. (1997a). Attention deficit/hyperactivity disorder. In E. J. Mash & L. G. Terdal (Eds.), *Assessment of childhood disorders* (3rd ed., pp. 71–129). New York: Guilford.

Barkley, R. A. (1997b). *Defiant children: A clinician's manual for assessment and parent training.* New York: Guilford.

Barkley, R. A. (1997c). *ADHD and the nature of self-control.* New York: Guilford.

Barnes, H. L., & Olson, D. H. (1985). Parent-adolescent communication and the circumplex model. *Child Development, 56,* 438–447.

Bates, J. E., Bayles, K., Bennett, D. S., Ridge, B., & Brown, M. M. (1991). Origins of externalizing behavior problems at eight years of age. In D. J. Pepler & K. H. Rubin (Eds.), *The development and treatment of childhood aggression* (pp. 93–120). Hillsdale, NJ: Lawrence Erlbaum.

Bayley, N. (1993). *Bayley Scales of Infant Development—Second edition manual.* San Antonio, TX: The Psychological Corporation.

Beck, A. T., Rush, A. J., Shaw, B. F., & Emery, G. (1980). *Cognitive therapy of depression.* New York: Guilford.

Beidel, D. C., & Randall, J. (1994). Social phobia. In T. H. Ollendick, N. J. King, & W. Yule (Eds.), *International handbook of phobic and anxiety disorders in children and adolescents* (pp. 111–129). New York: Plenum.

Beitchman, J. H., & Brownlie, E. B. (1996). Childhood speech and language disorders. In L. Hechtman (Ed.), *Do they grow out of it?: Long-term outcomes of childhood disorders* (pp. 225–253). Washington, DC: American Psychiatric Press.

Beitchman, J. H., & Young, A. R. (1997). Learning disorders with a special emphasis on reading disorders: A review of the past 10 years. *Journal of the American Academy of Child and Adolescent Psychiatry, 36,* 1020–1032.

Beitchman, J. H., Zucker, K. J., Hood, J. E., daCosta, G. A., & Akman, D. (1991). A review of the short–term effects of child sexual abuse. *Child Abuse and Neglect, 15,* 537–556.

Berg, I., & Jackson, A. (1985). Teenage school refusers grow up: A follow-up study of 168 subjects, ten years on average after inpatient treatment. *British Journal of Psychiatry, 147,* 366–370.

Berninger, V. W. (1994). *Reading and writing acquisition: A developmental neuropsychological perspective.* Madison, WI: Brown and Benchmark.

Bibace, R., & Walsh, M. E. (1980). Development of children's concepts of illness. *Pediatrics, 66,* 912–917.

Bierman, K. L., & Welsh, J. A. (1997). Social relationship deficits. In E. J. Mash & L. G. Terdal (Eds.), *Assessment of childhood disorders* (3rd ed, pp. 328–365). New York: Guilford.

Birmaher, B., Ryan, N. D., Williamson, D. E., Brent, D. A., Kaufman, J., Dahl, R. E., Perel, J., & Nelson, B. (1996). Childhood and adolescent depression: A review of the past 10 years. Part I. *Journal of the American Academy of Child and Adolescent Psychiatry, 35,* 1427–1439.

Black, B., Leonard, H. L., & Rapoport, J. L. (1997). Specific phobia, panic disorder, social phobia, and selective mutism. In J. M. Wiener (Ed.), *Textbook of child and adolescent psychiatry* (2nd ed, pp. 491–506). Washington, DC: American Psychiatric Press.

Bonner, B. L., Kaufman, K. L., Harbeck, C., & Brassard, M. R. (1992). Child maltreatment. In C. E. Walker & M. C. Roberts (Eds.), *Handbook of clinical child psychology* (2nd ed, pp. 967–1008). New York: Wiley.

Borkowski, J. G., Weyhing, R. S., & Can, M. (1988). Effects of attributional retraining on strategy-based reading comprehension in learning-disabled students. *Journal of Educational Psychology, 80,* 46–53.

Botvin, G. J., Baker, E., Renick, N., Filazzola, A. D., & Botvin, E. M. (1984). A cognitive-behavioral approach to substance abuse prevention. *Addictive Behaviors, 9*, 137–147.

Brazelton, T. B. (1962). A child oriented approach to toilet training. *Pediatrics, 29*, 121–128.

Brazelton, T. B., & Cramer, B. G. (1990). *The earliest relationship: Parents, infants, and the drama of early attachment.* New York: Addison-Wesley.

Brown, J. H., & Christensen, D. N. (1986). *Family therapy: Theory and practice.* Monterey, CA: Brooks/Cole.

Brown, S. A., Mott, M. A., & Stewart, M. A. (1992). Adolescent alcohol and drug abuse. In C. E. Walker & M. C. Roberts (Eds.), *Handbook of clinical child psychology* (2nd ed, pp. 667–693). New York: Wiley.

Bruck, M. (1985). The adult functioning of children with specific learning disabilities: A follow-up study. In I. Sigel (Ed.), *Advances in applied developmental psychology* (Vol. 1, pp. 91–129). Norwood, NJ: Ablex.

Bryson, S. E., Clark, B. S., & Smith, I. M. (1988). First report of a Canadian epidemiological study of autistic syndromes. *Journal of Child Psychology and Psychiatry, 29*, 433–445.

Bukstein, O. G., & Van Hasselt, V. B. (1995). Substance use disorders. In V. B. Van Hasselt & M. Hersen (Eds.), *Handbook of adolescent psychopathology: A guide to diagnosis and treatment* (pp. 384–406). New York: Lexington.

Butler, R. J., Brewin, C. R., & Forsythe, W. T. (1986). Maternal attributions and tolerance for nocturnal enuresis. *Behaviour Research and Therapy, 24*, 307–312.

Campbell, M. (1988). Fenfluramine treatment of autism. Annotation. *Journal of Child Psychology and Psychiatry, 29*, 1–10.

Campbell, S. B., Schliefer, M., & Weiss, G. (1978). Continuities in maternal reports and child behaviors over time in hyperactive and comparison groups. *Journal of Abnormal Child Psychology, 6*, 33–45.

Cantwell, D., & Baker, L. (1989). Stability and natural history of DSM-III childhood diagnoses. *Journal of the American Academy of Child and Adolescent Psychiatry, 28*, 691–700.

Carlson, G. A., & Abbott, S. F. (1995). Mood disorders and suicide. In H. I. Kaplan & B. J. Sadock (Eds.), *Comprehensive textbook of psychiatry* (6th ed, pp. 2367–2391). Baltimore, MD: Williams and Wilkins.

Carlson, G. A., & Kashani, J. (1988). Phenomenology of major depression from childhood through adulthood: Analysis of three studies. *American Journal of Psychiatry, 145*, 1222–1225.

Cartledge, G., & Milburn, J. F. (1995). *Teaching social skills to children and youth: Innovative approaches* (3rd ed.). Boston: Allyn & Bacon.

Chatlos, J. C. (1991). Adolescent drug and alcohol addiction: Diagnosis and assessment. In N. S. Miller (Ed.), *Comprehensive handbook of drug and alcohol addiction* (pp. 211–233). New York: Marcel Dekker.

Chess, S., & Thomas, A. (1996). *Temperament: Theory and practice.* New York: Brunner/Mazel.

Christophersen, E. R., & Rapoff, M. A. (1992). Toileting problems in children. In C. E. Walker & M. C. Roberts (Eds.), *Handbook of clinical child psychology* (2nd ed, pp. 399–411). New York: Wiley.

Cloninger, C. R., Dinwiddie, S. H., & Reich, T. (1989). Epidemiology and genetics of alcoholism. In A. Tasman, R. E. Hales, & A. J. Frances (Eds.), *American Psychiatric Press review of psychiatry* (pp. 293–308). Washington, DC: American Psychiatric Press.

Compas, B. E. (1997). Depression in children and adolecents. In E. J. Mash & L. G. Terdal (Eds.), *Assessment of childhood disorders* (3rd ed, pp. 197–229). New York: Guilford.

Conners, C. K. (1991). *Conners' Rating Scales manual.* North Tonawanda, NY: Multi-Health Systems.

Conners, C. K. (1995). *Conners Continuous Performance Test.* North Tonawanda, NY: Multi-Health Systems.

Coryell, W., & Norton, S. G. (1981). Briquet's syndrome (somatization disorder) and primary depression: Comparison of backgrounds and outcome. *Comprehensive Psychiatry, 22,* 249–256.

Creer, T. L., Renne, C. M., & Chai, H. (1982). The application of behavioral techniques to childhood asthma. In D. C. Russo & J. W. Varni (Eds.), *Behavioral pediatrics: Research and practice* (pp. 27–66). New York: Plenum.

Deblinger, E., & Heflin, A. H. (1996). *Treating sexually abused children and their nonoffending parents: A cognitive behavioral approach.* Thousand Oaks, CA: Sage.

Del Medico, V. D., Weller, E., & Weller, R. (1996). Childhood depression. In L. Hechtman (Ed.), *Do they grow out of it?: Long-term outcomes of childhood disorders* (pp. 101–119). Washington, DC: American Psychiatric Press.

Dolgin, M. J., & Jay, S. M. (1989). Pain management in children. In E. J. Mash & R. A. Barkley (Eds.), *Treatment of childhood disorders* (pp. 383–404). New York: Guilford.

Donovan, J. E., & Jessor, R. (1983). Problem drinking and the dimension of involvement with drugs: A Guttman scalogram analysis of adolescent drug use. *American Journal of Public Health, 73,* 543–552.

Douglas, J. W. B. (1973). Early disturbing events and later enuresis. In I. Kolvin, R. C. MacKeith, & S. R. Meadow (Eds.), *Bladder control and enuresis* (pp. 109–117). Philadelphia: Lippincott.

Drummond, D. C. (1990). The relationship between alcohol dependence and alcohol related problems in a clinical population. *British Journal of Addiction, 85,* 357–366.

Dunn, L. M. (1981). *Peabody Picture Vocabulary Test—Revised* (PPVT-R). Circle Pines, MN: American Guidance Service.

Durand, V. M. (1990). *Severe behavior problems: A functional communication training approach.* New York: Guilford.

Dykens, E. M., Hodapp, R. M., & Evans, D. W. (1994). Profiles and development of adaptive behavior in males with fragile X syndrome. *Journal of Autism and Developmental Disorders, 23,* 135–145.

Eisen, A. R., & Kearney, C. A. (1995). *Practitioner's guide to treating fear and anxiety in children and adolescents: A cognitive-behavioral approach.* Northvale, NJ: Jason Aronson.

Eisen, A. R., Spasaro, S. A., Kearney, C. A., Albano, A. M., & Barlow, D. H. (1996). Measuring parental expectancies in a childhood anxiety disorders sample: The Parental Expectancies Scale. *The Behavior Therapist, 19,* 37–38.

Elliot, C. H., Jay, S. M., & Woody, P. (1987). An observational scale for measuring children's distress during medical procedures. *Journal of Pediatric Psychology, 12,* 543–551.

Ewing, J. A. (1984). Detecting alcoholism: The CAGE questionnaire. *Journal of the American Medical Association, 252,* 1905–1907.

Eyberg, S. M. (1992). Parent and teacher behavior inventories for the assessment of conduct problem behaviors in children. In L. VandeCreek, S. Knapp, & T. L. Jackson (Eds.), *Innovations in clinical practice: A source book* (Vol. 11, pp. 261–270). Sarasota, FL: Professional Resource Exchange.

Fairburn, C. G., Jones, R., Peveler, R. C., Hope, R. A., & O'Connor, M. (1993). Psychotherapy and bulimia nervosa: The longer-term effects of interpersonal psychotherapy, behaviour therapy and cognitive behaviour therapy. *Archives of General Psychiatry, 50,* 419–428.

Farrell, M., & Strang, J. (1991). Substance use and misuse in childhood and adolescence. *Journal of Child Psychology and Psychiatry, 32,* 109–128.

Farrington, D. P. (1990). Long term criminal outcomes of hyperactivity-impulsivity-attention deficit (HIA) and conduct problems in childhood. In L. N. Robins & M. Rutter (Eds.), *Straight and devious pathways from childhood to adulthood* (pp. 62–82). New York: Cambridge University Press.

Farrington, D. P. (1991). Childhood aggression and adult violence: Early precursors and later-life outcomes. In D. J. Pepler & K. H. Rubin (Eds.), *The development and treatment of childhood aggression* (pp. 189–197). Hillsdale, NJ: Lawrence Erlbaum.

Feinstein, C., & Wiener, J. M. (1997). Developmental disorders of learning, motor skills, and communication. In J. M. Wiener (Ed.), *Textbook of child and adolescent psychiatry* (2nd ed, pp. 281–300). Washington, DC: American Psychiatric Press.

Fielding, D. M., & Doleys, D. M. (1988). Elimination problems: Enuresis and encopresis. In E. J. Mash & L. G. Terdal (Eds.), *Behavioral assessment of childhood disorders* (2nd ed, pp. 586–623). New York: Guilford.

Finkelhor, D. (1984). *Child sexual abuse: New theory and research.* New York: Free Press.

Flakierska, N., Lindstrom, M., & Gillberg, C. (1988). School refusal: A 15–20–year follow-up of 35 Swedish urban children. *British Journal of Psychiatry, 152,* 834–837.

Fletcher, K. E. (1996). Childhood posttraumatic stress disorder. In E. J. Mash & R. A. Barkley (Eds.), *Child psychopathology* (pp. 242–276). New York: Guilford.

Foreyt, J. P., & Mikhail, C. (1997). Anorexia nervosa and bulimia nervosa. In E. J. Mash & L. G. Terdal (Eds.), *Assessment of childhood disorders* (3rd ed, pp. 683–716). New York: Guilford.

Foster, S. L., & Robin, A. L. (1988). Family conflict and communication in adolescence. In E. J. Mash & L. G. Terdal (Eds.), *Behavioral assessment of childhood disorders* (2nd ed, pp. 717–775). New York: Guilford.

Foster, S. L., & Robin, A. L. (1989). Parent-adolescent conflict. In E. J. Mash & R. A. Barkley (Eds.), *Treatment of childhood disorders* (pp. 493–528). New York: Guilford.

Foster, S. L., & Robin, A. L. (1997). Family conflict and communication in adolescence. In E. J. Mash & L. G. Terdal (Eds.), *Assessment of childhood disorders* (3rd ed, pp. 627–682). New York: Guilford.

Frauenheim, J. G. (1978). Academic achievement characteristics of adult males who were diagnosed as dyslexic in childhood. *Journal of Learning Disabilities, 11,* 476–483.

Frick, P. J., Lahey, B. B., Loeber, R., Tannenbaum, L., Van Horn, Y., Christ, M. A. G., Hart, E. L., & Hanson, K. (1993). Oppositional defiant disorder and conduct disorder: A meta-analytic review of factor analyses and cross-validation in a clinic sample. *Clinical Psychology Review, 13,* 319–340.

Friedman, A. S., & Utada, A. (1989). A method for diagnosing and planning the treatment of adolescent drug abusers (the Adolescent Drug Abuse Diagnosis [ADAD] instrument). *Journal of Drug Education, 19,* 285–312.

Garner, D. M., & Garfinkel, P. E. (1979). The Eating Attitudes Test: An index of the symptoms of anorexia nervosa. *Psychological Medicine, 9,* 273–279.

Garner, D. M., & Garner, M. V. (1992). Treatment of eating disorders in adolescents: Research and recommendations. In C. E. Walker & M. C. Roberts (Eds.), *Handbook of clinical child psychology* (2nd ed, pp. 623–641). New York: Wiley.

Gilbert, B. O., & Dollinger, S. J. (1992). Neurotic disorders of childhood: Obsessive-compulsive, phobic, conversion, dissociative, and post-traumatic stress disorder. In C. E. Walker & M. C. Roberts (Eds.), *Handbook of clinical child psychology* (2nd ed, pp. 359–374). New York: Wiley.

Gillberg, C., Gillberg, I. C., & Steffenburg, S. (1992). Siblings and parents of children with autism: A controlled population-based study. *Developmental and Medical Child Neurology, 34,* 389–398.

Ginsburg, G. S., Silverman, W. K., & Kurtines, W. K. (1995). Family involvement in treating children with phobic and anxiety disorders: A look ahead. *Clinical Psychology Review, 15,* 457–473.

Goodwin, D. W. (1985). Alcoholism and genetics: The sins of the fathers. *Archives of General Psychiatry, 42,* 171–174.

Greenspan, S. I. (1997). Clinical assessment in infancy and early childhood. In J. M. Wiener (Ed.), *Textbook of child and adolescent psychiatry* (2nd ed, pp. 67–78). Washington, DC: American Psychiatric Press.

Griffin, W. A. (1993). *Family therapy: Fundamentals of theory and practice.* New York: Brunner/Mazel.

Grigorenko, E. L., Wood, F. B., Meyer, M. S., Hart, L. A., Speed, W. C., & Shuster, A. (1997). Susceptibility loci for distinct components of developmental dyslexia on chromosomes 6 and 15. *American Journal of Human Genetics, 60,* 27–39.

Hammen, C., & Rudolph, K. D. (1996). Childhood depression. In E. J. Mash & R. A. Barkley (Eds.), *Child psychopathology* (pp. 153–195). New York: Guilford.

Hansen, J. C., & L'Abate, L. (1982). *Approaches to family therapy.* New York: Macmillan.

Harrell, T. H., & Wirtz, P. W. (1990). *Adolescent Drinking Index.* Odessa, FL: Psychology Assessment Resources.

Hawkins, J. D., Kosterman, R., Maguin, E., Catalano, R. F., & Arthur, M. W. (1997). Substance use and abuse. In R. T. Ammerman & M. Hersen (Eds.), *Handbook of prevention and treatment with children and adolescents* (pp. 203–237). New York: Wiley.

Hechtman, L. (Ed.) (1996a). *Do they grow out of it?: Long-term outcomes of childhood disorders.* Washington, DC: American Psychiatric Press.

Hechtman, L. (1996b). Attention-deficit/hyperactivity disorder. In L. Hechtman (Ed.), *Do they grow out of it?: Long-term outcomes of childhood disorders* (pp. 17–38). Washington, DC: American Psychiatric Press.

Hendren, R. L., & Mullen, D. (1997). Conduct disorder in childhood. In J. M. Wiener (Ed.), *Textbook of child and adolescent psychiatry* (2nd ed, pp. 427–440). Washington, DC: American Psychiatric Press.

Herrero, M. E., Hechtman, L., & Weiss, G. (1994). Antisocial disorders in hyperactive subjects from childhood to adulthood: Predictive factors and characteristics of subgroups. *American Journal of Orthopsychiatry, 64,* 510–521.

Herzog, D. B., & Beresin, E. V. (1997). Anorexia nervosa. In J. M. Wiener (Ed.), *Textbook of child and adolescent psychiatry* (2nd ed, pp. 543–561). Washington, DC: American Psychiatric Press.

Hetherington, E. M., Bridges, M., & Insabella, G. M. (1998). What matters? What does not? Five perspectives on the association between marital transitions and children's adjustment. *American Psychologist, 53,* 167–184.

Hodapp, R. M., & Dykens, E. M. (1996). In E. J. Mash & R. A. Barkley (Eds.), *Child psychopathology* (pp. 362–389). New York: Guilford.

Holland, A. J., Sicotte, N., & Treasure, J. (1988). Anorexia nervosa: Evidence for a genetic basis. *Journal of Psychosomatic Research, 32,* 561–571.

Hops, H., & Greenwood, C. R. (1988). Social skill deficits. In E. J. Mash & L. G. Terdal (Eds.), *Behavioral assessment of childhood disorders* (2nd ed, pp. 263–314). New York: Guilford.

Houston, M., & Wiener, J. M. (1997). Substance-related disorders. In J. M. Wiener (Ed.), *Textbook of child and adolescent psychiatry* (2nd ed, pp. 637–656). Washington, DC: American Psychiatric Press.

Houts, A. C., & Liebert, R. M. (1984). *Bedwetting: A guide for parents and children.* Springfield, IL: Charles C. Thomas.

Hynd, G. W., Hern, K. L., Novey, E. S., Eliopulos, D., Marshall, R., Gonzalez, J. J., & Voeller, K. K. (1993). Attention-deficit hyperactivity disorder and asymmetry of the caudate nucleus. *Journal of Child Neurology, 8,* 339–347.

Janoff-Bullman, R. (1985). The aftermath of victimization: Rebuilding shattered assumptions. In C. R. Figley (Ed.), *Trauma and its wake: The study of post-traumatic stress disorder* (pp. 15–35). New York: Brunner/Mazel.

Jarvis, P. E., & Barth, J. T. (1994). *The Halstead-Reitan Neuropsychological Battery: A guide to interpretation and clinical applications.* Odessa, FL: Psychological Assessment Resources.

Johnson, S. B. (1988). Chronic illness and pain. In E. J. Mash & L. G. Terdal (Eds.), *Behavioral assessment of childhood disorders* (2nd ed, pp. 491–527). New York: Guilford.

Johnston, L. D., O'Malley, P. M., & Bachman, J. G. (1995). *National survey results on drug use from Monitoring the Future Study, 1975–1994: Vol. 1. Secondary school students.* Rockville, MD: U. S. Department of Health and Human Services.

Kaffman, M., & Elizur, E. (1977). Infants who become enuretics: A longitudinal study of 161 kibbutz children. *Monographs of the Society for Research in Child Development, 42:2* (Serial no. 170).

Kagan, J., Reznick, J. S., & Snidman, N. (1988). Biological bases of childhood shyness. *Science, 240*, 167–171.

Kager, V. A., Arndt, E. K., & Kenny, T. J. (1992). Psychosomatic problems of children. In C. E. Walker & M. C. Roberts (Eds.), *Handbook of clinical child psychology* (2nd ed, pp. 303–317). New York: Wiley.

Kaminer, Y., Bukstein, O., & Tartar, R. E. (1991). The Teen-Addiction Severity Index: Rationale and reliability. *International Journal of the Addictions, 26*, 219–226.

Kandel, D. B. (1982). Epidemiological and psychosocial perspectives on adolescent drug use. *Journal of the American Academy of Child Psychiatry, 21*, 328–347.

Karp, C. L., & Butler, T. L. (1996). *Treatment strategies for abused children.* Thousand Oaks, CA: Sage.

Kashani, J. H., & McNaul, J. P. (1997). Mood disorders in adolescents. In J. M. Wiener (Ed.), *Textbook of child and adolescent psychiatry* (2nd ed, pp. 343–385). Washington, DC: American Psychiatric Press.

Katz, E. R., Kellerman, J., & Siegel, S. E. (1980). Behavioral distress in children with cancer undergoing medical procedures: Developmental considerations. *Journal of Consulting and Clinical Psychology, 48*, 356–365.

Kaufman, J., Birmaher, B., Brent, D., Rao, U., Flynn, C., Moreci, P., Williamson, D., & Ryan, N. (1997). Schedule for Affective Disorders and Schizophrenia for School-Aged Children—Present and Lifetime Version (K-SADS-PL): Initial reliability and validity data. *Journal of the American Academy of Child and Adolescent Psychiatry, 36*, 980–988.

Kazdin, A. E. (1988). Childhood depression. In E. J. Mash & L. G. Terdal (Eds.), *Behavioral assessment of childhood disorders* (2nd ed, pp. 157–195). New York: Guilford.

Kazdin, A. E. (1996). *Conduct disorders in childhood and adolescence* (2nd. ed.). Thousand Oaks, CA: Sage.

Kazdin, A. E., Rodgers, A., & Colbus, D. (1986). The Hopelessness Scale for Children: Psychometric characteristics and concurrent validity. *Journal of Consulting and Clinical Psychology, 54*, 241–245.

Kearney, C. A., & Silverman, W. K. (1993). Measuring the function of school refusal behavior: The School Refusal Assessment Scale. *Journal of Clinical Child Psychology, 22*, 85–96.

Kearney, C. A., & Silverman, W. K. (1995). Family environment of youngsters with school refusal behavior: A synopsis with implications for assessment and treatment. *American Journal of Family Therapy, 23*, 59–72.

Kearney, C. A., & Silverman, W. K. (1996). The evolution and reconciliation of taxonomic strategies for school refusal behavior. *Clinical Psychology: Science and Practice, 3*, 339–354.

Keller, M. B., Lavori, P. W., Endicott, J., Coryell, W., & Klerman, G. L. (1983). "Double depression": Two year follow-up. *American Journal of Psychiatry, 140*, 689–694.

Kendall, P. C., & Wilcox, L. E. (1979). Self-control in children: Development of a rating scale. *Journal of Consulting and Clinical Psychology, 47*, 1020–1029.

Kendall-Tackett, K. A., Williams, L. M., & Finkelhor, D. (1993). Impact of sexual abuse on children: A review and synthesis of recent empirical studies. *Psychological Bulletin, 113*, 164–180.

Klinger, L. G., & Dawson, G. (1996). Autistic disorder. In E. J. Mash & R. A. Barkley (Eds.), *Child psychopathology* (pp. 311–339). New York: Guilford.

Klorman, R., Salzman, L. F., & Borgstedt, A. D. (1988). Brain event-related potentials in evaluation of cognitive deficits in attention deficit disorder and outcome of stimulant therapy. In L. Bloomingdale (Ed.), *Attention deficit disorder* (3rd ed, pp. 49–80). New York: Pergamon.

Knobloch, H., & Pasamanick, B. (Eds.) (1974). *Gesell and Amatruda's developmental diagnosis* (3rd ed.). New York: Harper & Row.

Koegel, L. K., & Koegel, R. L. (1996). The child with autism as an active communicative partner: Child-initiated strategies for improving communication and reducing behavior problems. In E. D. Hibbs & P. S. Jensen (Eds.), *Psychosocial treatments for child and adolescent disorders: Empirically based strategies for clinical practice* (pp. 553–572). Washington, DC: American Psychological Association.

Kosc, L. (1974). Developmental dyscalculia. *Journal of Learning Disabilities, 7,* 164–177.

Kovacs, M. (1992). *Children's Depression Inventory (CDI) manual.* North Tonawanda, NY: Multi-Health Systems.

Kovacs, M. (1996). Presentation and course of major depressive disorder during childhood and later years of the life span. *Journal of the American Academy of Child and Adolescent Psychiatry, 35,* 705–715.

Krug, D. A., Arick, J. R., & Almond, P. J. (1981). The Autism Screening Instrument for Educational Planning: Background and development. In J. E. Gilliam (Ed.), *Autism: Diagnosis, instruction, management, and research* (pp. 64–78). Springfield, IL: Charles C. Thomas.

La Greca, A. M. (1988). Adherence to prescribed medical regimens. In D. K. Routh (Ed.), *Handbook of pediatric psychology* (pp. 299–320). New York: Guilford.

La Greca, A. M., & Stone, W. L. (1993). Social Anxiety Scale for Children-Revised: Factor structure and concurrent validity. *Journal of Clinical Child Psychology, 22,* 17–27.

Lambert, N., Leland, H., & Nihira, K. (1992). *AAMD Adaptive Behavior Scales—School Edition* (2nd ed.). Odessa, FL: Psychological Assessment Resources.

Leiter, R. G. (1969). *Leiter International Performance Scale.* Los Angeles, CA: Western Psychological Services.

Lewinsohn, P. M. (1974). A behavioral approach to depression. In R. J. Friedman & M. M. Katz (Eds.), *The psychology of depression: Contemporary theory and research* (pp. 157–178). New York: Wiley.

Lewis, B. A. (1990). Familial phonological disorders: Four pedigrees. *Journal of Speech and Hearing Disorders, 55,* 160–170.

Lewis, D. O. (1997). Conduct and antisocial disorders in adolescence. In J. M. Wiener (Ed.), *Textbook of child and adolescent psychiatry* (2nd ed, pp. 441–458). Washington, DC: American Psychiatric Press.

Lewis, D. O., Yeager, C. A., Lovely, R., Stein, A., & Cobham-Portorreal, C. S. (1994). A clinical follow-up of delinquent males: Ignored vulnerabilities, unmet needs, and the perpetuation of violence. *Journal of the American Academy of Child and Adolescent Psychiatry, 33,* 518–528.

Loeber, R. (1996). Developmental continuity, change, and pathways in male juvenile problem behaviors and delinquency. In J. D. Hawkins (Ed.), *Delinquency and crime: Current theories* (pp. 1–27). Port Chester, NY: Cambridge University Press.

Loeber, R., & Stouthamer-Loeber, M. (1998). Development of juvenile aggression and violence: Some common misconceptions and controversies. *American Psychologist, 53,* 242–259.

Lovaas, O. I. (1977). *The autistic child: Language development through behavior modification.* New York: Irvington.

Lyon, G. R. (1996). Learning disabilities. In E. J. Mash & R. A. Barkley (Eds.), *Child psychopathology* (pp. 390–435). New York: Guilford.

MacKeith, R. C. (1972). Is maturation delay a frequent factor in the origins of primary nocturnal enuresis? *Developmental Medicine and Child Neurology, 14,* 217–223.

Maisto, A. A., & German, M. L. (1986). Reliability, predictive validity, and interrelationships of early assessment indices used with developmentally delayed infants and children. *Journal of Clinical Child Psychology, 15,* 327–332.

Maloney, M. J., McGuire, J., Daniels, S. R., & Specker, B. (1989). Dieting behavior and eating attitudes in children. *Pediatrics, 84,* 482–489.

Mash, E. J., & Dozois, D. J. A. (1996). Child psychopathology: A developmental-systems perspective. In E. J. Mash & R. A. Barkley (Eds.), *Child psychopathology* (pp. 3–60). New York: Guilford.

Masten, A. S., & Coatsworth, J. D. (1998). The development of competence in favorable and unfavorable environments: Lessons from research on successful children. *American Psychologist, 53,* 205–220.

Matson, J. L. (1989). *Treating depression in children and adolescents.* New York: Pergamon.

Mayer, J., & Filstead, W. J. (1979). The Adolescent Alcohol Involvement Scale: An instrument for measuring adolescent use and misuse of alcohol. *Journal of Studies of Alcohol, 40,* 291–300.

Mayfield, D., McLeod, G., & Hall, P. (1974). The CAGE questionnaire: Validation of a new alcoholism screening instrument. *American Journal of Psychiatry, 131,* 1121–1123.

McGrath, P. A. (1987). The multidimensional assessment and management of recurrent pain syndromes in children. *Behaviour Research and Therapy, 25,* 251–262.

McMahon, R. J., & Estes, A. M. (1997). Conduct problems. In E. J. Mash & L. G. Terdal (Eds.), *Assessment of childhood disorders* (3rd ed, pp. 130–193). New York: Guilford.

Minuchin, S. (1974). *Families and family therapy.* Cambridge, MA: Harvard University Press.

Minuchin, S., Rosman, B. L., & Baker, L. (1978). *Psychosomatic families: Anorexia nervosa in context.* Cambridge, MA: Harvard University Press.

Mitchell, J., McCauley, E., Burke, P. M., & Moss, S. J. (1988). Phenomenology of depression in children and adolescents. *Journal of the American Academy of Child and Adolescent Psychiatry, 27,* 12–20.

Mizes, J. S. (1995). Eating disorders. In M. Hersen & R. T. Ammerman (Eds.), *Advanced abnormal child psychology* (pp. 375–391). Hillsdale, NJ: Lawrence Erlbaum.

Moberg, D. P. (1991). The Adolecent Drug Involvement Scale. *Journal of Adolescent Chemical Dependency, 2*, 75–88.

Monahon, C. (1993). *Children and trauma: A parent's guide to helping children heal.* New York: Lexington.

Montague, M., Applegate, B., & Marquard, K. (1993). Cognitive strategy instruction and mathematical problem-solving performance of students with learning disabilities. *Learning Disabilities Research and Practice, 8,* 223–232.

Moos, R. H., & Moos, B. S. (1986). *Family Environment Scale manual* (2nd ed.). Palo Alto, CA: Consulting Psychologists Press.

National Institute on Drug Abuse. (1982). *Marijuana and youth* (Publication ADM 82–1186). Washington, DC: Department of Health and Human Services.

Newcomb, M. D., & Bentler, P. M., (1986). Cocaine use among adolescents: Longitudinal associations with social context, psychopathology, and use of other substances. *Addictive Behaviors, 11,* 263–273.

Newcomb, M. D., & Richardson, M. A. (1995). Substance use disorders. In M. Hersen & R. T. Ammerman (Eds.), *Advanced abnormal child psychology* (pp. 411–431). Hillsdale, NJ: Lawrence Erlbaum.

Nihira, K., Leland, H., & Lambert, N. (1992). *AAMD Adaptive Behavior Scales—Residential and Community* (2nd ed.). Odessa, FL: Psychological Assessment Resources.

Offord, D. R., & Bennett, K. J. (1994). Conduct disorder: Long-term outcomes and intervention effectiveness. *Journal of the American Academy of Child and Adolescent Psychiatry, 33,* 1069–1078.

Ollendick, T. H. (1983). Reliability and validity of the Revised Fear Survey Schedule for Children (FSSC-R). *Behaviour Research and Therapy, 21,* 685–692.

Olson, D. H., Portner, J., & Lavee, Y. (1985). *FACES III.* St. Paul, MN: University of Minnesota.

Patterson, G. R. (1982). *Coercive family processes.* Eugene, OR: Castalia.

Patton, G. C. (1988). The spectrum of eating disorders in adolescence. *Journal of Psychosomatic Research, 32,* 579–584.

Piers, E. V. (1984). *Piers-Harris Children's Self-Concept Scale: Revised manual 1984.* Los Angeles, CA: Western Psychological Services.

Prinz, R. J., Foster, S. L., Kent, R. N., & O'Leary, K. D. (1979). Multivariate assessment of conflict in distressed and nondistressed mother-adolescent dyads. *Journal of Applied Behavior Analysis, 12,* 691–700.

Quay, H. C., & Peterson, D. R. (1982). *Revised Behavior Problem Checklist.* Coral Gables, FL: University of Miami, Department of Psychology.

Rahdert, E. R. (1991). *The adolescent assessment/referral system: Manual.* Rockville, MD: National Institute on Drug Abuse.

Raphael, T. E. (1982). Teaching children question-answering strategies. *The Reading Teacher, 36,* 186–191.

Raven, J. C. (1995). *Raven's Progressive Matrices.* San Antonio, TX: The Psychological Corporation.

Rehm, L. P. (1977). A self-control model of depression. *Behavior Therapy, 8,* 787–804.

Reynolds, C. R., & Paget, K. D. (1981). Factor analysis of the Revised Children's Manifest Anxiety Scale for blacks, whites, males, and females with a national normative sample. *Journal of Consulting and Clinical Psychology, 49,* 352–359.

Reynolds, W. M. (1987). *Reynolds Adolescent Depression Scale.* Odessa, FL: Psychological Assessment Resource.

Robin, A. L., Bedway, M., Siegel, P. T., & Gilroy, M. (1996). Therapy for adolescent anorexia nervosa: Addressing cognitions, feelings, and the family role. In E. D. Hibbs & P. S. Jensen (Eds.), *Psychosocial treatments for child and adolescent disorders: Empirically based strategies for clinical practice* (pp. 239–259). Washington, DC: American Psychological Association.

Robin, A. L., & Canter, W. (1984). A comparison of the Marital Interaction Coding System and community ratings for assessing mother-adolescent problem-solving. *Behavioral Assessment, 6,* 303–314.

Robins, L. N. (1966). *Deviant children grown up.* Baltimore, MD: Williams & Wilkens.

Robins, L. N., & Rutter, M. (Eds.). (1990). *Straight and devious pathways from childhood to adulthood.* New York: Cambridge University Press.

Rosen, J. C., & Leitenberg, H. (1985). Exposure plus response prevention treatment of bulimia. In D. M. Garner & P. E. Garfinkel (Eds.), *Handbook of psychotherapy for anorexia nervosa and bulimia* (pp. 193–209). New York: Guilford.

Ross, D. M., & Ross, S. A. (1982). *Hyperactivity: Current issues, research, and theory* (2nd ed.). New York: Wiley.

Ross, R. T., Begab, M. J., Dondis, E. H., Giampiccolo, J., & Meyers, C. E. (1985). *Lives of the retarded: A forty-year follow-up study.* Stanford, CA: Stanford University Press.

Rourke, B. P., & Conway, J. A. (1997). Disabilities of arithmetic and mathematical reasoning: Perspectives from neurology and neuropsychology. *Journal of Learning Disabilities, 30,* 34–46.

Routh, D. K., & Ernst, A. R. (1984). Somatization disorder in relatives of children and adolescents with functional abdominal pain. *Journal of Pediatric Psychology, 9,* 427–437.

Rubin, K. H., & Stewart, S. L. (1996). Social withdrawal. In E. J. Mash & R. A. Barkley (Eds.), *Child psychopathology* (pp. 277–307). New York: Guilford.

Sadava, S. W. (1987). Interactionist theories. In H. T. Blane & K. E. Leonard (Eds.), *Psychological theories of drinking and alcoholism* (pp. 90–130). New York: Guilford.

Schaefer, C. E. (1993). What is play and why is it therapeutic? In C. E. Schaefer (Ed.), *The therapeutic powers of play* (pp. 1–16). Northvale, NJ: Jason Aronson.

Scharff, L. (1997). Recurrent abdominal pain in children: A review of psychological factors and treatment. *Clinical Psychology Review, 17,* 145–166.

Schopler, E., Reichler, R., & Renner, B. (1988). *The Childhood Autism Rating Scale (CARS).* Los Angeles, CA: Western Psychological Services.

Shedler, J., & Block, J. (1990). Adolescent drug use and psychological health: A longitudinal inquiry. *American Psychologist, 45,* 612–630.

Shepherd, M. J., & Uhry, J. K. (1993). Reading disorder. *Child and Adolescent Psychiatric Clinics of North America, 2,* 193–208.

Silverman, W. K., & Albano, A. M. (1996). *Anxiety disorders interview schedule for DSM-IV: Child version.* San Antonio, TX: The Psychological Corporation.

Smith, C., & Steiner, H. (1992). Psychopathology in anorexia nervosa and depression. *Journal of the American Academy of Child and Adolescent Psychiatry, 31,* 841–843.

Spanier, G. B. (1976). Measuring dyadic adjustment: New scales for assessing the quality of marriage and similar dyads. *Journal of Marriage and the Family, 38*, 15–28.

Sparrow, S. S., Balla, D. A., & Cicchetti, D. V. (1984). *Vineland Adaptive Behavior Scales.* Circle Pines, MN: American Guidance Service.

Spielberger, C. D. (1973). *Manual for the State-Trait Anxiety Inventory for Children.* Palo Alto, CA: Consulting Psychologists Press.

Sprich-Buckminster, S., Biederman, J., Milberger, S., Faraone, S. V., & Lehman, B. K. (1993). Are perinatal complications relevant to the manifestation of ADD? Issues of comorbidity and familiality. *Journal of the American Academy of Child and Adolescent Psychiatry, 32*, 1032–1037.

Stanovich, K. E. (1994). Romance and reality. *The Reading Teacher, 47*, 280–291.

Steffenburg, S., Gillberg, C., Hellgren, L., Andersson, L., Gillberg, I. C., Jakobsson, G., & Bohman, M. (1989). A twin study of autism in Denmark, Finland, Iceland, Norway, and Sweden. *Journal of Child Psychology and Psychiatry, 30*, 405–416.

Stein, M. B. (Ed.) (1995). *Social phobia: Clinical and research perspectives.* Washington, DC: American Psychiatric Press.

Stevenson, J. (1992). Evidence for a genetic etiology in hyperactivity in children. *Behavior Genetics, 22*, 337–343.

Stevenson, K. (1989). Guidelines for peer review of child and adolescent psychiatric treatment including substance abuse disorder and eating disorders. In M. M. DuPrat, & K. Stevenson (Eds.), *Child and adolescent psychiatric illness: Guidelines for treatment resources, quality assurance, peer review, and reimbursement* (pp. 29–72). Washington, DC: American Academy of Child and Adolescent Psychiatry.

Striegel-Moore, R. H. (1993). Etiology of binge eating: A developmental perspective. In C. G. Fairburn & G. T. Wilson (Eds.), *Binge eating: Nature, assessment, and treatment* (pp. 144–172). New York: Guilford.

Striegel-Moore, R. H., Silberstein, L. R., & Rodin, J. (1986). Toward an understanding of risk factors for bulimia. *American Psychologist, 41*, 246–263.

Strober, M. (1995). Family-genetic perspectives on anorexia nervosa and bulimia nervosa. In K. D. Brownell & C. G. Fairburn (Eds.), *Eating disorders and obesity: A comprehensive handbook* (pp. 212–218). New York: Guilford.

Sunday, S. R., Einhorn, A., & Halmi, K. A. (1992). Relationship of perceived macronutrient and caloric content to affective conditions about food in eating-disordered, restrained, and unrestrained subjects. *American Journal of Clinical Nutrition, 55*, 362–371.

Szymanski, L. S., & Kaplan, L. C. (1997). Mental retardation. In J. M. Wiener (Ed.), *Textbook of child and adolescent psychiatry* (2nd ed, pp. 183–218). Washington, DC: American Psychiatric Press.

Taylor, H. G. (1988). Learning disabilities. In E. J. Mash & L. G. Terdal (Eds.), *Behavioral assessment of childhood disorders* (2nd ed, pp. 402–450). New York: Guilford.

Taylor, H. G. (1989). Learning disabilities. In E. J. Mash & R. A. Barkley (Eds.), *Treatment of childhood disorders* (pp. 347–380). New York: Guilford.

Thompson, R. J., Gustafson, K. E., George, L. K., & Spock, A. (1994). Change over a 12-month period in the psychosocial adjustment of children and adolescents with cystic fibrosis. *Journal of Pediatric Psychology, 19,* 189–203.

Thorndike, R. L., Hagen, E. P., & Sattler, J. M. (1986). *The Stanford-Binet Intelligence Scale: Fourth edition, Guide for administering and scoring.* Chicago: Riverside Publishing.

Tisher, M., & Lang, M. (1983). The Children's Depression Scale: Review and further developments. In D. P. Cantwell & G. A. Carlson (Eds.), *Childhood depression* (pp. 181–203). New York: Spectrum.

Tobler, N. (1986). Meta-analysis of 143 adolescent drug prevention programs: Quantitative outcome results of program participants compared to control or comparison group. *Journal of Drug Issues, 4,* 537–567.

Torgesen, J. K., & Bryant, B. R. (1994). *Test of Phonological Awareness (TOPA).* Austin, TX: Pro-Ed.

Tsai, L. Y., & Ghaziuddin, M. (1997). Autistic disorder. In J. M. Wiener (Ed.), *Textbook of child and adolescent psychiatry* (2nd ed, pp. 219–254). Washington, DC: American Psychiatric Press.

Varni, J. W., Thompson, K. L., & Hanson, V. (1987). The Varni/Thompson Pediatric Pain Questionnaire. I. Chronic musculoskeletal pain in juvenile rheumatoid arthritis. *Pain, 28,* 27–38.

Vik, P. W., Brown, S. A., & Myers, M. G. (1997). Adolescent substance use problems. In E. J. Mash & L. G. Terdal (Eds.), *Assessment of childhood disorders* (3rd ed, pp. 717–748). New York: Guilford.

Volkmar, F. R., Klin, A., Marans, W. D., & McDougle, C. J. (1996). Autistic disorder. In F. R. Volkmar (Ed.), *Psychoses and pervasive developmental disorders in childhood and adolescence* (pp. 129–190). Washington, DC: American Psychiatric Press.

Walker, C. E., Kenning, M., & Faust-Campanile, J. (1989). Enuresis and encopresis. In E. J. Mash & R. A. Barkley (Eds.), *Treatment of childhood disorders* (pp. 423–448). New York: Guilford.

Walsh, T., & Menvielle, E. (1997). Disorders of elimination. In J. M. Wiener (Ed.), *Textbook of child and adolescent psychiatry* (2nd ed, pp. 613–620). Washington, DC: American Psychiatric Press.

Waslick, B., & Greenhill, L. (1997). Attention-deficit/hyperactivity disorder. In J. M. Wiener (Ed.), *Textbook of child and adolescent psychiatry* (2nd ed, pp. 389–410). Washington, DC: American Psychiatric Press.

Wechsler, D. (1989). *Manual for the Wechsler Preschool and Primary Scale of Intelligence—Revised* San Antonio, TX: The Psychological Corporation.

Wechsler, D. (1991). *Manual for the Wechsler Intelligence Scale for Children—Third Edition (WISC-III).* San Antonio, TX: The Psychological Corporation.

Weeks, G., & L'Abate, L. (1982). *Paradoxical psychotherapy: Theory and practice with individuals, couples, and families.* New York: Brunner/Mazel.

Weiss, G., Hechtman, L., Milroy, T., & Perlman, T. (1985). Psychiatric status of hyperactives as adults: A controlled prospective 15-year follow-up of 63 hyperactive children. *Journal of the American Academy of Child Psychiatry, 24,* 211–220.

Wenar, C. (1994). *Developmental psychopathology: From infancy through adolescence* (3rd ed). New York: McGraw-Hill.

Werry, J. S. (1996). Pervasive developmental, psychotic, and allied disorders. In L. Hechtman (Ed.), *Do they grow out of it?: Long-term outcomes of childhood disorders* (pp. 195–223). Washington, DC: American Psychiatric Press.

Werry, J. S., & Aman, M. G. (1993). *Practitioner's guide to psychoactive drugs for children and adolescents.* New York: Plenum.

White, H. R., & Labouvie, E. W. (1989). Towards the assessment of adolescent problem drinking. *Journal of Studies on Alcohol, 50,* 30–37.

White, S., & Santilli, G. (1988). A review of clinical practices and research data on anatomical dolls. *Journal of Interpersonal Violence, 3,* 430–442.

Widom, C. S. A. (1989). Does violence beget violence?: A critical examination of the literature. *Psychological Bulletin, 106,* 3–28.

Wilkinson, G. S. (1993). *Wide Range Achievement Test (WRAT-3) manual.* Odessa, FL: Psychological Assessment Resources.

Wilson, G. T., Fairburn, C. G., & Agras, W. S. (1997). Cognitive-behavioral therapy for bulimia nervosa. In D. M. Garner & P. E. Garfinkel (Eds.), *Handbook of treatment for eating disorders* (2nd ed, pp. 67–93). New York: Guilford.

Wilson, G. T., Heffernan, K., & Black, C. M. D. (1996). Eating disorders. In E. J. Mash & R. A. Barkley (Eds.), *Child psychopathology* (pp. 541–571). New York: Guilford.

Wing, L. (1989). Autistic adults. In C. Gillberg (Ed.), *Diagnosis and treatment of autism* (pp. 419–432). New York: Plenum.

Winters, K. C. (1992). Development of an adolescent alcohol and other drug abuse screening scale: Personal Experience Screening Questionnaire. *Addictive Behavior, 17,* 479–490.

Wirt, R. D., Lachar, D., Klinedinst, J. K., & Seat, P. D. (1984). *Multidimensional description of child personality: A manual for the Personality Inventory for Children.* Los Angeles, CA: Western Psychological Services.

Wolfe, V. V., & Birt, J. (1997). Child sexual abuse. In E. J. Mash & L. G. Terdal (Eds.), *Assessment of childhood disorders* (3rd ed, pp. 569–623). New York: Guilford.

Wolfe, V. V., & Wolfe, D. A. (1988). The sexually abused child. In E. J. Mash & L. G. Terdal (Eds.), *Behavioral assessment of childhood disorders* (2nd ed, pp. 670–714). New York: Guilford.

Wong, B. Y. L. (1996). *The ABCs of learning disabilities.* New York: Academic.

Wong, V. (1993). Epilepsy in children with autistic spectrum disorder. *Journal of Child Neurology, 8,* 316–322.

Yamaguchi, K., & Kandel, D. B. (1984). Patterns of drug use from adolescence to young adulthood: II. Sequences of progression. *American Journal of Public Health, 74,* 668–672.

Zametkin, A. J., Liebenauer, L. L., Fitzgerald, G. A., King, A. C., Minkunas, D. V., Herscovitch, P., Yamada, E. M., & Cohen, R. M. (1993). Brain metabolism in teenagers with attention-deficit hyperactivity disorder. *Archives of General Psychiatry, 50,* 333–340.

Zocolillo, M. (1993). Gender and the development of conduct disorder. *Development and Psychopathology, 5,* 65–78.

INDEX

TO THE OWNER OF THIS BOOK:

I hope that you have found *Casebook in Child Behavior Disorders* useful. So that this book can be improved in a future edition, would you take the time to complete this sheet and return it? Thank you.

School and address: ————————————————————————

Department: ——————————————————————————

Instructor's name: —————————————————————————

1. What I like most about this book is: ——————————————

———————————————————————————————————

———————————————————————————————————

2. What I like least about this book is: ——————————————

———————————————————————————————————

———————————————————————————————————

3. My general reaction to this book is: ———————————————

———————————————————————————————————

4. The name of the course in which I used this book is: ——————

———————————————————————————————————

5. Were all of the chapters of the book assigned for you to read? ————

   If not, which ones weren't? ———————————————————

6. In the space below, or on a separate sheet of paper, please write specific suggestions for improving this book and anything else you'd care to share about your experience in using the book.

———————————————————————————————————

———————————————————————————————————

———————————————————————————————————

———————————————————————————————————

Optional:

Your name: _____ Date: _____

May Brooks/Cole quote you, either in promotion for *Casebook in Child Behavior Disorders*, or in future publishing ventures?

Yes: _____ No: _____

Sincerely,

Christopher A. Kearney